BLOCKBUSTERS!

Robert Tanitch

B T BATSFORD • LONDON

For BRIAN DALLAMORE
and family

ALSO BY ROBERT TANITCH:
A Pictorial Companion to Shakespeare's Plays
Ralph Richardson, a Tribute
Olivier
Leonard Rossiter
Ashcroft
Gielgud
Dirk Bogarde
Guinness
Sean Connery
John Mills
Brando
Clint Eastwood
The Unknown James Dean
Oscar Wilde on Stage and Screen

A catalogue record for this book is available from the British Library.

ISBN 0 7134 8691 0

Printed in Spain

Volume © B T Batsford 2000

First published in 2000 by
B T Batsford
9 Blenheim Court
Brewery Road
London N7 9NT

A member of the Chrysalis Group plc

Contents

Foreword

BLOCKBUSTERS! is a chronicle of some of the most successful box-office films of the 20th century.

The very first "blockbuster" was, in fact, a bomb, which was dropped by the American Air Force on Germany in 1942 during World War II. Hollywood did not actually use the word "blockbuster" to describe highly successful films until the epics of the 1950s.

Taking one film for each year, since 1930, when records were first kept, the book becomes a record of the public's changing and unchanging taste over a 70-year period, covering all genres: horror, comedy, crime, Biblical epics, historical films, war films, cartoons, musicals, westerns, disaster movies, science-fiction, comic books, sea adventures, marital dramas, ghost stories and sentimental tearjerkers.

In the 1930s, during the Depression, audiences queued in large numbers for monsters, sexual innuendo, maritime brutality, earthquakes, hurricanes, dwarfs, and epic 19th century romantic dramas. In the 1990s they wanted to see ghosts, terminators, aliens, prehistoric monsters, the sinking of a ship on its maiden voyage and the White House being blown up.

In the intervening years, chariot-racing, the love-life of an Egyptian queen, torrid sex dramas in the Old West, a fight with giant squid under the sea, idyllic island adventures, sweeping Arabian sands, burning buildings, nannies, Dalmatians, train robbers, singing nuns, boxers, gyrating teenagers, sharks, cute dogs, Mafioso killings, exorcism, divorce, interplanetary wars, ghosts and, indeed, ghostbusters have all proved immensely popular; even babies have been known to catch the public's fancy and drawn queues round the block.

Robert Tanitch would like to express his appreciation to Roger Huggins, Tina Persaud, Simon Rosenheim, Joel Finler, Alan Frank, Jerald Samuel, Kobal staff, Time Warner Company, everyone at the BFI library and viewing service and members of the staff at Westminster Central Library.

1930 • Dracula

CREDITS

Count Dracula	Bela Lugosi
Mina	Helen Chandler
John Harker	David Manners
Renfield	Dwight Frye
Van Helsing	Edward Van Sloan
Dr Seward	Herbert Bunston
Studio	Universal
Director	Tod Browning
Producer	Carl Laemmle Jr
	Tod Browning
Screenplay	Garret Forte
Photography	Karl Freund
Music	Peter Ilich Tchaikovsky
	Richard Wagner

AWARDS

ACADEMY AWARDS
None

ACADEMY NOMINATIONS
None

BEST PICTURE

All Quiet on the Western Front

STARS OF 1930

Marie Dressler
Marlene Dietrich
Jean Harlow
Greta Garbo
Norma Shearer

1930 Blockbusters

Whoopee
Check and Double Check
All Quiet on the Western Front
Min and Bill
The Big House

THE WORLD

- Unemployment reaches 2 million in UK
- 107 Nazis elected to Reichstag
- Worst flood in history in China
- Amy Johnson flies solo to Australia

BRAM STOKER in 1890 had a nightmare, produced, so he said, by a dinner of dressed crab. Seven years later, having done his research, he published the most famous Gothic horror story of them all. The story has inspired more than 50 films and is the perfect horror entertainment.

Stoker's novel, which has been described as "a kind of incestuous necrophiliac, oral-anal-sadistic all-in male wrestling," first appeared in London in 1927 as a play by Hamilton Deane (uniformed nurses were in attendance for the faint-hearted). It then transferred to New York, the Hungarian actor Bela Lugosi playing the lead.

Universal Studios did not think the film would be a box-office hit and it would not have been made but for the great persistence of the 21-year-old producer, Carl Laemmele. Lugoisi, despite his success on Broadway and on the road (he had toured for two years) was not the first choice. The studio had wanted Lon Chaney, "the man of a thousand faces," star of *The Hunchback of Notre Dame*, *The Phantom of the Opera* and *London After Midnight* (in which he had played a vampire disguised as a policeman), but Chaney had died in 1930.

> " To die, to be really dead, must be glorious. There are far worse things waiting man than death. "
>
> *Count Dracula*

Tod Browning's film version was billed as "the strangest love story a man has ever known" and was released on Valentine's Day. "We hope," said the filmmakers with gross insincerity, "the memories of Dracula won't give you bad dreams." The advertisements had been warning people for weeks that it would "make your blood run cold."

Lugosi, wearing a long cloak and elegantly dressed, made a slow entrance. His hair was sleek and Brylcreamed, his face was pale and mask-like, his eyes were hypnotic, his nose was aquiline, his eyebrows were heavy, his lips were pinched and rouged. The make-up was the embodiment of evil: suave, weird, sinister, macabre. (His face would later be used as a model for the Devil in Walt Disney's *Fantasia*.) He had no charm, but plenty of heavy-handed sexual intensity. The acting was silent film acting, larger-than-life, stylised, theatrical and heavily accented. There were lots of pauses: "I am Dracula… I never drink wine." There were no fangs; he was not as repulsively ugly nor as frightening as Max Schrek in the 1923 classic, FW Murnau's *Nosferatu*. He was a cardboard villain.

The misty, eerie, atmospheric opening sequence, with its spooky spectral coach driver, had the feel of a silent film, which was intensified by the German expressionistic lighting by Karl Freund. Set designer Charles D Hill's huge baronial hall and its crumbling staircase, with its cobwebs, beetles, bats, rats and armadillos, had a magnificent decaying grandeur. Once Dracula left Transylvania and arrived in 1930s Britain, the film became merely a photograph of the play. The camera was static. The dialogue was dead. The bat on a string at the end of a fishing-rod wasn't very convincing. The lack of a proper score hampered the production. A few bars from *Swan Lake* and the odd howling wolf were not enough.

The nocturnal violence and sexual horrors were kept off-screen. As Dracula moved in for the bite, there was always a fade-out. The best moment came when Van Helsing realises that Dracula's figure was not reflected in the mirror of the lid of his cigarette case. Edward Van Sloan, in his spectacles, looked as evil as Lugosi. David

"I am Dracula… I never drink wine." Helen Chandler and Bela Lugosi as Dracula

Manners was an impotent hero. Helen Chandler was an anaemic heroine, although she did have one chilling moment when it seemed as if she was actually going to bite her fiancé. The most interesting performance was by Dwight Frye as the clean-cut, all American boy, Renfield, transformed into an insect-eating, raving madman, a performance straight out of a 1920s melodrama, in the Peter Lorre manner. Todd Browning would go on to make the notorious *Freaks* (1932) using people with genuine deformities.

Dracula launched the American horror movie and was a major turning point in Bela Lugosi's career. He achieved instant movie stardom and was doomed to play in the vampire genre for the rest of his life. He would still be playing Dracula on stage in 1930.

A Spanish language version of *Dracula* was shot simultaneously on the same set at the end of the day after the Americans had vacated the studio. Many people thought the Spanish version, directed by George Melford and starring Carmen Villarias, was the better film.

Dracula is an exciting melodrama, not as good as it ought to be but a cut above the ordinary trapdoor and winding sheet mystery film.

Time

The picture can at least boast to be the best of the many mystery films.

The New York Times

Dracula isn't mysterious. It is just plain spooky and bloodthirsty… Brrrrrr! We enjoyed it.

The New York Daily News

Lugosi outdoes any of the performances of the undead count which we have seen him give on the stage.

Hollywood Filmograph

1931 • Frankenstein

CREDITS

Henry Frankenstein	Colin Clive
Elizabeth	Mae Clarke
Victor Moritz	John Boles
The Monster	Boris Karloff
Dr Waldman	Edward Van Sloan
Baron Frankenstein	Frederick Kerr
Fritz	Dwight Frye
Studio	Universal
Director	James Whale
Producer	Carl Laemmle Jr
Screenplay	Garrett Fort
	Francis Edwards Faragoh
	John Balderton
	Robert Florey
Photography	Arthur Edeson
Music	David Broekman

AWARDS

ACADEMY AWARDS
None

ACADEMY NOMINATIONS
None

BEST PICTURE

Cimarron

STARS OF 1931

Marie Dressler
Jean Harlow
James Cagney
Richard Dix
Greta Garbo

1931 Blockbusters

Trader Horn
Cimarron
City Lights
A Free Soul
Daddy Long Legs

THE WORLD

- Japan occupies Manchuria
- Spain declared a republic
- Opening of the Empire State Building
- Invention of the electric razor

THE FILM began with Edward Van Sloan appearing in front of a theatre curtain and addressing the audience directly: "It is one of the strangest stories ever told," he said. "It deals with two great mysteries of creation, life and death. I think it will thrill you, I think it will shock you, it might even horrify you."

Frankenstein, or *The Modern Prometheus*, a macabre Gothic romance by the 21-year-old Mary Shelley, a sensational success when it was first published in 1813, had already been filmed in 1910 by Thomas Edison and in 1915 as *Life Without a Soul*. James Whale's version was based on Peggy Webling's 1927 play and it remains the most famous horror film of all horror films, a landmark, which had its original audiences screaming and fainting in large numbers.

Henry Frankenstein, a scientist, had the insane ambition to create life. His henchmen stole bodies from graveyards and gallows. By mistake he used a criminal's abnormal brain and created a monster, which he brought to life during a thunder storm with the aid of a rising electrical contraption, which looked as if it had been inspired by Fritz Lang's *Metropolis*.

Universal Studios had originally offered the role to Bela Lugosi, but he had turned it down, refusing to play a non-speaking part. Boris Karloff, tall, gaunt, lumbering, stumbling, was no savage but a gentle, vulnerable giant with a child-like innocence. The make-up by Jack Pierce, based on cadavers, was unforgettable: Roman hair cut, flat head, stitched face, sucked-in cheeks, and a bolt through the neck. Pierce also made him 18 inches taller with lifts and 65 pounds heavier with stones in his pockets. Karloff was lantern-jawed, long-armed (achieved by making the sleeves shorter), stiff-legged and heavy-booted. The Monster became an instant 20th century icon.

Audiences felt compassion, even affection for the helpless, confused, tormented outcast, terrified by the hostility he met. The Monster emerged as a tragic figure, a figure of inarticulate pathos, humane and noble. The trailer described him as "fiendish". That was the last thing he was. Karloff always referred to him as The Creature. The performance, notable for its grave dignity and subtlety, made him a household name and typecast him for the rest of his acting career.

Cinematically and theatrically, the tableaux and the lighting owed much to German Expressionism. There were striking images in the graveyard and during the torch-lit man-hunt. The most famous scene was with the little girl (Marilyn Harris) at the water's edge throwing flowers into the water, a scene influenced by *Der Golem*. What exactly happened to the girl was left to the audience's imagination, but it would have been unlikely that Karloff's Creature had raped and strangled her. It was more likely that he had thrown her into the water, thinking she would float like the flowers.

The film, released in a print tinted in ghoulish green, was billed as *Frankenstein, The Man Who Made a Monster*, but that did not stop audiences thinking of Frankenstein as the Monster's name. Henry Frankenstein (a role earmarked for Leslie Howard) was acted by Colin Clive, who had played Captain Stanhope in

> " I want the picture to be a very modern, materialistic treatment, something of *Doctor Caligari*, something of Edgar Allan Poe, and, of course, a good deal of me. "
>
> *James Whale*

"It's Alive!" Boris Karloff as The Monster and Mae Clarke as the bride in Frankenstein.

Whale's highly successful London production of *Journey's End*. Clive, with his clipped English accent, so typical of the period, brought the same neurotic-in-jodhpurs quality to Frankenstein that he had brought to Stanhope: "It's alive! It's alive! It's alive! I know what it feels like to be God!" he screamed. "You'll see whether I'm crazy or not!" Clive was completely upstaged by Karloff.

Frankenstein and *Dracula* were reissued as a double-bill and sold to the public on "we dare you to see it" campaign. Ambulances were parked outside cinemas and nurses stood in the lobbies with first-aid equipment.

A sequel followed: *The Bride of Frankenstein*. This time Karloff got top billing. Elsa Lanchester played Mary Shelley and the Monster's bride. Karloff would also appear in *Son of Frankenstein* (1939) and *House of Frankenstein* (1940). He played Frankenstein in *Frankenstein* (1970). Bela Lugosi played The Monster in *The Ghost of Frankenstein* (1942.)

No matter what one may say about the melodramatic ideas here, there is no denying that it is far and away the most effective thing of its kind.
The New York Times

A rather crudely constructed bloodcurdler which will thrill those who find their pleasures in things morbid.
Bioscope

You'll want to shriek with fright and run home and hide under the bed.
Kansas City Journal Post

As a horrifier it is a tremendous success, but I doubt very much it will be equally successful as a financial venture.
Hollywood Spectator

1932 • King Kong

CREDITS

Ann Darrow	Fay Wray
Carl Denham	Robert Armstrong
Jack Driscoll	Bruce Cabot
Englehorn	Frank Reicher
Weston	Sam Hardy
Native Chief	Noble Johnson
Studio	RKO
Director	Merian C Cooper
Producer	Ernest B Schoedsack
Screenplay	James Creelman
	Ruth Rose
Photography	Eddie Linden
Music	Max Steiner

AWARDS

ACADEMY AWARDS
None

ACADEMY NOMINATIONS
None

BEST PICTURE

Grand Hotel

STARS OF 1932

Marie Dressler
Janet Gaynor
Joan Crawford
Charles Farrell
Greta Garbo

1932 Blockbusters

Grand Hotel
Shanghai Express
Tarzan, The Ape Man
Red Dust
42nd Street

THE WORLD

- 14 million unemployed in USA
- Great Hunger March of Unemployed to London
- Roosevelt elected US President
- Opening of Sydney Harbour Bridge

KING KONG is the definitive monster and *King Kong*, the film, was and still is the best monster movie ever made, appealing to a mass market at the height of the Depression. Audiences queued four abreast. Some 12,000 were turned away at the premiere.

A film producer (Robert Armstrong) set off for a remote, uncharted island. "I'm going to give the public what they want," he declared. "I'm going to make the greatest picture in the world, something nobody has seen or heard of." He arrived on Skull Island (Conan Doyle's Lost World) with his latest star (Fay Wray), whom he had picked up in the street when she was starving, the only reference to the Depression. The island natives abducted her and gave her as a present to Kong. The 50-foot ape immediately fell in love with the five-foot blonde. The story was one of the world's great, unrequited love stories.

Kong drummed on his chest. Wray screamed and carried on screaming for the rest of the movie, pausing only once to swoon at the sight of his phallus, the eighth wonder of the world. His face was seven feet from hairline to tip of chin. His nose was two feet wide at the nostrils. His eyes were ten inches long. His chest was 36 feet. His legs were 15 feet. His arms were 23 feet and they could reach 75 feet. His mouth was six feet wide. How could Wray's leading man (Bruce Cabot) begin to compete? Kong battled with pterodactyls, tyrannosaurs, brontosaurs and snakes to defend and keep her for himself. Fay Wray lived through an experience other woman could only dream about: an erotic, surreal, black nightmare.

Kong was knocked out by a smoke bomb and brought back to New York in chains to make an exhibition of himself to gratify the public's curiosity. At his premiere, he broke his chains, chewed up a few first nighters, strode through the city, destroyed the elevated railway and tossed the railway carriage and passengers into the street. There was a memorable shot of him peering into a Manhattan bedroom, looking for Wray, his face filling the whole window frame. When he found her, he climbed with her to the top of the Empire State Building via the outside wall. The Empire State Building had opened the previous year and at 1449 feet, it was the biggest erection in the world.

Kong, balancing precariously, grabbed at the circling aeroplanes, which were machine-gunning him. Finally, he toppled to his death. Max Steiner's score made certain Kong emerged a tragic figure, who didn't deserve his fate.

Fay Wray, star of Eric von Stroheim's *The Wedding March*, became the horror movie's first sex symbol: a half-naked woman in a gorilla's paw, screaming her head off. It was, in essence, a silent film performance. "I felt I did too much screaming," she admitted much later when she was in her nineties. Wray had initially been told she was going to have the tallest, darkest leading man in Hollywood. She thought RKO Studio meant Cary Grant.

The action was essentially visual. The production was a technical tour de force, its stunning special effects achieved by animation, miniatures, stop-frame photography and back projection. The scenes in the jungle were excellent value with dinosaurs chasing the crew through the misty waters and undergrowth. The monsters were the stars. Kong was the creation of animator Willis O'Brien.

> It wasn't the airplanes that killed him. It was Beauty killed the Beast. ""

"The Eigth Wonder of the World." King Kong and Fay Wray

The most spectacular film since the talkies and a masterpiece of technical ingenuity that marks a milestone in the development of the screen.

Picturegoer

The picture emerges as an interesting and effective stunt, produced with considerable imagination.

The New York Herald Tribune

The director has succeeded up to a point in stifling that laughter which comes from even the most unsophisticated when reason is knocked so violently and effectively unconscious.

The Times

On the night I saw this film there was a great deal of laughter provoked by palpable absurdity.

Tatler

Its horrors are never far removed from laughter, the treatment is frequently banal and in places the machinery creaks badly. But as entertainment for the masses it is terrific.

Kong, I fear, is a one picture star. He will never play opposite Garbo.

The Sunday Dispatch

1933 • I'm No Angel

CREDITS

Tira	Mae West
Jack Clayton	Cary Grant
Benny Pinkowitz	George Ratoff
Big Bill Barton	Edward Arnold
Kirk Lawrence	Kent Taylor
Studio	Paramount
Director	Wesley Ruggles
Producer	William LeBaron
Screenplay	Mae West
	Harlan Thompson
Photography	Leo Tover
Music	Harvey Brooks

AWARDS

ACADEMY AWARDS
None

ACADEMY NOMINATIONS
None

BEST PICTURE

Cavalcade

STARS OF 1933

Marie Dressler
Will Rogers
Janet Gaynor
Eddie Cantor
Wallace Beery

1933 Blockbusters

State Fair
Cavalcade
Dangerous Lady
She Done Him Wrong
Gold-diggers of 1933

THE WORLD

• Hitler appointed Chancellor of Germany
• Roosevelt's New Deal
• Prohibition repealed in USA
• Discovery of polythene

I'M NO ANGEL, a sophisticated sexual comedy, was a reworking of *The Lady and The Lions* by Mae West to suit her special talents and was produced and screened before the censors could stop her. It followed hard on the heels of *She Done Him Wrong*, an adaptation of *Diamond Lil*, her Broadway success, in which she had played Lady Lou, "one of the finest women (pause) that walked these streets." The new script was in the same vein, but better.

I'm No Angel was, West said, "just a story about a girl who lost her reputation and never missed it." It began in a small-time circus where a side-show singer was so broke she agreed to put her head in the lion's mouth. (West actually went into the cage with the lions despite the fact that their trainer had been mauled only the day before.) Tira, lion-tamer and man-tamer, quickly progressed from tent to penthouse with the help of a large number of admirers. "It's not the men in my life that counts," she explained, "it's the life in my men." Her philosophy was "Find 'em, fool 'em, forget 'em... take all you can get and give as little as possible." She ended up in court suing a rich young man for breach of promise. He was so bemused by her style that he let her win the case. The young man was played by 29-year-old Cary Grant, who had already appeared with her in *She Done Him Wrong*.

> " Love is a wonderful thing – at least I've heard it highly praised. "
>
> *Mae West*

The court scene was classic comedy. Tira decided to cross-examine the witnesses herself. She dangled her necklace, rolled her hips and flirted with judge and jury. One juror rang her up to congratulate her, but he was a bit slow off the mark; the judge has already come and gone. "Thanks," she drawled, "don't forget to come up and see me sometime." The line, and its many variations, became her signature tune.

Mae West, the former Baby Vamp of burlesque, had come from the theatre where she had once been jailed for 10 days on a charge of obscenity when she produced *Sex on Broadway*, a play which she had also written and directed. She was the mistress of camp, a good-natured, blowsy, Junoesque 40-year-old, who satirised her own sexuality. She tapped her curls, tossed her head and prowled across the screen in a languorous, voluptuous manner, which managed to be both quick and slow at the same time. "I'm tired from tossing my hips," she complained to her black servant. "Beulah, peel me a grape."

West was more than ample distraction from the Depression. There was always a knowing, come-hither glint in her eye and plenty of eye-shadow and mascara. She wore huge hats with wide brims, boas and dresses that emphasised her full bosom and hour-glass figure. She had bravado. Sailors and pilots named their inflatable emergency life-jackets after her.

West, "torso-tossin' in tights, tiaras and teagown" (as the posters put it) was a parody of sex. She wrote her own dialogue, too. The one-line innuendoes were superbly delivered. "When I'm good, I'm very good, but when I'm bad, I'm better." She was quick on the uptake. "Do you mind if I get personal?" asked a potential beau. "I don't mind if you get familiar," she replied.

"I've changed my mind," said a guy. "Does it work any better?" she snapped. "I'll never forget you," said another beau. "Nobody does!" she boasted. "If only I could trust you," pleaded a lover. "Hundreds have," she assured him.

"And don't forget to come up and see me sometime." Mae West tosses her hips in court in I'm No Angel.

Mae West, "a rough diamond in a platinum setting," was equally at home in a boudoir and a rowdy music hall. She had a Restoration comedy bawdiness. The Motion Picture Production Code and League of Decency, established under Joseph Breen in 1934, found her too risqué and started to cut out the double entendres. Once her laconic wit was deleted, her film career declined.

Mae West is today the biggest conversation provoker, free space grabber and all-round box-office bet in the country. She is as hot an issue as Hitler.

Variety

Mae West is definitely amusing but not in such large doses as here.

Picturegoer

My chief objection to this picture is its low moral tone.

Hollywood Reporter

1934 • It Happened One Night

CREDITS

Peter	Clark Gable
Ellie	Claudette Colbert
Andrews	Walter Connolly
Shapeley	Roscoe Karns
Danker	Alan Hale
Studio	Columbia
Director	Frank Capra
Producer	Harry Cohn
Screenplay	Robert Riskin
Photography	Joseph Walker

AWARDS

ACADEMY AWARDS

Best Film	Harry Cohn
Best Direction	Frank Capra
Best Actor	Clark Gable
Best Actress	Claudette Colbert
Best Writing	
Adaptation	Robert Riskin

ACADEMY NOMINATIONS

None

BEST PICTURE

It Happened One Night

STARS OF 1934

Will Rogers
Clark Gable
Janet Gaynor
Wallace Beery
Mae West

1934 Blockbusters

Tarzan and His Mate
The Thin Man
Belle of the Nineties
The Barretts of Wimpole Street
Manhattan Melodrama

THE WORLD

- Hitler becomes Reichsführer
- Night of the Long Knives
- Bonnie and Clyde shot dead
- John Dillinger shot dead
- Discovery of nuclear fission

"TOGETHER for the first time!" said the posters. It was a near thing. Neither Clark Gable nor Claudette Colbert wanted to do it. Gable was there only under duress, on loan from MGM as punishment for having been a bad boy. Colbert, on loan from Paramount, was only there because she had asked for double her salary and Columbia, amazingly, had given it to her. Nobody expected this film to succeed. Colbert thought she had made the worst picture in the world. It opened to modest interest from critics and public alike, but gradually it caught on, especially in the rural areas.

The episodic story, set in Middle America and shot mainly on location, was a slight, sentimental novelette, based on *Night Bus* by Samuel Hopkins Adams. A society heiress ran away to marry the man of her choice, a worthless playboy and fortune-hunting celebrity aviator. Her father put a reward of 10,000 dollars on her head. On an all-night bus she met an ace-reporter, who has just been sacked. When he realised who she was, he saw her as his meal ticket and agreed to help her in return for an exclusive story. On the journey, they were initially at odds, a clash of egos and class. "You're just a headline to me," she said. But when her luggage was stolen and they ran out of money, mutual antagonism gave way to mutual dependence.

> "I believe it was the only picture in which Gable was ever allowed to play himself: the fun-loving, boyish, attractive, he-man rogue that was the real Gable."
>
> *Frank Capra*

Ellie represented the idle rich, a spoiled brat, who was so used to getting her way that she presumed buses would wait for her and that she could buy off anybody. Peter represented the jobless working-class. The cynical, hard-drinking, hot-headed journalist, reversing long-distance telephone charges to his irate editor, was a character who might have stepped out of Moss Hart and Charles MacArthur's play, *The Front Page*.

Gable, who had been cast until then in brutal, callous roles, found it a relief to be playing comedy and a down-to-earth, likeable chap. There was a scene in which Peter gave Ellie a demonstration of how to thumb a lift when hitch-hiking. Car after car whizzed by, ignoring him completely. Finally, Ellie showed him how to do it. She lifted her skirt to reveal a shapely leg and a car stopped immediately, proving her point that "the limb is mightier than the thumb."

In order to save money, the couple shared a motel room. Their twin beds were coyly separated by a makeshift curtain, a blanket hanging on a string, which Peter nicknamed "The Walls of Jericho". Contrary to expectations raised by the movie's title, nothing happened in the night. Peter did not take advantage of Ellie's offer. In fact, despite all the sexual innuendo, the comedy remained utterly chaste to the very end. "The Walls of Jericho" only came down after they were married, and then off-screen, too, heralded by the sound of a trumpet and a black-out.

It Happened One Night, one of the many 'bus movies' of the early 1930s, has been described as the first screwball comedy, although strictly speaking it is neither wacky nor witty enough to justify the term. The film succeeded because of the chemistry of the stars and because the audience was able to identify with them. There was just one glimpse of the Depression when a starving mother on the bus fainted

Clark Gable and Claudette Colbert discover "the limb is mightier than the thumb".

and Ellie spontaneously gave the woman all the journalist's money, leaving them broke and having to survive on a diet of raw carrots.

Colbert, good-looking, slim, intelligent, had class. Gable, physically strong and sexy, had roguish charm. When he took off his shirt to reveal a bare torso, there was (it was reported) an immediate slump in the underwear business. Men all over the US threw away their vests.

Audiences during the Depression era wanted escapism and the affectionate, Capracorn mixture of *The Taming of the Shrew* and *Cinderella* (poor boy gets rich girl) was very appealing. The film was praised for its good humour, warmth, sincerity and unpretentiousness. It had all Frank Capra's relaxed professionalism. Capra would go on to make the populist and didactic *Mr Deeds Goes to Town*, *Mr Smith Goes to Washington* and *It's a Wonderful Life*, all three equally simplistic yet much better films and socially and economically more pertinent.

Both play as though they really liked their characters, and therein lies much of its charm.
Variety

She [Claudette Colbert] combines irresistible sex appeal with a sense of humour and portrays the character with a naturalness which is wholly captivating.
Picturegoer

His [Frank Capra's] great talent is in making ordinary people do extraordinary things in a quite ordinary way.
The Observer

The film is conceived in a delightful vein of mingled romance and high comedy, and never departs from this vein for a single instant. It is brilliantly directed by Mr Frank Capra,
Tatler

1935 • Mutiny on the Bounty

CREDITS

Bligh	Charles Laughton
Christian	Clark Gable
Byam	Franchot Tone
Smith	Herbert Mundin
Ellison	Eddie Quillan
Bacchus	Dudley Digges
Burkitt	Donald Crisp
Studio	MGM
Director	Frank Lloyd
Producer	Irving Thalberg
	Albert Lewin
Screenplay	Talbot Jenings
	Jules Furthman
	Carey Wilson
Photography	Arthur Edeson
Music	Herbert Stothart

AWARDS

ACADEMY AWARDS

Best Picture	Irving Thalberg with Albert Lewin

ACADEMY NOMINATIONS

Best Actor	Clark Gable, Charles Laughton and Franchot Tone
Best Director	Frank Lloyd
Best Screenplay	Jules Furthman, Talbot Jennings and Carey Wilson
Best Film Editing	Margaret Booth
Best Score	MGM Music Department

BEST PICTURE

Mutiny on the Bounty

STARS OF 1935

Shirley Temple
Will Rogers
Fred Astaire and Ginger Rogers
Clark Gable
Joan Crawford

1935 Blockbusters

David Copperfield
Broadway Melody of 1936
China Seas
Roberta
Captain Blood

THE WORLD

- Dust storm in USA
- Persecution of Jews in Germany
- Italy invades Abyssinia
- Death of TE Lawrence

"SHE ISN'T very big" said a new recruit. "It isn't size that matters," said a knowing sailor, who has been to sea before. HMS *Bounty* left Portsmouth in December 1787. (The sequence was beautifully photographed by Arthur Edeson and edited by Margaret Booth.) Her mission was to sail to Tahiti and procure breadfruit trees for transplanting to the West Indies as cheap food for slaves. Neither ship nor breadfruit reached the West Indies.

Captain Bligh's character was immediately established when a corpse received the appointed 20 lashes in full view of officers and men. Bligh ruled by fear. There were daily lashings, splayings and keel haulings. The film cast him as an unbridled monster, a single-minded pervert, who flogged not to punish but to break a man's spirit. Men were clapped into irons at the drop of a tricorn. One man was sent to the top of masthead during a raging storm. Bligh's brutality (always expressed in long shots or reaction shots, never in close-up) was the only real motive for mutiny. He accused the crew of stealing food he had stolen himself. Finally, the majority of the sailors, under Fletcher Christian's command, had had enough. They seized the ship and put Bligh and 18 loyal men in an open boat.

> "It doesn't matter there are no women in the cast. People are fascinated with cruelty and that's why *Mutiny* will have appeal.
>
> *Irving Thalberg*

Bligh was defiant: "Casting me adrift 35,000 miles from a port of call. Send me to my doom, eh? Well, you're wrong, Christian. I'll take this boat as she floats to England if I must. I'll live to see you, all of you hanging from the highest yardarm of the British fleet." Bligh brought his crew 35,000 miles to safety. "We have," he said, "beaten the sea itself." It was one of the supreme feats of seamanship.

Bligh was a self-made man. Christian was a gentleman. Byam, a fictional character, was an aristocrat. Gable, despite his fears that his regular fans would laugh at him in costume and without his moustache, looked good in breeches and ponytail. Byam (played by Franchot Tone) looked no less romantic and handsome. Laughton looked mean, common and decidedly ugly.

Byam was court martialled on his return to England. Condemned to death, he made an impassioned speech in which he denounced the tyranny that had driven the men to mutiny. His message was clear: "A kind word would do more than a cat o' nine tails." He was later reprieved by King George III and the film ended, as it had begun, on a patriotic note, with sturdy singing of "Rule Britannia."

Charles Laughton (who had just had a big success in *The Private Lives of Henry VIII*) did for Bligh what Shakespeare did for *Richard III* and what he himself had already done for Dr Moreau, Mr Barrett and Javert. He was always good playing bullies and *Mutiny on the Bounty* was one of his most memorable virtuoso roles. His vicious, demented, glowering tyrant has been imitated so much that Laughton now seems as if he is caricature. History has been kinder to Bligh than his performance.

It might have been better if more time had been spent with Bligh in the open boat (a scene to recall Theodore Gericault's *The Raft of the Medusa*) and less time in Tahiti, an overlong, romantic idyll among the palm trees with the crew wandering around in their underwear, kissing the girls and having babies. The only person who didn't have any sex was Bligh.

"The ship's company will remember that I am your captain, your judge and your jury.
Byron Russell and Charles Laughton prepare for mutiny on the Bounty

Grim, brutal, sturdily romantic, made out of horror and desperate courage, it is as savagely exciting and rousingly dramatic a photoplay as has come out of Hollywood in recent years… *Mutiny on the Bounty* contains the stuff of half a dozen adventure pictures. It is superlatively thrilling.
The New York Times

[Charles Laughton] a refined and dreadful study of perversion.
The Times

Not for the unduly sensitive and certainly not for children…. The film could well be considerably shortened – much of the continuity during the last half hour or so is especially heavy and discontinuous – but the film has a vividness and intensity which compel one to remember it.
Monthly Film Bulletin

1936 • San Francisco

CREDITS

Blackie Norton	Clark Gable
Father Mullins	Spencer Tracy
Mary Blake	Jeanette MacDonald
Jack Burley	Jack Holt
Mrs Burley	Jessie Ralph

Studio	MGM
Director	WS Van Dyke
Producers	John Emerson
	Bernard Hyman
Screenplay	Anita Loos
Photography	Oliver T Marsh
Music	Edward Ward

AWARDS

ACADEMY AWARDS

Best Sound Recording

ACADEMY NOMINATIONS

Best Picture	John Emerson
Best Director	W.S. Van Dyke
Best Actor	Spencer Tracy
Best Original Story	Robert Hopkins
Best Assistant Director	Joseph Newman

BEST PICTURE

The Great Ziegfeld

STARS OF 1936

Shirley Temple
Fred Astaire and Ginger Rogers
Clark Gable
Robert Taylor
Joe E Brown

1936 Blockbusters

The Great Ziegfeld
After The Thin Man
Modern Times
Show Boat
Mr Deeds Goes to Town

THE WORLD

- Abdication of King Edward VIII
- Accession of King George VI
- Start of Spanish Civil War
- Burning of Crystal Palace
- Queen Mary's maiden voyage

THE CITY of San Francisco was described in the film as probably the wickedest, most corrupt, most Godless city in America, so it was no real surprise when it went the way of Sodom and Gomorrah. Its destruction was evidently no geological flaw, but clearly the work of God. The earthquake was a memorable sequence, thanks to the skill of Arnold Gillespie and James Basevi, who provided a brilliantly edited montage of shots of collapsing edifices, caving walls, crashing chandeliers, raining bricks, toppling statues, splitting streets, bursting water mains, flaring fires and dynamited buildings. People were buried under rubble and looters were shot. The individual touches, such as the spinning wheel of a crushed wagon, which didn't stop spinning until the earth stopped quaking, might have been the work of Sergei Eisenstein. Some people thought the movie earthquake was bigger and better than the real thing.

> Earthquake: 18 April, 1906. 5.13 am

Anita Loos's screenplay, based on a story by Robert Hopkins, ended on a positive note. When the citizens of San Francisco, who had just lost their husbands, wives, children and homes, learned that the raging fires had finally been put out, they immediately launched into "The Battle Hymn of the Republic" and strode off arm in arm to build a new and modern city, in a manner which would have made any Russian cinematic propagandist proud.

Blackie Norton, the self-styled king of the Barbary Coast, operated a gambling saloon and beer garden called *Paradise*. He had a reputation for being unscrupulous with women and ruthless with men. He was a cheerful, popular philistine and atheist, who became infatuated with Mary Blake, a good girl from Denver, the orphaned daughter of a country preacher. She had come to the big city to get a job. "Well, sister, what's your racket?" "I'm a singer." "Let's see your legs." "I said I'm a singer." "All right, let's see your legs." Blackie signed her up to sing in his music hall. His rival, Jack Hurley, engaged her to sing at The Tivoli Opera House. Torn between variety and opera and uncertain whether to marry Blackie or Jack, the impasse was resolved only by the earthquake, which conveniently killed off Jack and transformed Blackie's character. He went down on his knees to thank God when he found that Mary was still alive. The reformation was hardly convincing, even though it had been established early on that he had done good deeds and was fighting for decent fire regulations.

Clark Gable was everybody's idea of a cynical, smiling, charming, flashy rogue, but he did not play Blackie for the real villain he was clearly meant to be. Spencer Tracy, acting in a subtler key, was cast as a priest, Blackie's life-long friend, who refused to allow him to exploit Mary and drag her down to his level. Father Mullins, battling for two souls, packed an unexpected punch early on in the gymnasium when the two men were sparring.

Jeanette MacDonald, a colourless performer, sang arias from *Faust* and *La Traviata*, hymns ("Nearer My God to Thee") and music hall ditties ("San Francisco"). The last song set off the earthquake. There was a scene-stealing performance by Jessie Ralph as a rich old lady, a former Irish washerwoman, who had married into the aristocracy. One scene was directed by Van Dyke's mentor, DW Griffith, but nobody knows which one.

The killing of large numbers of people has always been good for the box office. Major disaster movies of the 1930s included *The Last Days of Pompeii* (1935), *In Old Chicago* (1937), *The Hurricane* (1937) and *The Rains Came* (1939).

"The gambler, the singer and the priest fought for the soul of San Francisco."
Spencer Tracy as the priest and Jeanette MacDonald as the singer in San Francisco.

The earthquake is a shattering spectacle, one of the truly great cinematic illusions.
The New York Times

There is a recurrent discrepancy between the incidents and the characters they are meant to display, as though the director, having the earthquake up his sleeve, saw no need for precise characterisation.
The Times

It is a cunningly screened pattern of cinematic hokum.
The New York Herald Tribune

San Francisco offers cinemaddicts views of two unusual phenomena: the San Francisco earthquake and Jeanette MacDonald acting with her teeth. Of the two, the latter is the more appalling.
Time

1937 • The Hurricane

CREDITS

Marama	Dorothy Lamour
Terangi	Jon Hall
Madame De Laage	Mary Astor
Father Paul	C Aubrey Smith
Dr Kersaint	Thomas Mitchell
Governor De Laage	Raymond Massey
Warder	John Carradine
Captain Nagle	Jerome Cowan
Studio	Goldwyn
Director	John Ford
Producer	Merritt Hulburd
Screenplay	Dudley Nichols
	Oliver HP Garrett
Photography	Bert Glennon
Music	Alfred Newman

AWARDS

ACADEMY AWARDS

Best Sound
  Recording   Thomas Moulton

ACADEMY NOMINATIONS

Best Supporting
  Actor   Thomas Mitchell
Best Score   Samuel Goldwyn
          Studio Music Department

BEST PICTURE

The Life of Emil Zola

STARS OF 1937

Shirley Temple
Clark Gable
Robert Taylor
Bing Crosby
William Powell

1937 Blockbusters

Saratoga
Lost Horizon
In Old Chicago
The Good Earth
Maytime

THE WORLD

• Germans bomb Guernica
• Hindenburg explodes
• Duke of Windsor marries Mrs Simpson
• Japan invades China

THE HURRICANE was based on the novel by Charles Nordhoff and James Norman Hall, the authors of *Mutiny on the Bounty*. The setting was the South Seas. A young native (John Hall), while visiting Tahiti, was socked in the face by a white racist. He socked him back and broke the man's jaw. He was sentenced to six months in jail and hard labour. Unable to stand prison life, he attempted to escape and was sentenced to an additional year. He went on trying to escape. Soon he had added a further 16 years to his sentence.

The French Governor (Raymond Massey) of the island where he lived was a stickler for honour and duty and refused to intervene on his behalf, saying the law must be upheld. He was deaf to the entreaties of his doctor (Thomas Mitchell), his priest (C Aubrey Smith) and his wife (Mary Astor), who at regular intervals throughout the film got together to have a moral debate. "I am not a representative of the well-meaning point of view," said the Governor. "I represent the law."

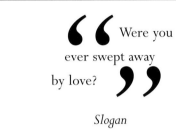

" Were you ever swept away by love? "

Slogan

Meanwhile, the young man, having escaped yet again, was making a 600-mile journey in a tiny open boat, battling all the while with the sea, storms, sharks, hunger and thirst. He arrived back home just in time for the hurricane. The governor, when he learned that he had returned, got very angry that nobody had told him. "I had a feeling something queer was going on behind my back," he said.

"I've never been on the island during a storm," said his wife. "Do they get very bad?" This was the cue for the hurricane to start rattling the shutters and turning out the lights. Palm trees were torn up, coral reefs were ripped, forests were mown down, houses were toppled and boats were smashed by 50-feet tidal waves. The wind whistled and howled. The sea roared. The natives shrieked. The church bell tolled. The doctor managed to deliver a baby boy in an open boat. The priest remained at his organ and he, his parishioners and the church building, took a terrible pounding from the sea. None of them survived. The young native managed to save his wife, his daughter and the governor's wife by tying them to a tree.

The cast, hosed down with water, blown apart by wind machines, their faces whipped by sand, were battered and bruised. The magnificent hurricane was the work of James Basevi, who had been responsible for the earthquake in *San Francisco*, the fire in *In Old Chicago*, the typhoon in *Suez* and the locusts in *The Good Earth*. The Samoan natives said Basevi's storm was worst than the real one in 1915.

Newcomer John Hall, defying the law and the elements, remained in remarkably good shape, despite his ordeal. Part Tahitian and nephew of the co-author, he was not much of an actor and would go on to spend much of his film career in South Seas sagas, as would Dorothy Lamour, who played his wife. She got top billing, although she had little to do, except wear a sarong. The sarong became Lamour's trademark. Three years later she appeared in another disaster movie, *Typhoon*. Thomas Mitchell's doctor, unshaven and permanently drunk, was a dummy run for his role in John Ford's *Stagecoach*.

The Hurricane was remade in 1979 with Jason Robards, Mia Farrow, Trevor Howard and Max Von Sydow.

Dorothy Lamour and Jon Hall swept away by love and a hurricane.

One of the most thrilling spectacles the screen has produced this year. That hurricane is a whopper.

The New York Times

The film was made for the storm and for 20 minutes or so it raged, sometimes actual, sometimes faked and always impressive.

Sight and Sound

The Hurricane is not a film which calls for any subtleties in acting and it does not get them. It is, in effect, a storm in a teacup, but it can at least plead it is a very large one.

The Times

The biggest, the best, the noisiest, the most spectacular cataclysm ever screened.

The Observer

1938 • Snow White and the Seven Dwarfs

CREDITS

Snow White	Adriana Caselotti
Prince Charming	Harry Stockwell
The Queen	Lucille La Verne
Magic Mirror	Moroni Olsen
Sneezy	Billy Gilbert
Sleepy	Pinto Colvig
Grumpy	Pinto Colvig
Happy	Otis Harlan
Bashful	Scotty Mattraw
Doc	Roy Atwell
Studio	Walt Disney
Director	David Hand,
Perce Pearce, Larry Morey,	
William Cottrell, Wilfred Jackson,	
	Ben Sharpsteen
Producer	Walt Disney
Animators	Hamilton Luske,
Vladimir Tytla, Fred Moore	
	Norman Ferguson
Screenplay	Ted Sears
Otto Englander, Earl Hurd	
Dorothy Ann Blank,	
Richard Creedon, Dick Rickard	
Merrill De Maris, Webb Smith	
Music	Frank Churchill
Paul Smith, Leigh Harline	
	Paul Smith

AWARDS

ACADEMY AWARDS

Special and Honorary Award	Walt Disney

ACADEMY NOMINATIONS

Best Score	Walt Disney Music

BEST PICTURE

You Can't Take It with You

STARS OF 1938

Shirley Temple
Clark Gable
Sonja Henie
Mickey Rooney
Spencer Tracy

1938 Blockbusters

Test Pilot
The Adventures of Robin Hood
Alexander's Ragtime Band
You Can't Take It with You
Sweethearts

THE WORLD

- Germany annexes Austria
- IRA bombings in England
- Orson Welles produces *The War of the Worlds* on radio
- Discovery of nylon in USA

SNOW WHITE AND THE SEVEN DWARFS, a delightful and unique entertainment, was based on the Brothers Grimm's classic fairy tale. It was Walt Disney's first full-length cartoon and his most ambitious film to date. No one had ever attempted a seven-reel cartoon before and Hollywood expected the film to be a disaster. On the drawing board for three years (1934–37), Hollywood christened it "Disney's Folly".

Snow White was given a chocolate-box, plump-cheeked prettiness. She sang *Some Day My Prince Will Come* at her wishing well with eye-batting, winsome innocence. The Prince immediately arrived on cue. "I have only one song for you," he sang. His face was vacuous and his body was without bone and muscle. They both looked like drawings in a second-rate picture book.

Snow White's role in life was to wash, sow, sweep and cook; and indeed she was never happier than when she was scrubbing the steps and doing the

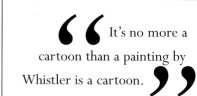

> ❝ It's no more a cartoon than a painting by Whistler is a cartoon. ❞
>
> *Walt Disney*

housework. She behaved like a bossy nanny and treated the dwarfs like naughty children. She always had a smile and a song. She preached that housework need never be chore if you whistled while you work. The cleaning of the cottage by the animals was delightfully inventive: cobwebs were rolled into knitting balls, deers' antlers were used as a clothes-horse and the squirrels cleaned the plates with their bushy tails. A nice touch was the mouse, irate at having the dust swept into his home, a hole in the wall.

The Queen looked like an elegant front cover of *Vogue* by Erté. Dressed in a purple flowing cloak she resembled the Duchess of Windsor. "Magic Mirror on the wall, who is the fairest one of all?" she asked. The mirror always told the truth and she was not amused to hear that Snow White was the fairest. The Queen was the typical wicked, cruel stepmother of fairy tale, cackling at the thought of burying the heroine alive. She brewed a magic potion, which included a mummy's dust, an old hag's cackle, a scream of fright, a blast of wind and a thunderbolt. The brew might not have been in the *Macbeth* league, but it was good enough to transform her body and voice into that of an old crone. She shrivelled up and sprouted warts, claws and snaggled teeth. Her transformation frightened even her pet raven, who hid in a skull. The Queen came to a terrible end during a raging storm when, trying to roll a boulder on her pursuers, she fell from a craggy precipice into a deep ravine off-screen. The two smiling vultures, who had been her constant companions, were delighted and swooped down to take their pickings.

The production was a tribute to the Disney Studio's extraordinary craftsmanship. Marge Champion, a dancer, was engaged so the artists could study Snow White's movements when she danced with the dwarfs. The Dwarfs – Doc, Happy, Sneezy, Dopey, Grumpy, Bashful, Sleepy – and the extraordinary number of animals were all treated in an individual way. The slow-coach tortoise was a delectable running gag.

All the best fairy stories are frightening. Snow White's flight through the forest at night, with the branches grabbing at her, the trees full of eyes and the swamp full of logs, which looked like crocodiles, was the Grimm stuff of nightmares. There was a memorable image in the castle dungeon of a skeleton reaching out through the bars of his cell for a jug of water, which had been deliberately placed just outside his reach. In Stockton, England, as late as 1954, the local Council insisted that children had to be accompanied by an adult.

Walt Disney and Shirley Temple at Academy Award Ceremony

Snow White and the Seven Dwarfs was tuneful. Twenty-five songs were written but only eight were included. The delightful *Soup Song* was deleted because it was felt it held up the story. (It is included in the video version.) The cartoon is witty, inventive and enchants children and adults alike. Orson Welles in *Citizen Kane* and Frederic Fellini in *Juliet of the Spirits* paid homage to its artistry.

Walt Disney received a special and honorary award from the Academy. The citation recognised the film "as a significant screen innovation which has charmed millions and pioneered a great new entertainment field for the motion picture cartoon." Nine-year-old Shirley Temple presented him with the award: one full-size Oscar and seven smaller ones.

Snow White and the Seven Dwarfs .remains a very powerful, emotional experience for any age in any era.
Voice

The animals he has done before but never has he [Walt Disney] made them so enchanting and so strangely moving.
Sight and Sound

Another *Snow White* will sound the Disney death-knell.
Current History

1939 • Gone with the Wind

CREDITS

Rhett Butler	Clark Gable
Scarlett O'Hara	Vivien Leigh
Ashley	Leslie Howard
Melanie	Olivia de Haviland
Mammy	Hattie McDaniel
Prissy	Butterfly McQueen
Gerald O'Hara	Thomas Mitchell
Belle Watling	Ona Munson
Aunt Pitty Pat	Laura Hope Crews
Dr Meade	Harry Davenport
Yankee Deserter	Paul Hurst
Studio	Selznick
Director	Victor Fleming
Producer	David O Selznick
Screenplay	Sidney Howard
Photographer	Ernest Haller
	Ray Rennahan
Music	Max Steiner

AWARDS

ACADEMY AWARDS

Best Picture	David O. Selznick
Best Director	Victor Fleming
Best Actress	Vivien Leigh
Best Supporting Actress	Hattie McDaniel
Best Screenplay	Sidney Howard
Best Colour Photography	Ernest Haller
Best Art Direction	William Cameron Menzies
Best Editing	Hal C. Kern
Best Interior Decoration	Lyle Wheeler

ACADEMY NOMINATIONS

Best Actor	Clark Gable
Best Supporting Actress	Olivia de Haviland
Best Original Score	Max Steiner
Best Sound Recording	Thomas T. Moulton
Best Special Effects	Jack Cosgrove, Fred Albin, Arthur Johns

BEST PICTURE

Gone with the Wind

STARS OF 1939

Mickey Rooney, Tyrone Power
Spencer Tracy, Clark Gable
Shirley Temple

1939 Blockbusters

*The Wizard of Oz • Union Pacific
Mr Smith Goes to Town
Jesse James • Idiot's Delight*

THE WORLD

- Germany invades Poland
- Second World War begins
- Italy invades Albania
- USSR invades Finland

MARGARET MITCHELL's much-loved novel of the American Civil War, a glorification of the South and an elegy to it, was published in 1936 and sold 1.38 million copies. It remained on the best-seller list for two years, winning the Pulitzer Prize. The film, also much-loved, had all the popular ingredients for box-office success: romantic melodrama, strong characters, stars with sex appeal and spectacular tableaux. Epic yet intimate, it was a testament to David O Selznick's assurance, command and conviction that *Gone With the Wind* could be as significant as *Birth of a Nation*.

Selznick began filming before he had cast the part of Scarlett O'Hara. His two years international search for the ideal actress received worldwide publicity. Actresses who were considered for the role included Jean Arthur, Tallulah Bankhead, Joan Bennett, Claudette Colbert, Joan Crawford, Bette Davis, Irene Dunn, Paulette Goddard, Jean Harlow, Katharine Hepburn, Miriam Hopkins, Carole Lombard and Norma Shearer. There was a great deal of resentment when an English actress landed the role.

Scarlett (Fiddle-de-de) O'Hara, an artful, egotistical Southern belle, flirted with all the men. She was a devious, selfish, capricious, tempestuous, wilful, scheming bitch, who had a romantic obsession for Ashley Wilkes, her neighbour.

At three hours and 40 minutes, *Gone With the Wind* was the longest film Hollywood had yet produced and the first to need an interval.

Clark Gable, synonymous with romantic adventurers in the 1930s, was the public's overwhelming choice for Rhett Butler, rogue, gambler, murderer, blockade runner and war profiteer. (Margaret Mitchell's own choice had been Basil Rathbone.) Gable didn't want to play Rhett for precisely the reason that he was the public's choice, feeling that he could never measure up to their individual expectations. Rhett Butler was no gentleman and Scarlett was no lady. "You need to be kissed often by somebody who knows how to do it," he told her. They were two of a kind. He thought a good whipping would do her good. When she refused to sleep with him, he raped her. Margaret Mitchell never saw his behaviour as marital rape, only as mutual pleasure; and that was how the scene was interpreted on screen.

Leslie Howard hadn't wanted to play the aesthetic and disillusioned Ashley, feeling he had already played far too many gentle and ineffectual characters. Olivia de Haviland, as the charitable and frail Melanie, made her too-good-to-be-true saintliness totally convincing. Her warmth and honesty enriched the role. Hattie McDaniel, cast as the larger-than-life Mammmy, was the first black person to win an Academy Award. Margaret Mitchell always insisted that Prissy (the silly, cowardly, lying servant girl with the high-pitch, squeaky voice, played by Butterfly McQueen) was based on a real person. The racism of the novel was toned down in the film and the Ku Klux Klan were kept off the screen.

What gave *Gone with the Wind* its strength was that the romantic fiction was always surrounded by authentic period settings and props. The historical events served as counterpoints to the personal drama. The most famous single sequence was the crane shot of the dead and wounded soldiers lying in the Atlanta railway yard. But there were other memorable moments: Rhett bidding $150 dollars to dance with Scarlett at a fund-raising ball when she was in widow's weeds (for the death of her first husband)

> " Forget it, Louis, no Civil War picture ever made a nickel. "
>
> *Irving Thalberg to Louis B. Mayer*

"Do you never shirk from marrying men you don't love?" Clark Gable and Vivien Leigh in Gone with the Wind.

and their escape from burning Atlanta, then the largest fire ever staged on film and achieved by burning the studio's backlot.

The ending, with Rhett finally walking out on Scarlett, was unforgettable. "If you go, where shall I go? What shall I do?" she cried. "Frankly, my dear, I don't give a damn." The censors in the Hays Code office wanted to cut the line but they were persuaded to keep it in and merely fined Selznick $5000 dollars for the profanity. The riposte was the perfect curtain. But Scarlett had the last word: "I'll go home. I'll think of some way to get him back. After all, tomorrow is another day."

Gone with the Wind, seven months in the shooting, went through three directors – George Cukor, Victor Fleming and Sam Wood – and six writers, including Scott Fitzgerald and Ben Hecht. Gable complained that Cukor was spending more time on the actresses than on him and got him fired. When Fleming took over, he hammed up the melodrama. Cukor, meanwhile, continued to coach Leigh and de Haviland in secret. Wood stepped in when Fleming had a nervous breakdown brought on by Leigh's tantrums and Selznick's constant interference. Fleming and Wood split the direction. Fleming, thinking the film would be the biggest white elephant of all time, rejected the opportunity to buy lucrative shares in the production.

The most eagerly awaited premiere took place in Atlanta, Georgia. In London, *Gone with the Wind* played for four years right through the Second World War. It would go on to be one of the biggest blockbusters again on its re-releases in 1948 and 1968.

The picture is an event, the greatest ever to date in motion picture production… No actor and a role were ever so perfectly wed as Clark Gable and Rhett Butler.
Hollywood Reporter

Is it the greatest motion picture ever made? Possibly not, although it is the greatest motion mural we have ever seen and the most ambitious film-making venture in Hollywood's spectacular history.
The New York Times

Mightiest achievement in the history of the motion picture.
Film Daily

Gone with the Wind is a first-rate piece of Americana.
Time

It is a monumental picture! Standing alone in its class, *Gone with the Wind* defies a reviewer to put into print its fabulous achievement.
The New York Herald Tribune

1940 • Boom Town

CREDITS

Big John McMasters	Clark Gable
Square John Sand	Spencer Tracy
Betsy Bartlett	Claudette Colbert
Karen Vanmeer	Hedy Lamarr
Luther Aldrich	Frank Morgan
Harry Compton	Lionel Atwill

Studio	MGM
Director	Jack Conway
Producer	Sam Zimbalist
Screenplay	John Lee Mahin
Photography	Harold Rosson
Music	Franz Waxman

AWARDS

ACADEMY AWARDS

None

ACADEMY NOMINATIONS

Best Cinematography Harold Rosson
Best Special
 Effects Arnold Gillespie

BEST PICTURE

Rebecca

STARS OF 1940

Mickey Rooney
Tyrone Power
Spencer Tracy
Clark Gable
Shirley Temple

1940 Blockbusters

Pinocchio
Northwest Mounted Police
The Road to Singapore
The Great Dictator
The Philadelphia Story

THE WORLD

- Winston Churchill Prime Minister
- Evacuation of Dunkirk
- Battle of Britain
- Italy declares war on Britain
- Trotsky assassinated in Mexico

BOOM TOWN was a big, oil-gushing, cliché-ridden, rags-to-riches saga, which was at its best in its early parts which had the feel of an old pioneer film. The most dramatic moment was a blazing oil-well, which was put out by blowing it up with nitroglycerine, a dangerous business.

Big John McMasters (Clark Gable) and Square John Sand (Spencer Tracy), two wildcat oil prospectors, looking for oil in unlikely places in 1918, joined forces. The sprawling story followed their failures and successes, their friendship and enmity. It tended to be very repetitive. They got rich. They got poor. They got rich. The audience was never emotionally involved. Big John's marital problems were not interesting and Square John's efforts to solve them were ludicrous. Gable, who had worked as a tool-dresser in the Oklahoma oilfields in his teens, was cast as the bad guy, a womaniser, who was constantly unfaithful to his loyal and long-suffering wife (Claudette Colbert). Tracy was the good guy, noble and stoic, standing by the woman he loves, even though she had married McMaster rather than him. He was even willing to marry McMasters' mistress (Hedy Lamarr), a calculating femme fatale he loathed, naively thinking that it would stop her affair with McMasters.

> " The guy's good. There's nobody in the business who can touch him, and you're a fool to try. And the bastard knows it, so don't fall for that humble stuff. "
>
> *Clark Gable on Spencer Tracy*

McMasters found a monopoly in defiance of the anti-trust laws and was indicted. In court he was accused of being "a typical economic royalist and Bourbon industrialist," who for reasons of self-indulgence had sought to ride roughshod over New York City. Sand turned up, unexpectedly, to speak up in his favour: "He is an oil man with the right idea what to do with our oil. It's always been his breed who has opened up the country and made it what it is."

Sand also gave the court a rousing speech in favour of capitalism. "Is it getting to be out of line in these United States for a man like him to make a million dollars with his brain and his hands? Because if this is true, we had better rewrite the land of opportunity stuff." The speech (well delivered by Tracy) was the sort of thing cinema-goers might have expected in a Frank Capra film, although the speech wouldn't have been in favour of capitalism and it would have come as a climax to all that had gone on before and not had the tacked-on feeling it had here.

There was plenty of easy knockabout comedy for the fans: Gable and Tracy fell flat on their faces into oozing mud and later appeared in long underwear. They also had an extended fist fight, a bit of rough and tumble, a scene straight out of a screwball comedy, in which neither of them got really hurt.

Boom Town was the third and last film Tracy made with Gable, the other two being *San Francisco* and *Test Pilot*. Tracy, fed up with second billing, vowed he would never take second billing again.

Here is man and woman stuff in a balance calculated with shrewdest showmanship to hit all classes of universal entertainment.
Daily Variety

The story no doubt is nonsensical but its impetus is irresistible, and there is no time to ponder the narrative values.
The Times

More colourful action in the oil fields and less agitation indoors might have made *Boom Town* a great picture.
The New York Times

If there was ever a box-office natural — it's it.
Hollywood Reporter

"Don't call me shorty!" Spencer Tracy and Clark Gable as two wildcatters in Boom Town.

1941 • Sergeant York

CREDITS

Sergeant York	Gary Cooper
Pastor	Walter Brennan
Grace	Joan Leslie
Major Buxton	Stanley Ridges
Pusher Ross	George Tobias
Mother York	Margaret Wycherly
George York	Dickie Moore

Studio	Warner Bros
Director	Howard Hawks
Producer	Jesse L Lasky, Hal B Wallis
Screenplay	Abem Finkel
	Harry Chandlee, Howard Koch
	John Huston
Photography	Sol Polito
	Arthur Edeson
Music	Max Steiner

AWARDS

ACADEMY AWARDS

Best Actor	Gary Cooper
Best Editing	William Holmes

ACADEMY NOMINATIONS

Best Picture	Jesse L. Lasky and Hal B. Wallis
Best Director	Howard Hawks
Best Supporting Actor	Walter Brennan
Best Supporting Actress	Margaret Wycherley
Best Original Screenplay	Harry Chandlee, Abem Finkel, John Huston and Howard Koch
Best Black and White Cinematography	Sol Polito
Best Score for Drama	Max Steiner
Best Black and White Interior Decoration	John Hughes and Fred MacLean
Best Sound Recording	Nathan Levinson

BEST PICTURE

How Green Was My Valley

STARS OF 1941

Mickey Rooney • Clark Gable
Abbott and Costello • Bob Hope
Spencer Tracy

1941 Blockbusters

Fantasia
How Green Was My Valley
The Road to Zanzibar
Ball of Fire
The Little Foxes

THE WORLD

- Germany invades Soviet Union
- Japan bombs Pearl Harbor
- USA declares war on Japan
- All Jews in Germany required to wear yellow star

SERGEANT YORK was made at a time when the United States was only thinking about involvement in another war. It was released shortly before Pearl Harbour and made a powerful call to arms, jolting the nation out of its isolationism. The story had a strong religious message. Jingoism was given God's blessing.

Sergeant York, one of the most decorated heroes of the First World War, had killed 25 and captured 132 Germans single-handed. Marshal Foche said it was the greatest thing accomplished by any private soldier of all the armies in Europe. How did he do it? "I guess he must have surrounded them," said one wag. "I reckon the Good Lord was protecting me," said York.

Jesse L Lansky had seen York in the 1919 Armistice Day Parade and had wanted to make a film of his story; but York had always refused to make capital out of his heroism. He was only persuaded to change his mind when he was told that it was his patriotic duty. The screenplay was based on his War Diaries.

York, born in an isolated valley in the Cumberland Mountains of Tennessee, was, initially, an immature country yokel, a well-known hell-raiser, bar-room brawler and boisterous drunk until he got religion when lightening struck and hurled his twisted rifle from his hand. (York was utterly mortified by this big Hollywood embellishment, feeling it trivialised his conversion.) When war was declared he beame a conscientious objector. He believed in the Bible and the ten commandments. His application for exemption was denied.

The question was whether he would fight? His commanding officer gave him leave to think about it. He went back to the mountains to ponder if there was any difference between defending God and defending his country. "What are we fighting for?" he asked his mother. "I don't rightly know," she replied. Finally, in an uncomfortable parallel, he found there wasn't much difference between shooting turkeys back home and shooting Germans in Europe.

York, aged 54, attended the premiere, escorted by a guard of honour. He expressed the wish that the film would contribute to national unity in the hour of danger. His belief had remained intact. He still denounced war but recognised there were just wars. "I killed," he said, "to save lives." He gave the money he earned to building a Bible school.

Gary Cooper, a big, lanky fellow, six feet two inches tall, brown hair, blue eyes, naturally taciturn, was York's first choice. Cooper didn't feel he could do justice to the biography of a living man. It was put to him that he had a patriotic duty to make the film. His performance was admired for its conviction, integrity, humility and nobility. *Sergeant York* established him as a folk hero and won him his first Oscar. (His second was for *High Noon*). He dedicated the Oscar to York, saying it wasn't Cooper who had won the award but York and all that he had done, to the best of his ability, was to try and be York.

Walter Brennan appeared as priest and mentor, leading the congregation in a

> ❝ Sergeant York and I had quite a few things in common even before I played him on the screen. We both were raised in the mountains – Tennessee for him, Montana for me – and I learned to ride and shoot as a natural part of growing up. ❞
>
> *Gary Cooper*

"People back home used to say I could shoot a rifle before I was weaned. They were exaggerating some. Gary Cooper as Sergeant York.

rousing hymn, "Give us that old time religion. It can take us all to heaven." Sixteen-year-old Joan Leslie played his sweetheart. Margery Wycherly, who played his mother, had very little dialogue; it was practically a silent film performance. Her fine, crusty old face didn't need dialogue.

President Theodore Roosevelt attended a preview. "I was really thrilled," he told York. "Of course, I didn't care so much for the killing and I guess you feel that way about it, too." York said, "Of course." But it was Sol Polito's photography of the soldiers coming out of the trenches and being mown down which stayed chiefly in the memory.

The performance of Gary Cooper in the title role holds the picture together magnificently, and even the most unfavourable touches are made palatable because of him. He is the gaunt, clumsy yokel, the American hayseed to the life.
The New York Times

Sergeant York, one of the greatest entertainments of all time. A Yankee Doodle Dandy that I urge everyone to see.
Walter Winchell

I came out of the film feeling that Sergeant York would be better employed felling trees than felling Germans.
Tribune

1942 • Mrs Miniver

CREDITS

Mrs Miniver	Greer Garson
Clem Miniver	Walter Pidgeon
Carol Beldon	Teresa Wright
Lady Beldon	Dame May Whitty
Foley	Reginald Owen
Mr Ballard	Henry Travers
Vin Miniver	Richard Ney
Vicar	Henry Wilcoxon
Toby Miniver	Christopher Severn
German Flyer	Helmut Dantine

Studio	MGM
Director	William Wyler
Producer	Sidney Franklin
Screenplay	Arthur Wimperis
George Froeschel, James Hilton	
	Claudine West
Photography	Joseph Ruttenberg
Music	Herbert Stothart

AWARDS

ACADEMY AWARDS

Best Picture	Sidney Franklin
Best Direction	William Wyler
Best Actress	Greer Garson
Best Supporting Actress	Teresa Wright
Best Screenplay	Arthur Wimperis,
George Froeschel, James Hilton	
	and Claudine West
Best Black and White	
Cinematography	Joseph Ruttenberg

ACADEMY NOMINATIONS

Best Actor	Walter Pidgeon
Best Supporting Actor	Henry Travers
Best Supporting	
Actress	Dame May Whitty
Best Film Editing	Harold F. Kress
Best Sound Recording	
	Douglas Shearer
Best Special Effects	A. Arnold
Gillespie, Warren Newcombe	
	Douglas Shearer

BEST PICTURE

Mrs Miniver

STARS OF 1942

Abbott and Costello • Clark Gable
Gary Cooper • Mickey Rooney
Bob Hope

1942 Blockbusters

Bambi
Random Harvest
Yankee Doodle Dandy
Rear the Wild Wind

THE WORLD

- Battle of Stalingrad
- Rommel defeated at El Alamein
- First 'Blockbuster' bomb dropped
  on Stuttgart

MRS MINIVER, which had gone into production before Pearl Harbour, was patriotic propaganda designed to strengthen American support for the British allies in the Second World War. The film, strong on courage and faith, was admired by both Prime Minister Churchill and President Roosevelt. Churchill said that the film was more valuable than six divisions. Joseph Goebbels, Head of Nazi propaganda, said it was exactly the sort of film the Germans should be making.

The story, based on articles by Jan Struther in *The Times*, started just before the outbreak of war and ended with the first big air-raids. It told a story of love, separation and bereavement. Today, Mrs Miniver may seem a quaint, dated, period piece, slightly absurd and dreadfully patronising to the working classes, but in the dark days of the war, it had a powerful emotional appeal.

The Minivers were an average middle-class family in "happy, easy-going England, who found themselves fighting desperately for their way of life and for life itself." Mrs Miniver, reading *Alice in Wonderland* in a home-made air-raid shelter while bombs fell all around her, was a symbol of the courageous British mother and stolid housewife during the Blitz.

> " As I saw it, *Mrs Miniver* was perfect propaganda for the British because it was a story about a family, about the kind of people audiences care about. "
>
> *William Wyler*

Greer Garson, so serene, so glam, so ladylike, looked very dreamy and was far too young for the role and, indeed, had not wanted to play it, not liking the idea of having a grown-up son. She was 34. Richard Ney, who played her son, was 27. (They began an affair and married shortly after the film was released.)

Pipe-smoking Mr Miniver (a stolid if somewhat dull Walter Pidgeon) took his boat to help in the evacuation of 400,000 soldiers at Dunkirk. "Wouldn't have missed it for the world," he said with classic British understatement. The sequence was shot with miniature models, and was not any the less moving for that, the number of little ships growing with each static still.

While her husband was away doing his bit, Mrs Miniver found a German pilot (Hemlmut Dantine) in the kitchen and dealt with him single-handed. Initially, she was compassionate, almost motherly towards the poor young man, who could have been her own son, but he gradually turned into a raving Nazi swinehund, boasting how 30,000 people had been killed in two hours in Rotterdam. When Mrs Miniver complained they were innocent women and children, he retorted hysterically that they were not innocent. "They were against us!" Mrs Miniver did what any British woman would have done in the circumstances. She slapped his face.

Vin Miniver was rebelling against the British class system. "You must excuse my son," said his dad, "he's just down from Oxford." Vin fell in love with the daughter of the village matriarch, who disapproved of her daughter marrying beneath her. The matriarch was acted by Dame May Whitty as if she were a formidable relation of Queen Mary. Mrs Miniver argued that in war, time was so precious for the young that marriage was the right thing. The old lady's change of mind and character were totally predictable.

On the night of their engagement, Vin was called into action and took part in the Battle of Britain. His fiancée knew that he might be killed any day, any hour. "We

"This is the people's war. It is our war. Greer Garson and Walter Pidgeon in Mrs Miniver.

mustn't waste time with fear," she said. "If I must lose him, there will be a lifetime for tears." The screenplay cunningly led the audience to believe that they could expect the death of the young man, but it was the two-week bride (nice Teresa Wright), who was killed, riddled with machine-gun bullets while travelling in a car with Mrs Miniver.

The film ended in the village's bombed-out church where the vicar preached a rousing Churchillian sermon: "There's scarcely a household which hasn't been struck… Why in all conscience should they be the ones to suffer? Why these? Are they our soldiers? Are they our fighters? Why should they be sacrificed? This is not only a war of soldiers in uniforms, it is a war of all the people and it must be fought not only on the battlefields but in the cities and the valleys, in the factories and on the farms, in the home and the heart of every man, woman and child who loves freedom. They will inspire us with an unbreakable determination to free ourselves and those who come after us from the tyranny and terror that threaten to strike us down. This is the people's war. It is our war. We are the fighters. Fight it then." It only remained for the congregation to sing "Onward Christian Soldiers" and the soundtrack to play Elgar's *Land of Hope and Glory.* The sermon was later printed on leaflets and dropped over allied and enemy lines.

The most moving, sensitive and inspirational film that has come out of the war yet in any country.
The Observer

There has been nothing to touch the understated eloquence of this magnificent and moving dramatisation of The Battle of Britain.
The New York Herald Tribune

William Wyler directs these family affairs with such warmth and good taste that *Mrs Miniver* packs more emotional wallop than any other fictional war film to date.
Life

A great war picture that photographs the inner meaning instead of the outward realism of the Second World War.
Time

1943 • This is the Army

CREDITS

Jerry Jones	George Murphy
Eileen Dibble	Joan Leslie
Johnny Jones	Lt Ronald Reagan
Maxie Twardofsky	George Tobias
Sgt McGee	Alan Hale
Eddie Dibble	Charles Butterworth
Irving Berlin	Irving Berlin
Kate Smith	Kate Smith
Studio	Warner Bros
Director	Michael Curtiz
Producer	Jack L Warner
	Hal B Wallis
Screenplay	Casey Robinson
	Capt Claude Binyon
Photography	Bert Glennon
Music	Ray Heindorf

AWARDS

ACADEMY AWARDS

Best Score (Musical) Ray Heindorf

ACADEMY NOMINATIONS

Best Interior Decoration (Color)
John Hughes,
Lt. John Koenig
George James Hopkins
Best Sound Recording
Nathan Levinson

BEST PICTURE

Casablanca

STARS OF 1943

Betty Grable
Bob Hope
Abbott and Costello
Bing Crosby
Gary Cooper

1943 Blockbusters

For Whom the Bell Tolls
The Song of Bernadette
Stage Door Johnny
A Guy Named Joe
Casablanca

THE WORLD

- Italy surrenders to Allies
- Mussolini deposed.
- Fascist Party ends
- Casablanca Conference

IRVING BERLIN's *This Is the Army*, a patriotic all-male revue performed by men of the armed forces, opened on Broadway on the 4 July 1942. It was specifically designed to be a money-raiser and morale-booster. The show followed the same pattern as Irving Berlin's First World War all-male revue, *Yip! Yip! Yaphunk*, and included some of the old material.

The film was divided into three distinct parts. It began in an army camp in the First World War with soldiers putting on their own show and it was such a success that they transferred it to Broadway. The first part closed with the GIs getting their marching orders while they were still on stage and exiting down the centre aisle through the auditorium to the waiting trucks which would take them to the docks and France and the war. There had been a similar scene in Irving Berlin's 1938 film, *Alexander's Ragtime Band*, a patriotic tribute to songwriter George M Cohan played by James Cagney.

The second part, set just after America's entry into the Second World War, opened with Kate Smith singing "God Bless America". The third part was the show itself. The songs included the rousing "This Is the Army, Mr Jones", the heartsick "I Left My Heart at the Stage Door Canteen", the stylish black number, "What the Well-Dressed Man in Harlem Will Wear" (which had boxer Joe Louis in punching form) and the slushy "What Does He Look Like?"

Irving Berlin, no singer, dressed in First World War uniform, sang "Oh! How I Hate To Get Up in the Morning", a song he had sung in "Yip! Yip! Yaphunk". The transvestite items, which had been such a feature of the stage show, were reduced for reasons of film censorship and for propaganda reasons. Nobody wanted the enemy to think the US army was a bunch of sissies.

Lt. Ronald Reagan played a young soldier whose best mate had died at Pearl Harbour and he didn't want to get married while there was any chance that his wife would end up a war widow. His girlfriend (Joan Leslie) pointed out that it was their patriotic duty to get married: "We're free people fighting to be free, free to marry, free to raise a family… We're all in this together, women as well as men… I want to be part of you… If we want to get married, let's get married." The young man had no choice but to get married. She had brought along an army chaplain.

This Is the Army was recognised by the President as making a notable and effective stimulation to civilian morale. Its message was loud and clear: in wartime, singers, dancers and comedians have as important a part to play as the fighting men. Wherever the film was shown, it was accompanied by military bands and 4000 lb Blockbuster bombs. It became every filmgoers' patriotic duty to see the film, hence its enormous success.

This Is the Army, produced on a non-profit basis, raised nearly $10 million for Army Emergency Relief and Irving Berlin received a Medal of Merit for his work on the stage and screen versions.

> **"** War is a pretty grim business, and sometimes a song or a smile is just as vital to an army as food. Teach your men to fight, naturally, but don't discourage their attempts to entertain one another. As a matter of fact, encourage them. **"**
>
> *Commanding Officer in the film*

The cast of This is the Army *was the only integrated Second World War company in the US armed forces.*

This is the Army is still the freshest, the most enchanting, the most endearing, the most rousing musical tribute to the American fighting man that has come out of the Second World War.
The New York Times

It's democracy in action to the hilt. It's showmanship and patriotism combined to a super-duper Yankee Doodle degree.
Variety

It offers cinemaudiences the rare pleasure of feeling generous towards a generous job.
Time

1944 • Going My Way

CREDITS

Father O'Malley	Bing Crosby
Father Fitzgibbon	Barry Fitzgerald
Jenny Linden	Rise Stevens
Father Timothy	Frank McHugh
Ted Haines Jr	James Brown
Carol James	Jean Heather
Haines Sr	Gene Lockheart
Studio	Paramount
Director	Leo McCarey
Producer	Leo McCarey
Screenplay	Frank Butler
	Frank Cavett
Photography	Lionel Lindon
Music	James van Heusen

AWARDS

ACADEMY AWARDS

Best Picture	Leo McCarey
Best Direction	Leo McCarey
Best Actor	Bing Crosby
Best Supporting Actor	
	Barry Fitzgerald
Best Screenplay	
Frank Butler and Frank Cavett	
Best Original Story	Leo McCarey
Best Song	
'Swinging on a Star' by James Van Heusen and Johnny Burke	

ACADEMY NOMINATIONS

Best Actor:	Barry Fitzgerald
Best Supporting Actor:	
	Barry Fitzgerald
Best Black and White Cinematography:	Lionel Linden
Best Film Editing:	Leroy Stone

BEST PICTURE

Going My Way

STARS OF 1944

Bing Crosby
Gary Cooper
Bob Hope
Betty Grable
Spencer Tracy

1944 Blockbusters

Meet Me in St Louis
Since You Went Away
Thirty Seconds Over Tokyo
Hollywood Canteen
The White Cliffs of Dover

THE WORLD

• Normandy invasion (D-Day landings)
• Hitler conscripts children over 10
• Paris liberated
• Attempt to assassinate Hitler fails

GOING MY WAY was something of a departure for Bing Crosby, who was cast as a young, athletic, music-loving, golf-playing, Catholic priest: a regular guy, who wore a clerical collar and a Maurice Chevalier boater. Father 'Chuck' O'Malley was appointed curate to St Dominic's, a poverty-stricken church in a New York slum parish. The church's debts were so bad that it was in danger of being pulled down to make way for a car park. It was O'Malley's assignment to reorganise things and persuade the cold-blooded businessman, who owned the mortgage, to save the church.

Father Fitzgibbon, who had been in charge of St Dominic's for 45 years, was set in his ways and resented O'Malley's arrival. Irish actor Barry Fitzgerald's memorable "little-old-guy" performance – testy, stubborn, absent-minded – was a sly bit of scene-stealing. The appeal of Leo McCarey's production was in the friction between the progressive young man and the staid old man and the clash of their acting styles. Crosby didn't act. Fitzgerald didn't stop acting. He was nominated by the Academy for best

> Would you like to swing on a star
> Carry moonbeams in a jar
> And be better off than you are,
> Or would you rather be a mule?

Lyric by Johnny Burke

actor and best supporting actor, the first and only time this has happened. *Life Magazine* described "his performance was one of the finest things in 50 years of motion pictures."

There was an affecting scene when Fitzgibbon came back from seeing his Bishop having been informed for the first time that he had been put out to pasture and his junior was in charge. He behaved like a little boy and ran away. There was also a delightful moment when Chuck sang the old man to sleep and as he tiptoed out of the bedroom, Fitzgibbon wished him a good night. The sparring was both comic and touching. Many cinemagoers were sorry they didn't repeat their partnership the following year in *The Bells of St Mary's*.

Bing Crosby, America's most popular crooner of the 1930s (his records sold by the million) became America's most popular film star in the 1940s. He had a natural warmth and his sincerity came to be seen as a symbol of stability during the Depression and the war years. He sang in a relaxed, casual manner. "Going My Way" (a song to show religion could be bright) was sung three times when once was more than enough. He had a song for every occasion. He was able to shame a couple, who were living in sin, into marriage, merely by singing to them.

O'Malley also saved the souls of a gang of street urchins, who had been terrorising the district. He won their confidence by buying them hot dogs and taking them to baseball games and to the movies. He turned them into sweet choir boys, who quickly graduated from "Three Blind Mice" to Gounod's *Ave Maria*. In no time at all they were teaming up with one of The New York Met's leading opera singers (played by soprano Risë Stevens), a former girlfriend of O'Malley's, and auditioning "Going My Way". The music publishers turned the song down. "Schmalz," they said, "wasn't selling this season." Very sensibly, they preferred "Swinging on a Star".

O'Malley transformed the young hoodlums into Botticelli angels. The boys (who had never looked like Dead End Kids in the first place) were played by the Robert Mitchell Boy's Choir, supplemented by Stanley Clements in his familiar role of tough juvenile.

"What made you become a priest?" Barry Fitzgerald and Bing Crosby in Going My Way.

Clements had a nice vaudeville routine when he was slapping the face of his best mate, who wanted to opt out of the choir.

The film ended with the dedication of the new church and the reunion of Father Fitzgibbon with his 90-year-old mother. The choir sang his favourite, old Irish lullaby, *Too-ra-loo-ra-loora*. There were those who found the ending nauseating but they were in the minority.

Going My Way, a resolute tearjerker, warm and human, was hugely popular, largely because of Crosby's following. The Roman Catholic Church was delighted with the free propaganda. Pope Pius XII gave a private audience to Crosby and thanked him for his portrayal.

Many Catholics and non-Catholics are likely to gag at some of the sentimentality.
Commonwealth

McCarey. a director of remarkable ability which he obstinately lavishes on second-rate material, wrings genuine pathos from the tritest situations.
The Sunday Times

I should not feel safe in recommending it to anyone but a simple-hearted sentimentalist with a taste for light music.
Punch

I knew he [Bing Crosby] could play golf like a pro; he can act like one, too.
The New Statesman

1945 • The Bells of St Mary's

CREDITS

Father O'Malley	Bing Crosby
Sister Benedict	Ingrid Bergman
Bogardus	Henry Travers
Joe Gallagher	William Gargan
Sister Michael	Ruth Donnelly
Dr McKay	Rhys Williams
Mrs Breen	Una O'Connor
Studio	Rainbow
Director	Leo McCarey
Producer	Leo McCarey
Screenplay	Dudley Nichols
Photography	George Barnes
Music	Robert Emmett Dolan

AWARDS

ACADEMY AWARDS

Best Sound Recording
Stephen Dunn

ACADEMY NOMINATIONS

Best Picture	Leo McCarey
Best Actor	Bing Crosby
Best Actress	Ingrid Bergman
Best Director	Leo McCarey
Best Film Editing	Harry Marker
Best Score in Drama or Comedy	
	Robert Emmett Dolan
Best Song	

'Aren't You Glad You're You' by
James Van Heusen
and Johnny Burke

BEST PICTURE

The Lost Weekend

STARS OF 1945

Bing Crosby
Van Johnson
Greer Garson
Betty Grable
Spencer Tracy

1945 Blockbusters

The Valley of Decision
Leave Her to Heaven
Spellbound
Anchors Aweigh
The Lost Weekend

THE WORLD

- Second World War ends in Europe
- Atomic bombs dropped on Hiroshima and Nagasaki
- Death of Franklin D Roosevelt
- Nuremberg War Crimes Trials

THE BELLS OF ST MARY'S was more Catholic propaganda. It followed the same sentimental and humorous route as *Going My Way*, only it wasn't as good and it didn't ring as true. Bing Crosby repeated his role of the nonchalant, trouble-shooting, singing padre. This time he was appointed chaplain to St Mary's, another rundown and overcrowded New York city school in a tough parish.

"Have you ever been up to your neck in nuns before?" warned his housekeeper. The last incumbent had evidently left in a wheelchair. The very first thing Father 'Chuck' O'Malley did was to give all the children a holiday. There was the inevitable clash between him and the Sister Superior but their misunderstandings were too slight to be dramatic. They both employed trickery and deceit, each exploiting their pet pupil. He taught a girl how to write an essay by singing "Aren't You Glad You're You?" She taught a boy how to box and predictably she got a sock in the jaw. There was one nice visual gag, showing O'Malley reading the Bible and Sister reading a boxing manual. She believed in maintaining academic standards, whereas he believed every pupil should pass his examinations, even if this meant lowering the standard.

When she walks on screen and says "Hello," people ask, "Who wrote that wonderful line of dialogue?"

Leo McCarey on Ingrid Bergman

Crosby was his usual whimsical, unflappable *Dial-O-For-O'Malley* self, a man, who liked people, who liked music and believed in broad-minded Christianity rather than dogma. He managed to reunite a husband and wife, who had been separated for 13 years, just by crooning "In the Land of the Beginning" to them. Crosby was the only crooner to win an Academy Award as an actor.

Ingrid Bergman had a natural serenity and charm as Sister Benedict, an idealised nun, who could wield a baseball bat and sing a folk song in Swedish. She thought O'Malley had been responsible for her losing her job. She was so grateful when (contrary to her doctor's advice) he told her that the only reason she was being sent away was because she had tuberculosis. She was so relieved. "Thank you, Father, you've made me so happy." Bergman's flawless complexion glowed with pleasure.

One of O'Malley's tasks was to persuade an irascible millionaire to change his mind about pulling down the school and turning it into a parking lot. The quickest method to reach him was through his heart. He, in fact, had a bad heart, and O'Malley persuaded the doctor to frighten him with thoughts of death. (Neither the priest nor the doctor saw anything wrong in this approach.) The millionaire was instantly transformed from Scrooge to Philanthropist, helping stray dogs over busy streets and ladies on to buses. The only way Henry Travers could play the character was as a bewildered simpleton, who suddenly appreciated it was more blessed to give than to receive when it was tax deductible.

The most enchanting scene was the Nativity Play as performed by kindergarten children. The five-year-old director (acted by Bobby Dolan, son of the film's musical director) also played Jesus and the Narrator. He firmly rejected O'Malley's suggestion that they should sing "Silent Night", opting instead for "Happy Birthday, Jesus".

"Did anyone ever tell you that you have a dishonest face — for a priest, I mean?" Bing Crosby and Ingrid Bergman in The Bells of St. Mary's.

The picture subtly and without malice illustrates the Catholic Church's unique and infallible flair for wheedling financial aid and from the most stubborn anti-Christian.
Kine Weekly

I was haunted by the film it might have been if they had substituted simple truth for cloying charm and if the characters had been allowed to be grave instead of facetious.
Sunday Graphic

The vulgarity goes without question, but when has the Church of Rome ever objected to vulgarity? Only the deeply irreligious, it would appear, are shocked.
The Spectator

1946 • The Best Years of Our Lives

CREDITS

Milly Stephenson	Myrna Loy
Al Stephenson	Frederic March
Fred Derry	Dana Andrews
Peggy Stephenson	Teresa Wright
Marie Derry	Virginia Mayo
Wilma Cameron	Cathy O'Donnell
Homer Parrish	Harold Russell
Butch Eagle	Hoagy Carmichael
Studio	Goldwyn
Director	William Wyler
Producer	Samuel Goldwyn
Screenplay	Robert E Sherwood
Photographer	Gregg Toland
Music	Hugo Friedhofer

AWARDS

ACADEMY AWARDS

Best Picture	Samuel Goldwyn
Best Direction	William Wyler
Best Actor	Frederic March
Best Supporting Actor	
	Harold Russell
Best Screenplay	
	Robert E. Sherwood
Best Editing	Daniel Mandell
Best Music Score of a Drama or a	
Comedy	Hugo Friedhofer

ACADEMY NOMINATIONS

Best Sound Recording
Gordon Sawyer

BAFTA AWARD

Best Film

BEST PICTURE

The Best Years of Our Lives

STARS OF 1946

Bing Crosby
Ingrid Bergman
Van Johnson
Gary Cooper
Bob Hope

1946 Blockbusters

The Jolson Story
Blue Skies
Saratoga Trunk
Notorious
The Road to Utopia

THE WORLD

- Iron Curtain descends – Cold War begins
- Chinese Civil War resumes
- UNESCO established
- Construction of first electronic digital computer

THE BEST YEARS OF OUR LIVES, powerful and popular, humorous and tragic, was socially relevant in the 1940s and designed to make Americans feel guilty about the way they were treating their war veterans.

Three servicemen – a soldier, a sailor and an airman – returning home at the end of the Second War World War, had difficulty readjusting to civilian life. Plagued by memories of the war and doubts about the future, they felt out of place both in the home and the workplace. The three men offered a cross-section of society and Robert E Sherwood's screenplay explored their problems with intelligence and compassion but made no attempt to provide any answers. The film was heartening, realistic and not afraid to preach.

The soldier (Frederic Marsh), a middle-aged sergeant, got promotion at the bank and became Vice President in charge of loans. The bank was portrayed as an inhuman, soulless place, denying citizens their rights. He had two key propaganda scenes. The first was when he questioned his boss's values. The second was when he made a drunken, satiric after-dinner speech to his fellow bankers and told them a parable about an officer, who was ordered to take a hill but since he didn't have any collateral, he didn't take the hill and the US lost the war. Marsh was at his best here rather than in his drunken, all-night binge, a scene which was very contrived and went on far too long. Dean White was excellent in a cameo role as a young farmer, a veteran with no collateral.

The sailor (Harold Russell) had lost both his hands and had to grapple, not only with articulated hooks and his frustration, but also with the well-intentioned consideration and distress of loved ones. He was engaged to "a swell girl" but was frightened she was only marrying him out of pity rather than love. He was played by a 32-year-old non-professional, an ex-paratroop sergeant, who had lost both his hands when a defective fuse exploded in his grasp. Russell was a natural actor, unaffected and affecting. His only previous screen experience had been in an army training film, *The Diary of a Sergeant*, in which he had demonstrated his skilful use of his prosthetic hands.

The airman (Dana Andrews), a much decorated ace-bomber, who still had nightmares, reliving the horrors of his bombing raids, came home to find his gin-soaked father and his blowsy mother-in-law living in the same old shack. He had married in haste and his wife has been unfaithful during his absence. He quickly discoverd that a good war record did not get him a job and he was back where he had started as a soda fountain jerk in a drug store.

Dana Andrews gave a convincing study of a man who had lost his self-esteem. He had a symbolic scene on an airfield surrounded by thousands of surplus aeroplanes waiting for the scrapyard. This scene carried more weight than the happy ending, which struck a false note. The airman fell in love with the sergeant's daughter. He told her: "It may take us years to get anywhere. We'll have no money, no decent place to live. We'll have to work, get kicked round." The daughter (Teresa Wright) looked absolutely radiant at the prospect.

Virginia Mayo played his wife, a shallow, brassy, steely good-time blonde, who worked in a night club and liked the idea of "a big hunk of heaven in uniform," but

> **"** I don't care if it doesn't make a nickel. I just want every man, woman and child in America to see it. **"**
>
> *Samuel Goldwyn*

"Last year, it was Kill Japs. This year, it's Make Money."
Harold Russell, Teresa Wright, Dana Andrews, Myrna Loy, Hoagy Carmichael and Frederic March in The Best Years of Our Lives.

when she found he was no longer the smooth operator she married, she quickly ditched him.

The acting was restrained throughout. The actresses wore their normal make-up. The actors wore no make-up. The clothes were grey, black and white. Gregg Toland's photography was particularly impressive in a famous deep focus shot which took in Russell at the piano in close-up, Andrews on the phone, right at the back of the screen, and Marsh somewhere in the middle trying to hear what Fred was saying to his daughter.

The essential humanity of the film will ensure a very wide appeal.
The Manchester Guardian

It is seldom that there comes a motion picture which can be wholly and enthusiastically endorsed not only as superlative entertainment but as food for quiet and humanising thought.
The New York Times

No piece of entertainment, however intelligent and thrilling, or beautiful, can justify so Wagnerian a length.
Tribune

In its sentiment, its code of accepted behaviour and its attitude towards a job of work done, it is wholly foreign to our [British] temperament. It would be the greatest mistake to judge this clever and beautifully acted film by our standard of decorum, because the people in it happen to speak our language.
The Observer

1947 • Duel in the Sun

CREDITS

Pearl Chavez	Jennifer Jones
Lewt McCanles	Gregory Peck
Jesse McCanles	Joseph Cotton
Senator McCanles	Lionel Barrymore
Scott Chavez	Herbert Marshall
The Sinkiller	Walter Huston
Mrs McCanles	Lillian Gish
Mrs Chavez	Tilly Losch
Sherrif	Charles Dingle
Sam Pierce	Charles Bickford
Sid	Scott McKay

Studio	Selznick International
Director	King Vidor
Producer	David O Selznick
Screenplay	David O Selznick
	Oliver HP Garrett
Photography	Lee Garmes
	Hal Rosson
	Ray Rennahan
Music	Dimitri Tiomkin

AWARDS

ACADEMY AWARDS

None

ACADEMY NOMINATIONS

Best Actress:　　　Jennifer Jones
Best Supporting Actress:
　　　　　　　　　　Lillian Gish

BEST PICTURE

Gentleman's Agreement

STARS OF 1947

Bing Crosby
Betty Grable
Ingrid Bergman
Gary Cooper
Humphrey Bogart

1947 Blockbusters

Welcome Stranger
Life with Father
Unconquered
The Egg and I
The Road to Rio

THE WORLD

- Independence of India and Pakistan
- House of UnAmerican Activities Committee begins hearings
- First British nuclear reactor built
- Dead Sea Scrolls found in Palestine

DUEL IN THE SUN, the most ballyhooed film since *Gone with the Wind*, was a vulgar parody of a torrid sex drama and so over-the-top that the censor demanded 47 cuts. Catholics, Protestants, Jews, The League of Decency, all condemned it, giving it excellent publicity. Boards in Memphis, Tennessee, Hartfield and Connecticut banned it. They didn't like the message of wrong triumphing over right. They didn't like lust being better than love, they didn't like the violence and the mockery of the church. Archbishop Cantwell said Catholics should not see it.

Duel in the Sun, based on the novel by Niven Busch and set in the hills of Tennessee, was the story of a half-bred Indian girl and the two brothers who loved her. She loved Jesse but lusted after Lewt. "I want to be a good girl," she said, trying ever so hard to resist him, but it was difficult when he was watching her take a swim in the nude and invading her bedroom and rapeing her. "I hate you!" she said but she kept coming back for more. "I want to go with you! I want you! Take me with you!" she screamed. But Lewt was only interested in a good time, not marriage. Torn between good and evil, Pearl succumbed to her passion. "I guess I'm trash, like my ma," she declared. Her ma, a dancer, had been shot *in flagrante delicto* with her lover by her father, a renegade Southern aristocrat.

> " A bizarre picture. I don't think the Old West was very like that. "
>
> *Gregory Peck*

Jennifer Jones, tiger-cat, sex-pot, glared, glowered, wore a low-cut dress and flashed her sex appeal in every scene. She seemed to spend most of her time on her knees, grovelling. The hell-fire preacher (written as caricature and played as such by Walter Huston) got quite carried away and described her as "a full-blossom woman to drive men crazy and curved in the flesh of temptation."

Gregory Peck played the lawless Lewt, a wild, vicious man, who had been spoiled by his dad and was given to murder, blowing up trains and shooting his brother. Lewt loved and despised Pearl. He also boasted he knew how to handle a sex-starved stallion, so, if anybody could have tamed Pearl, it really should have been him. Peck was basically too nice. He didn't do too much acting; he left that to Lionel Barrymore.

Barrymore was cast as a ruthless, belligerent, racist senator in a wheelchair, who was prepared to shoot unarmed men when his property was threatened by the railroad company. The sequence when his men rode to do battle with the railmen and the US cavalry arrived in the nick of time to stop the shooting was the high spot of the film. Barrymore had an unconvincing change of character and became a lonely old man in need of a friend. He claimed that it was "jealousy born of love that had made him cruel." Lillian Gish, who played his genteel and fragile wife, sang "Beautiful Dreamer" before she passed away.

Joseph Cotton played the good, decent Jesse, a lawyer, who had been banished by his father and had gone on to become Governor of the State. The final duel was not, as cinema-goers might have been expected, between him and Lewt, but between Pearl and Lewt. Having shot each other to ribbons, they died in each other's arms, but not before the wounded Pearl had crawled on her belly all over the rocks to reach him. "I love you," she said. "I love you," he said. "I had to do it," she said. "Of course, you did," he said. It was this preposterous, yet unforgettable, scene which earned *Duel in the Sun* its nickname, "Lust in the Dust."

Lust in the Dust. Jennifer Jones and Gregory Peck in Duel in the Sun.

King Vidor got the director's credit, but he quit before the shooting ended, fed up with David O Selznick's constant interference. Directors William Dieterle, Otto Brown, Reaves Eason, Josef von Sternberg, William Cameron Menzies and Chester Franklin all worked on the film at various times.

I would rate *Duel in the Sun* as the most dangerous film so far released this year, a film all set for popular success, a film to stir brooding ideas of violence in the hearts of too many people close-packed under our wet, grey skies.

Tribune

No redeeming virtue of decency, honesty, surprise, ingenuity, novelty or even fun.

News Chronicle

The whole thing fluctuates between the repellent and the ridiculous.

The Sunday Express

Wild stallions wouldn't drag me to see it again.

New Statesman and Nation

No film this year can match it for stupendous stupidity – and yet how entertaining it is!

Sunday Graphic

1948 • The Red Shoes

CREDITS

Boris Lermontov	Anton Walbrook
Victoria Page	Moira Shearer
Julian Craster	Marius Goring
Grisha Ljubov	Leonide Massine
Ivan Boleslawsky	Robert Helpmann
Sergei Ratov	Albert Basserman
Irina Boronskaja	Ludmilla Tcherina
Livy	Esmond Knight
Studio	Archers
Director	Michael Powell
	Emeric Pressburger
Producer	Michael Powell
	Emeric Pressburger
Screenplay	Michael Powell
	Emeric Pressburger
	Keith Winter
Photography	Jack Cardiff
Music	Brian Easdale

AWARDS

ACADEMY AWARDS

Best Score   Brian Easdale
Best Art Direction
   Hein Heckroth and Arthur Lawson

ACADEMY NOMINATIONS

Best Picture: Michael Powell
          and Emeric Pressburger
Best Screenplay
          Emeric Pressburger
Best Film Editing   Reginald Mills

BEST PICTURE

Hamlet

STARS OF 1948

Bing Crosby
Betty Grable
Abbott and Costello
Gary Cooper
Bob Hope

1948 Blockbusters

Gone with the Wind
The Paleface
Easter Parade
Red River
The Three Musketeers

THE WORLD

- Gandhi assassinated
- Russian blockade of West Berlin
- National Health introduced in UK
- Apartheid official policy in South Africa

THE RED SHOES, the first English film to be devoted to ballet, remains the most famous and most popular ballet film ever made. It success was precisely due to the dancing; yet the very things for which it was criticised – the backstage clichés, the melodramatic, novelette story-line and its corny theme of art versus romance – played no little part in its popularity.

Emeric Pressburger originally wrote *The Red Shoes* for Merle Oberon, Alexander Korda's mistress, but the production never got off the ground and he and Michael Powell retrieved the screenplay and offered it to a very reluctant Moira Shearer, premiere ballerina at the Sadler's Wells Company. (Ninette de Valois, artistic director, agreed to release her because she thought the publicity would be useful when the company went to America.) In England J Arthur Rank, facing bankruptcy, and with the film at 100% over budget, withdrew financial support while it was still in production. Korda came to the rescue, but when the film was ready, Rank refused to give it either a proper London premiere or a proper general release. "Nobody is going to go and see this nonsense," he said. In New York it played twice daily to full houses for 120 weeks.

An early dialogue between the great impresario, Boris Lermontov (Anton Walbrook) and a would-be ballerina, Victoria Page (Moira Shearer) set the scene and theme: "Why do you want to dance?" he asked. "Why do you want to live?" she replied. "I don't know exactly, but I must," he said. "That's my answer, too," she replied

> 66 I think the real reason why *The Red Shoes* was such a success was that we had all been told for ten years to go out and die for freedom and democracy, for this and that, and now that the war was over, *The Red Shoes* told us to go and die for art. 99
>
> *Michael Powell*

Page was forced to choose between her career and her marriage, when her composer-husband (Marius Goring) was sacked from the company. She chose marriage, but it wasn't long before she was back in the theatre. Her first night in Monte Carlo clashed with the first night of his opera in London. He insisted she gave up ballet. The last scene in the dressing room, a struggle between the impresario and composer for her soul, was a heterosexual replay of the Sergei Diaghilev, Vaslav Nijinsky and Romola de Pulazky triangle. Diaghilev, in love with Nijinsky, had sacked him when he married Romola.

The high spot of the film was an entirely original 13½-minute ballet to music by Brian Easdale, choreographed by Robert Helpmann, designed by Hein Heckroth and conducted by Sir Thomas Beecham. A wicked shoemaker made a pair of red shoes which gave the dancer great joy but they did not allow her to stop dancing. The dancer died of exhaustion. The ballet created its own world, which mirrored the off-stage psychological conflict. The two heroines fused. Impresario and composer were momentarily superimposed on to the dancers. The ballet – with its rapidly changing scene, time and costume, its ravishing colour, its striking pictorial design, its artistry, its imagination, its kitsch – was conceived entirely in film terms and thus was a true cinematic experience. Perhaps the most memorable single image was the ocean engulfing the stalls of Covent Garden. The sea was the audience applauding.

Mrs Tanqueray threw herself down a liftshaft, Tosca threw herself off the battlements, Anna Karenina threw herself under a train. Vicky Page threw herself off a balcony and

Robert Helpmann, Moira Shearer and Leonide Massine dance the ballet of The Red Shoes.

under a train. The suicide was much criticised for its gore and for being unbelievable, but the death was an extension of the ballet. The two heroines were indivisible, an artistic conceit. The red shoes took possession of the ballerina and drove her to her death. (The Hans Christian Andersen fairy tale was far gorier. The heroine's legs were chopped off by a woodsman with his axe.) After Page's death, the ballet went ahead without her, the spotlight taking on her role. This deeply affecting moment was based on real life: Anna Pavlova's death in 1931 had been marked in exactly the same way.

Anton Walbrook was totally convincing as the ruthless impresario, an attractive brute, a mixture of Svengali and Mephistopheles, a megalomaniac, who could have been inspired not only by Diaghilev, but also by Korda and even Michael Powell. With her natural beauty and Titian red hair, Moira Shearer was the most exciting British star since Vivien Leigh. There was a beautiful shot of her in a flowing evening gown mounting a seemingly endless flight of steps to Lermontov's villa, which could have been a scene out of a ballet. The role of the shoemaker was created and danced by Leonide Massine, former premier dancer at the Ballets Russes and successor to Nijinsky. Massine had also been sacked by Diaghilev when he got married.

The success of *The Red Shoes* inspired MGM to include a 19-minute ballet choreographed by Gene Kelly in Vincent Minnelli's *An American in Paris* in 1951, but there was no endeavour by Hollywood to make a true ballet film until *The Turning Point* in 1977.

The film is as individual as a painting, and its artistic success is unquestionable. By sheer beauty it will, I think, convert many who might normally resist a ballet film.

The Daily Express

There has never been a picture in which the ballet and its special, magic world, has been so beautifully and dreamily presented as the new British film, *The Red Shoes.*

The New York Times

Given a better story, this could have been a truly great film – possibly the greatest ballet film in the world.

Graphic

1949 • The Outlaw

CREDITS

Rio	Jane Russell
Billy	Jack Buetel
Pat Garrett	Thomas Mitchell
Doc Holliday	Walter Huston
Aunt Guadelupe	Mimi Aguglia
Studio	Howard Hughes
Director	Howard Hughes
Producer	Howard Hughes
Screenplay	Jules Furthman
Photography	Gregg Toland
Music	Victor Young

AWARDS

ACADEMY AWARDS
None

ACADEMY NOMINATIONS
None

BEST PICTURE

All the King's Men

STARS OF 1949

Bob Hope
Bing Crosby
Abbott and Costello
John Wayne
Gary Cooper

1949 Blockbusters

Jolson Sings Again
Battleground
The Sands of Iowa Jima
I Was a Male War Bride
Little Women

THE WORLD

- NATO alliance formed
- Mao Tse-tung declares People's Republic of China
- Creation of West and East Germany
- Republic of Ireland formed
- George Orwell's *1984* published

THE OUTLAW was a legend before it even got to the cinema. It was finished in 1941, but a lengthy argument with the Production Code Authority, an off-shoot of the Hayes Code, delayed its initial, restricted release until 1943. It was shown in one cinema in San Francisco. The cinema owner was arrested and the film broke box office records. Howard Hughes then withdrew it from general release until the end of the decade. The battle with the censor (which Hughes finally won, helping to diminish the power of the PCA) raised audience expectations, but by the time it arrived in the cinemas, denounced by cities, churches, critics and even the cinema industry itself, most people wondered what all the fuss had been about and felt that it hadn't been worth the wait. But that didn't stop the film from becoming the US's biggest blockbuster of the year.

> 66 How would you like to tussle with Russell? 99
>
> *Billboard Publicity*

The Outlaw was a second-rate B-Western, crudely acted, badly made, a caricature of cowboy horse-operas and so corny that it was greeted with gales of laughter. The British Board of Censors gave it a U certificate, the ultimate insult.

Far more interesting than the film was the publicity campaign organised by Russell Birdwell. The advertising was crude: "What are two great reasons for Jane Russell's rise to stardom?" Her cleavage was prominently displayed when she was on horseback fleeing from the Indians. The camera stayed on her 37½" bust, rather than on her pursuers. "Who wouldn't fight for a woman like this?" asked the posters, which showed Russell on a haystack sucking a piece of straw and described her as "mean, moody and magnificent... alluringly sultry and tempestuously romantic" and declared that "she gave the kind of savage dangerous love every woman longs to give."

The plot was based on the legend that Billy the Kid was not killed. Howard Hughes's screenplay centred on the sentimental and ambiguous relationship between Billy and Doc Holliday. Baby-face Billy flirted quite openly. "Doc, if you are not already fixed up, you can bunk with me." "No, thanks," said Doc, "I've got a girl." At times they were standing so unnaturally close to each other and the music was so romantic that you half expected them to go into a clinch.

Doc introduced Billy to Rio, a half-breed girl, not realising the two of them had already rolled about in the hay together. Doc asked her to do her best for the boy and she nursed him through his fever. "You're not going to die," she promised. "I'll keep you warm." And, true to her word, she got into bed with him, thinking, mistakenly he wasn't well enough to have sex. "Billy, you mustn't, you'll hurt yourself." The music on the soundtrack got very slushy. The camera, tactfully, took a long, long look at a blank wall. There was a great deal of innuendo in *The Outlaw*, but any sex always took place either off-screen or in dark shadow. Since Rio was a nice, respectable girl, she married Billy while he was still in a coma.

Sheriff Pat Garrett, Doc's former partner in crime, accused Billy of coming between him and Doc. Garrett behaved like a woman scorned: "Ever since you met him, you've treated me like a dog," he blubbed, "the best friend you've ever had." In real life Garrett shot Billy dead. In the film Garrett killed Doc and inscribed Billy's name on Doc's tomb. The Kid rode off into the sunset with Rio.

Jane Russell, chosen from numerous applicants during a nation-wide magazine publicity campaign, became the sex symbol for the 1940s. A former receptionist to a

Californian dentist's, she was 19 when she made the film and 27 when it was publically shown. Rio was merely a sex object, a small role in a low-cut dress with close-ups of a pouting mouth. Russell's acting was limited. (*The Tribune* critic said: "She can register three degrees of the sulky.") The equally inexperienced Jack Buetel wasn't much better as Billy and could generally be seen moving to his marker on the floor. The performances were as wooden and as artificial as its studio-bound sets. The older actors, Walter Huston and Thomas Mitchell as Doc and Garrett, hammed it up. The music on the soundtrack, alternating between the jaunty "I'm an Old Cowhand from the Rio Grande" and Tchaikovsky's *Pathetique*, signalled very loudly what the audience's reaction should be at any given point, just in case they weren't sure.

Howard Hawks, the original director, finally fed up with Howard Hughes's endless interference, quit just before the film was finished.

We dislike *The Outlaw* not because it is salacious but because it is not salacious enough, not frankly pornographic.
Tribune

A strong candidate for the floperoo of all time.
Time

It is blatant, vulgar, prurient and so silly as to amount to burlesque.
News Chronicle

As an actress Miss Russell remains strictly a torso.
The Daily Graphic

1950 • Samson and Delilah

CREDITS

Samson	Victor Mature
Delilah	Hedy Lamarr
The Saran of Gaza	George Sanders
Semadar	Angela Lansbury
Ahtur	Henry Wilcoxon
Miriam	Olive Deering
Saul	Russell Tamblyn
Studio	Paramount
Director	Cecil B DeMille
Producer	Cecil B DeMille
Screenplay	Harold Lamb
	Vladimir Jabotinsky
	Jesse Lasky Jr
	Fredric M Frank
Photography	George Barnes
Music	Victor Young

AWARDS

ACADEMY AWARDS

Best Colour Art Direction
    Hans Dreier and Walter Tyler
Best Set Decoration
    Sam Comer and Roy Moyer
Best Colour Costume Design
    Edith Head, Dorothy Jeakins,
    Eloise Jenssen, Gile Steele
    and Gwen Wakeling

ACADEMY NOMINATIONS

Best Colour Cinematography
    George Barnes
Best Score in Drama or Comedy
    Victor Young
Best Special Effects   Paul Lerpae
    and Deveraux Jennings

BEST PICTURE

All About Eve

STARS OF 1950

John Wayne
Bob Hope
Bing Crosby
Betty Grable
James Stewart

1950 Blockbusters

King Solomon's Mines
Cinderella
Annie Get Your Gun
Cheaper by the Dozen
Father of the Bride

THE WORLD

● Korean War starts
● China conquers Tibet
● First successful kidney transplant
● Arrest of Klaus Fuchs for selling
    atomic secrets

CECIL B DeMILLE was reputed to have said that every time he made a picture the critics' estimation of the public dropped by 10%. The trailer promised cinema-goers "shattering thrills, earth-shaking excitement and savage drama" and reminded them, just in case they didn't already know, that Samson was "the strongest man in all history, the mightiest colossus that ever lived, ensnared by a seductive beauty."

Biblical sex and Biblical spectacle were DeMille's trademark. When it came to moralising and gross debauchery, extravagance and vulgarity, he was the master showman. He had a gift for handling vast crowds and huge sets. Audiences went to his epics – *King of Kings* (1927), *Sign of the Cross* (1932), *Cleopatra* (1933), *The Crusades* (1935) – specifically for the sex and violence.

"I am sometimes accused," he said, "of gingering up the Bible with lavish infusions of sex and violence but I wish my accusers would read their Bible more closely, for in those pages are more violence and sex than I could ever portray on screen." He apologised for rewriting The Book of Judges. In his version, Delilah turned out to be the sister of Samson's wife.

> " I have one major criticism — you can't expect the public to get excited where the leading man's bust is bigger than the leading lady's. "
>
> *Groucho Marx*

Samson and Delilah was a big, brassy, gaudy, titillating extravaganza, totally lacking in taste. ("Manna for illiterates," said Paul Rotha.) The costumes were glossy. The helmets were shiny. The performances and accents were Hollywood. The film was balderdash, stodgily narrated and ponderously directed. "Saw the picture; loved the Book," said John Steinbeck.

Samson fought barehanded with a stuffed lion. He wrestled with Delilah ("Hey, one cat a time.") He killed 30 wedding guests. He hurled spears and masonry. He overturned chariots and crushed skulls. He picked up men and held them above his head. Single-handed, he fought a thousand Philistine soldiers with only the jawbone of an ass. He pulled down the Temple of Dagon. The Temple (which Paramount Studios had taken five months to build) was demolished over eight days. The destruction on screen lasted under three minutes. The spectacular demolition was the high spot of the film. Amazingly, nobody was hurt.

Delilah, the definitive temptress, sexy and bejewelled, was discovered sitting on a wall, throwing plum stones at Samson. "You're a bold little monkey," he said. "You could teach the devil a few tricks." She suggested he might like to tame her, but Samson preferred to marry her sister instead. "I could have loved you to make all other loves like ice," she told him. Scorned, all she wanted was revenge: "I'll make him curse the day he was born."

Delilah and Samson had a bit of a frolic by a pool. The seduction scene went on interminably. "I came to betray you," she confessed. He was impressed: "By the four winds, you have courage, Delilah." The big surprise was that the most famous haircut in the world took place off-screen. Shorn of his locks, he gave her a piece of his mind: "You Philistine gutter-rat." The language was never Biblical.

Victor Mature and Hedy Lamarr were chosen for the leading roles because they embodied the public's idea of manliness and sexiness. The stars offered brawn and

The most famous haircut in the world. Hedy Lamarr and Victor Mature as Delilah and Samson.

beauty. Mature, a clean-shaven, surly, saturnine hulk, was a straightforward sort of beefy guy, handsome and dumb, a bit of a mother's boy. ("You're not all bad," said his ma.) Lamarr, in slit-chiffon, bare-midriff, and off-the-shoulder costumes, was skimpily dressed for all occasions. DeMille had said his ideal Delilah would have had Jean Simmons's hair and eyes, Lana Turner's nose and Vivien Leigh's mouth. He had wanted body-builder Steve Reeves for Samson but Reeves refused to lose weight.

George Sanders, a master of waspish cynicism and dilettante repartee, was always on the point of saying something witty and although he was never given anything witty to say, he somehow managed to look satirical. With admirable sang froid, as the Temple comes crashing down around him, he raised his tumbler in toast to Delilah.

In a television remake in 1984, Mature played Samson's father.

The voluptuousness and savagery of the Bible story are translated into lukewarm sadism and sexless glamour.
News Chronicle

Samson appears bilious and flaccid and it is difficult to believe that he could pull down even the pulp coagulation of *papier mâché* that is passed off here as a formidable temple.
The New Yorker

She [Hedy Lamarr] came as near to my conception of that great harlot Delilah as a soft-centred chocolate.
The Daily Express

If you'll settle for gold-plated pageant, for muscular episodes and for graphic inducements to wolf-whistling, then *Samson and Delilah* is for you.
The New York Times

1951 • Quo Vadis

CREDITS

Marcus Vinicius	Robert Taylor
Lygia	Deborah Kerr
Petronius	Leo Genn
Nero	Peter Ustinov
Poppaea	Patricia Laffan
Peter	Abraham Sofaer
Paul	Finlay Currie
Eunice	Marina Berti
Ursus	Buddy Baer
Studio	MGM
Director	Mervyn LeRoy
Producer	Sam Zimbalist
Screenplay	John Lee Mahin
	S N Behrman
	Sonya Levien
Photography	Robert Surtees
	William V Skall
Music	Miklos Rozsa

AWARDS

ACADEMY AWARDS

None

ACADEMY NOMINATIONS

Best Picture   Sam Zimbalist
Best Supporting Actor
          Leo Genn and Peter Ustinov
Best Colour Cinematography
     Robert Surtees and William V. Skall
Best Film Editing   Ralph E. Winters
Best Score in Drama or Comedy
          Miklos Rozsa
Best Art/Set Decoration
     William A. Horning, Cedric Gibbons,
     Edward C. Carfango, Hugh Hunt
Best Costume Design in Color
          Herschel McCoy

BEST PICTURE

An American in Paris

STARS OF 1951

John Wayne
Martin and Lewis
Betty Grable
Abbott and Costello
Bing Crosby

1951 Blockbusters

Show Boat
The African Queen
David and Bathsheba
An American in Paris
A Streetcar Named Desire

THE WORLD

• Spies Guy Burgess and Donald
  Maclean defect to USSR
• British forces occupy Suez Canal
• JD Salinger's *The Catcher in the
  Rye* published

QUO VADIS was based on the best-selling novel by Nobel Prize winner Henry Sienkiewicz, published in 1896. It had already been filmed three times: a 20-minute version in Paris in 1902; a nine-reel Italian version in 1912 (which Auguste Rodin declared a masterpiece); and in 1926 in another Italian production with Emil Jannings as Nero.

"This Is The Big One!" screamed the advertisements, promising cinema-goers "splendour, savagery, spectacle you'll remember for a lifetime!" The trailer also promised the most colossal movie ever made with a cast of 29 principals, 110 speaking parts, 30,000 extras, a panoramic spectacle, infamous revelry, catacombs, a battle of the giants, the terror of the arena, the burning of Rome, roaring multitudes, marching armies, fighting gladiators and orgies. There were 63 lions, 47 bulls, 450 horsemen, 85 doves, 115 sets, 500 statues and 15,000 costumes. Audiences arrived in the cinema in much the same way that audiences had arrived at the Roman Coliseum. They came to see the lions eating the Christians.

> " *Whither goest thou?* "
>
> The Bible. St. John, Chapter 16, Verse 5

Quo Vadis, three years in the making, three hours to see, was a story of Christian persecution during the time of Emperor Nero, circa 64 AD. The Christianity was trite, the moralising a bore and the vision of Christ embarrassing. The appeal of the film was in the pageantry rather than in the romance and the question it raised: could a Christian slave girl save and redeem a pagan Roman commander who gloried in war and death? Could she convert him to Christianity?

Visually, the most thrilling sequence was two charioteers racing down the Appian Way, lashing their horses and each other. There were disappointments. The orgies are sexless and the burning of Rome did not blaze. A shot of the crowds in the square below Nero's palace, saluting vestal virgins, recalled the D.W. Griffith epic, *Intolerance*, but the camera was held for far too long in one position.

Robert Taylor, glamour boy of the 1930s and 1940s, played Marcus as an all-American commander. There was no reason why an American actor shouldn't play a Roman, but since all the other actors who played Romans were British, his American accent was incongruous. Taylor, handsome, sturdy and totally without humour, merely said his lines. Deborah Kerr, cast as Lygia, a Christian slave, a former princess of a defeated king, was always beautifully dressed and coiffured, even when she was tied to the stake, waiting to be killed by a bull. Lygia freely admitted she was attracted to Marcus's body and that she wanted him to see the Light for her sake rather than his. Kerr, always well-bred and serene, was an actress of greater range than the role suggested.

MGM thought Peter Ustinov might be too young to play Nero until he pointed out that the emperor had died at the age of 31 and that if they didn't hurry up and make the film, he would be too old for the part. In his autobiography, Ustinov said the only clue Mervyn LeRoy gave as to how he might act him was that Nero was the sort of guy who played with himself at nights. Ustinov was more clown than monster, a caricature rather than the real thing, and his outlandish mugging out-Laughtoned Charles Laughton in Cecil B DeMille's *The Sign of the Cross*. Ustinov's vain, florid, petulant, degenerate sensualist, postured, lolled, giggled, blubbed and warbled to his lyre while Rome sizzled. Ustinov chewed up the scenery and became an instant star.

Leo Glenn, cast as the cynical and wily Pretonius, had the best dialogue and gave the best performance. Nero was foolish enough to think Petronius's ironic flattery sincere,

"O Marcus, Marcus, you know I don't hate you." Robert Taylor as Marcus and Deborah Kerr as Lydia in Quo Vadis.

until he received Petronius's death-bed letter: "I can forgive you for murdering your wife, your mother, for burning our beloved Rome, but one thing I cannot forgive is the boredom of having to listen to your very second-rate songs, your mediocre performance. Adhere to your special gifts: murder, arson, terror. Mutilate your subjects, if you must, but I beg you do not mutilate the arts. Compose no more music. Brutalise the people, but do not bore them as you have bored your dear friend." Glenn's performance, suave and sharp, was beautifully understated.

No Hollywood epic in the 1950s would have been complete without Finlay Currie. Cast as Saint Peter, he had to deliver a ten-minute sermon in the catacombs on the life of Jesus for the benefit of cinema-goers who hadn't read the New Testament. Currie preached with such dignity and conviction that there was no need for the cringe-making close-ups of the enthralled faces of his congregation gazing heavenward.

Patricia Laffan played Nero's concubine, an ice-cold, camp, sexy villainess who was accompanied everywhere by two cheetahs. She was a bit of a man-eater herself and hankered after Marcus. When she couldn't get him, she threw his girlfriend to the bull.

Quo Vadis was dismissed as "diamond-studded hokum", "three hours of vulgarity, cliché and disgust" and "about as Roman as bubble-gum."

The whole achieves a richness and scale unprecedented in films of this genre, and should prove once and for all that spectacles can be made successfully without the excesses and vulgarities of Cecil B DeMille.

Saturday Review

Here is a staggering combination of cinema brilliance, of visual excitement and verbal boredom, of historical pretentiousness and sex… It was made for those who like grandeur and noise without punctuation.

The New York Times

The colour is magnificent, the crowd scenes stupendous, the taste poor and the length appalling.

Spectator

1952 • The Greatest Show on Earth

CREDITS

Holly	Betty Hutton
Sebastian	Cornel Wilde
Brad	Charlton Heston
Phyllis	Dorothy Lamour
Angel	Gloria Grahame
Buttons	Jimmy Stewart
FBI Man	Henry Wilcoxon
Klaus	Lyle Bettger
Henderson	Lawrence Tierney
Studio	Paramount
Director	Cecil B DeMille
Producer	Cecil B DeMille
Screenplay	Frederic M Frank
	Barrie Lyndon
	Theodore St John
	Frank Cavett
Photography	George Barnes
Music	Victor Young

AWARDS

ACADEMY AWARDS

Best Picture   Cecil B. DeMille
Best Motion Picture Story
    Frederic M. Frank,
    Theodore St. John
    and Frank Cavett

ACADEMY NOMINATIONS

Best Film Editing   Bauchens
Best Costume Design in Color
    Edith Head
    Dorothy Jeakins
    and Miles White

BEST PICTURE

The Greatest Show on Earth

STARS OF 1952

Martin and Lewis
Gary Cooper
John Wayne
Bing Crosby
Bob Hope

1952 Blockbusters

This Is Cinerama!
Ivanhoe
The Snows of Kilimanjaro
Hans Christian Andersen
Jumping Jacks

THE WORLD

- Accession of Queen Elizabeth II
- UK and US test hydrogen bomb
- Eisenhower elected US President
- Mau Mau rebellion in Kenya
- First contraceptive pill

THE GREATEST SHOW ON EARTH, strident and extremely dull, an elephantine mixture of Big Top spectacle and trite sentimentality, won Cecil B DeMille his first Academy award. The story-lines were poor. The dialogue was crass. The all-star cast played a supporting role to the circus, a cavalcade of acts, parades and pageants, provided by Ringling Bros and Barnum and Bailey Circus.

The manager of the circus (tough Charlton Heston) engaged a sensational French aerialist (good-looking Cornel Wilde, a daredevil flirt) to boost sales, which meant he had to move his girlfriend (an ear-piercing Betty Hutton) out of the centre ring to accommodate him. The manager had "sawdust in his veins" and loved the circus more than he did her. The two rival aeralists started competing and showing off to the crowds, taking more and more risks, performing more and more dangerous feats, until the Frenchman took a fall, broke his arm, crippled his hand and ended his career.

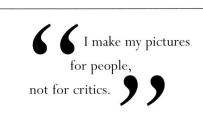

> I make my pictures for people, not for critics.
>
> *Cecil B DeMille*

The characters included a genuine clown, Emmett Kelly, and a fictional clown (James Stewart), who was, in fact, a surgeon in disguise, a fugitive from justice, given to quoting Oscar Wilde's "Each man kills the thing he loves." He had practised euthanasia on his wife and was on the run for her murder. He wore excessive clown make-up all the time, but the familiar Stewart drawl was an absolute give-away.

Dorothy Lamour was cast as an iron-jaw lady, a wise-cracking, gum-chewing beauty queen, hanging on to her non-existent part, literally by her teeth. Lamour wore a spiky sarong and sang an indifferent song. Bing Crosby and Bob Hope were seen briefly when the camera pans along a row of moronic, pop-corn eating, bubblegum-blowing spectators. Blink and you missed them. The best visual gag was the solemn, little boy, bored by the circus antics, sitting next to his big dad, who was roaring his head off.

The elephant trainer (a very bitter Lyle Bettger) got so jealous that his girlfriend (a very sultry Gloria Grahame) fancied the bare-chested and well-packaged Frenchman, her ex-boy friend, that he tried to murder her, using one of his elephants as an unwitting accomplice. Grahame, Lamour and Hutton, troupers all, did their own stunts. The only star who didn't do his own stunts was Cornel Wilde, an agrophobiac.

The Greatest Show on Earth, an extravagant, professional bit of brassy, spangled showmanship, was at is best in its more documentary moments when it dealt with setting up the circus, rolling out the canvas and then striking the whole thing when the show came down. There was one memorable shot of the tents being raised. DeMille was, as usual, a relentless narrator and provided an overblown commentary.

The film ended with a spectacular train crash and the animals prowling the wreckage. The circus manager, pinned under a girder, needed a blood transfusion. The surgeon sacrificed himself to save his life, performing the operation under the eyes of the detective who was about to arrest him. The blood was provided by the French aerialist. Needless to say the show went on the very next day. The elephants looked pretty fed-up as they lumbered across the screen.

Sawdust in their veins. Cornel Wilde, Betty Hutton and James Stewart in The Greatest Show on Earth.

Here it is right for DeMille to be vulgar, obvious, gaudy. For what else is circus? In this film any other approach would produce the same pretentiousness which vitiated his early epics… It's hokum, sure – but it's hokum from the hands of a master.

Saturday Review

In fact nothing is lacking to make this good wholesome family entertainment except perhaps taste, sense, and one or two other ingredients that hardly matter. After all the show must go on – though sometimes it is not easy to see why.

The Daily Telegraph

His influence towards loudness, extravagance and violence may well linger after the work of many an artist on the screen has been forgotten.

The Sunday Times

1953 • The Robe

CREDITS

Marcellus Gallio	Richard Burton
Diana	Jean Simmons
Demetrius	Victor Mature
Peter	Michael Rennie
Caligula	Jay Robinson
Justus	Dean Jagger

Studio	Twentieth Century Fox
Director	Henry Koster
Producer	Frank Ross
Screenplay	Philip Dunne
Photographer	Lyle Wheeler
Music	Alfred Newman

AWARDS

ACADEMY AWARDS

Best Colour Art Decoration
Lyle Wheeler
and George W. Davis
Best Set Decoration
Walter M. Scott and Paul S. Fox
Best Colour Costume Design
Charles LeMaire
and Emile Santiago

ACADEMY NOMINATIONS

Best Picture	Frank Ross
Best Actor	Richard Burton
Best Color Cinematography	
	Leon Shamroy

BEST PICTURE

From Here to Eternity

STARS OF 1953

Gary Cooper
Martin and Lewis
John Wayne
Alan Ladd
Bing Crosby

1953 Blockbusters

Shane
Peter Pan
How To Marry a Millionaire
Gentlemen Prefer Blondes
Mogambo

THE WORLD

- Death of Stalin
- Korean War ends
- Edmund Hilary and Sherpa Tenzing climb Everest
- Eisenhower US President

*T*HE ROBE was a milestone, the first film to be made in Cinemascope and designed specifically to bring back the crowds, who had deserted the cinema for television. (The 3D films, which you had to wear special spectacles to see, had failed to appeal to the public the previous year.) The Cinemascope screen was 68 feet by 24 feet, a triumph for spectacle, but not so good for the more intimate scenes. The most memorable moment, after the initial impact of the sheer size of the screen had worn off, was the shot of four white horses galloping straight at the camera.

The Robe, based on Lloyd C Douglas's mawkish best-seller (more than 10 million copies sold in all countries) was such old-fashioned religiosity that it could have been made at any time in the silent era. The action alternated between Rome (spick and span) and the Holy Land (very dusty). Henry Koster's direction was reverential, turgid and strangely uninvolving.

Marcellus, a dissolute and moody tribune, made an enemy of Caligula, when he outbid him for a Greek slave in the market place. Ordered to Jerusalem ("the worst pest-hole in the world") he arrived on the very day Jesus Christ was entering the city and was put in charge of the crucifixion. He won Christ's robe in a game of dice at the foot of the cross. Marcellus looked into Christ's eyes, heard Him speak and was splashed by His blood. On board ship he confused the beat of the hammer (keeping the oarsmen in time) with the hammering of the nails into the cross. He suffered terrible nightmares, became suicidal and was convinced he was bewitched. "No one can help me," he confided to his childhood sweetheart. "The truth is I am mad."

A soothsayer said he would never be cured until he found the robe (a symbol of his shame and conscience) and destroyed it. Marcellus returned to the Holy Land, met Peter, the Big Fisherman, and lots of Christians doing good deeds. He was converted to Christianity by a nice girl,who explained that Christ hadn't healed her so that she could show people that it was possible to remain unhealed and still be happy. Once he was back in Rome, Marcellus was put on trial for treason for refusing to renounce his new-found faith and was condemned to death by archery.

The sweetheart, who had been promised in marriage to Caligula, elected to die with him. She hadn't quite got the hang of Christianity. She promised to marry him, even if she had to share him with a thousand gods. The couple then, blissfully, marched down the aisle, hand in hand, to a marriage in heaven, accompanied by choirs singing away. It seemed as if they were taking a curtain call.

Jean Simmons looked very pretty standing by her man. Richard Burton, on the other hand, looked pretty stiff and uncomfortable in a role he found prissy and silly. Jay Robinson as Caligula ranted and raved in a shrill hysterical voice, determined to outdo Peter Ustinov's Nero in *Quo Vadis*. Robinson's warped, public school bully was classic camp. Ernest Thesiger's Tiberius was also camp, but in a minor key.

Victor Mature, a prime cut of muscular Christianity, played the Greek slave, Demetrius, who tried to find Jesus and warn Him that He was going to be arrested. Told he was too late by a man, who turned out to be Judas, he grabbed the robe and deserted. Back in Rome, he was tortured on the rack until Marcellus rescued him. Mature spends much of the time contorting his face and looking heavenward. He went on to make *Demetrius and the Gladiators* in 1954.

> " The shape of films to come – the modern miracle you can see without glasses. "
>
> *Slogan*

"No one can help me. The truth is I am mad." Jean Simmons and Richard Burton in The Robe.

Somehow it achieves
the impossible by
leaving us unmoved.
*The Evening
Standard*

The violent assault
on the senses
dissipated spiritual
intimacy.
The New York Times

The film, then, is the
usual vulgarising
stuff and to judge
cinemascope on this
evidence would be
unfair.
The Sunday Times

It will bring the
crowds back.
Daily Mirror

This will not beat the
film slump.
The Evening News

1954 • 20,000 Leagues Under the Sea

CREDITS

Ned Land	Kirk Douglas
Captain Nemo	James Mason
Prof Aronnax	Paul Lukas
Conseil	Peter Lorre
Studio	Walt Disney
Director	Richard Fleischer
Producer	Walt Disney
Screenplay	Earl Felton
Photography	Franz F Planer
	Ralph Hammeras
	Till Gabbani
Music	Paul J Smith
	JS Bach

AWARDS

ACADEMY AWARDS

Best Colour Art Direction
John Meehan
Best Set Decoration   Emile Kuri
Best Special Effects Disney Studios

ACADEMY NOMINATIONS

Best Film Editing   Elmo Williams

BEST PICTURE

On the Waterfront

STARS OF 1954

John Wayne
Martin and Lewis
Gary Cooper
James Stewart
Marilyn Monroe

1954 Blockbusters

White Christmas
The Caine Mutiny
Gone with the Wind (reissue)
The Glenn Miller Story
Rear Window

THE WORLD

- Vietnam divided into North and South
- Roger Bannister runs first four-minute mile
- Rationing ends in Britain
- Racial segregation in US schools declared illegal

20,000 LEAGUES UNDER THE SEA was one of Walt Disney's most ambitious, live-action movies with a big budget and big stars. There had already been three silent film versions of Jules Verne's prophetic novel in 1905, 1907 and 1916. It was generally agreed that Disney's version was the best.

A ship set sail in 1868 in search of a sea-monster, which was destroying ships. The ship was sunk and there were only three survivors: a French professor, his assistant and a master-harpooner. The sea-monster turned out to be a man-made submarine captained by a mad genius with an evil plan to destroy the world.

Captain Nemo, scientist, inventor, visionary, avenger, was no routine villain, even if he did play Bach fugues at his pipe-organ while dressed in a quilted smoking jacket. Nemo was a gourmet, who offered his prisoner-guests such delicacies as sauté of unborn octopus with cream from the sperm whale. But although he lived in the lap of luxury, he was not interested in personal wealth and he used his stolen treasure for ballast.

> " I am not what you call a cultured man. I have done with society. I do not obey its laws. "
>
> *Captain Nemo*

Nemo, a practising Nietzschean misanthrope, was bitter about man's stupidity and inhumanity to man. His wife and young son had been tortured to death. There were any number of close-ups of James Mason's bearded, brooding, anguished face. His performance had authority, style and he deserved Verne's tragic ending rather than a Disney rewrite.

Kirk Douglas (not one of his better performances) was cast as the banjo-playing master-harpooner, a grinning, brawling, womanising, cheeky, curly-haired, mugging Popeye sailor with a fine physique. He sang a sea shanty ("A Whale of a Time") and wiggled his bottom, which was pinched by a honking, whiskered, flipper-clapping, self-regarding performing seal. Douglas overdid it to such an extent that he made many people begin to regret that the cannibals had not caught him and eaten him. The chase was played for comedy rather than thrills. What little excitement there was came in his almost balletic fight with a tenacious giant squid with eight tentacles and two feelers.

Paul Lukas, cast as the foremost authority on undersea life, was very earnest, very boring, very cardboard and his foreign accent made heavy weather of the voiceover narration. Peter Lorre played his assistant, a piece of gross miscasting. Lorre (likened to "a plump tadpole" by one critic) was an actor who always found it impossible to be anything but sinister, even when he was saying lines such as "I thought we were friends."

The Nautilus submarine, manned by escaped prisoners who looked like automatons, has a battering ram snout, electric eyes, metallic ridges along its back and an enormous tail. It was, however, the red plush, opulently upholstered interior, designed by Emile Kuri, which made the most impression. Nemo had a fine library, a fine art collection, an ornamental marble fountain and a beautiful art deco observation window.

Most of the film was shot in a large tank on one of Disney's sound stages, which, no doubt, partly explained why the underwater scenes were never as thrilling as they might have been had the actors really been 20,000 leagues under the sea. The final image was an explosion of atomic bomb proportions with the familiar mushroom cloud. The voiceover hoped a new and better life would come in the future.

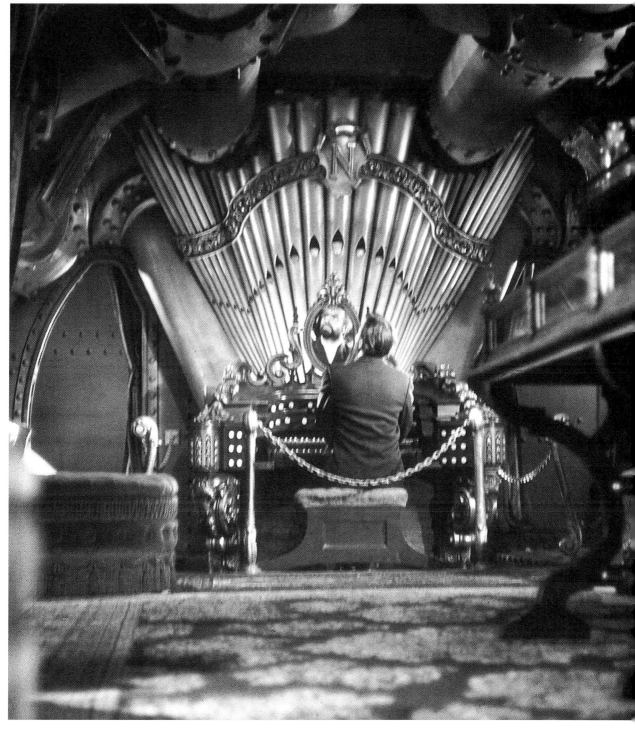

Captain Nemo plays Bach. James Mason in 20,000 Leagues Under the Sea.

Disney has at last succeed in making a good movie with human beings instead of animals and animation.
Saturday Review

A very special kind of picture-making combining ingenuity, imagination, story-telling and fiscal daring.
Variety

It is full of surprises. The biggest is that at least 120 of its 126 minutes are tedious.
The Daily Sketch

If you are a 15-year-old – or feel like it – this is for you.
News Chronicle

1955 • The Lady and the Tramp

CREDITS

Lady	Barbara Luddy
Tramp	Larry Roberts
Darling	Peggy Lee
Jock	Bill Thompson
Bull	Bill Thompson
Dachsie	Bill Thompson
Trusty	Bill Baucon
Beaver	Stan Freberg
Studio	Walt Disney
Director	Hamilton Luske
	Clyde Geronimi
	Wilfred Jackson
Producer	Walt Disney
Screenplay	Erdman Penner
	Joe Rinaldi
	Ralph Wright
	Don DaGradi
Music	Oliver Wallace

AWARDS

ACADEMY AWARDS
None

ACADEMY NOMINATIONS
None

BEST PICTURE

Marty

STARS OF 1955

James Stewart
Grace Kelly
John Wayne
William Holden
Gary Cooper

1955 Blockbusters

Mr Roberts
Battle Cry
Oklahoma!
Guys and Dolls
The Seven Year Itch

THE WORLD

• Warsaw Pact formed
• Ruth Ellis hanged
• Commercial TV starts in Britain
• James Dean dies

WALT DISNEY'S first Cinemascope cartoon was a human romance (boy meets girl) in canine terms (spoiled pedigree meets mongrel). Lady was a King Charles spaniel, who lived in the best part of town. Tramp was a mongrel terrier, who lived on the wrong side of the railway tracks. He was a raffish, ragged, street-smart, working-class mutt, a good-natured criminal, scrounging meals. She was a prim, proper, pampered, middle-class snob, who lived a sheltered and happy life until her master and mistress had a baby and she was no longer the centre of attraction.

Tramp was the voice of experience and he knew what humans were like. "When a baby moves in," he observed, "a dog moves out. A human heart has only so much room for love and affection." He saved Lady from being raped by some thuggish dogs. (The fight off-screen sounded ferocious.) He then proceeded to seduce her. "Let's build some memories," he said. They raided a hen house and he took her to an Italian restaurant for dinner by moonlight where they shared a spaghetti while the waiter played his accordion and sang "*Bella Notte*". They spent the night together under the moon. Tramp was not the sort of dog who wanted a collar-and-leash existence. He opened Lady's eyes to what life could be. "There's a great big chunk of world out there where the two of us could find adventure – all ours for the taking." But she couldn't do it.

The Disney animators reproduced the anatomy, personalities, mannerisms and actions of all the dogs most wittily. Lady had two elderly admirers: a very Scots Scottie and a fine old Southern bloodhound, who had lost his sense of smell. A Pekinese (voiced by Peggy Lee) was cast in the role of a sultry ex-burlesque queen in the Mae West mould. She sang a raunchy torch song, "He's a tramp, he breaks a heart everyday." Tramp's conquests were in the Errol Flynn league. The villains were two odious Siamese cats, who had their eyes on a goldfish and a budgie. There was also a monster red-eyed rat and he had his red-eyes on the baby.

The City Council issued an order that any unlicensed dog would be impounded. The pound (where the down-and-outs were liable to take the long walk) included an American Chihuahua, a German dachshund, a cockney bulldog and a Russian wolfhound. The last was an intellectual given to quoting from Maxim Gorky's *The Lower Depths*. The quartet sang "Home Sweet Home" and were a howling success.

Very daringly for the 1950s *The Lady and The Tramp* declared mixed marriages were OK. The story ended happily (or unhappily, depending on your point of view) with Tramp settling down to domestic bliss and a life where there was a fence round every tree and a collar (a badge of faith and respectability) round every neck. The film is a delight. The reviews, however, were mixed, many critics finding the cute dogginess too sugary for their taste.

> " One of the greatest love stories ever told. "
>
> *Slogan*

The picture seems likely to appeal to the exceptionally sentimental and unimaginative child.
Film Bulletin

Emphatically not for cat lovers.
The Financial Times

A delight for juveniles and lots of fun for adults.
Variety

Tramp and Lady enjoy a spaghetti at an Italian restaurant. ©*Walt Disney.*

1956 • The Ten Commandments

LET MY PEOPLE GO! But Cecil B DeMille, a religious man, a genuine believer, hardened his heart and kept audiences in the cinema for 339 minutes. He had already filmed *The Ten Commandments* in 1923. Forty years on, the old showman was still offering cinema-goers his staple diet: erotic licentiousness, lurid pageantry, colossal vulgarity, Lethean acting, fancy dress kitsch and gigantic boredom. It was his last film. He was 78. (Despite suffering a heart attack one Friday, he was back at work on the Monday.) He was, as usual, at his best with the spectacle, deploying vast numbers of extras and animals; he was not so good with the individual actor. The language was archaic, the performances stilted and the production pedestrian. The compositions were visually dull and looked like static theatrical tableaux of the Victorian era as painted by Alma-Tadema.

Before the film began, DeMille appeared on screen in front of a curtain to apologise for the fact that *The Book of Exodus* had omitted some 30 years covering Moses's boyhood and early manhood, but he assured the public that, with the help of some of the best historians in the business (including Philo and Josephus), he had been able to fill in the gap.

> " I wouldn't be as rash as to say I played Moses and found God, but one learns from it, certainly. You'd be a bloody fool if you couldn't.
>
> *Charlton Heston*

There were some excellent epic sequences, such as the toiling slaves building a city and the Egyptian chariots racing in pursuit of the exodus. The sheer scale of the migration was impressive. Extras were hired, not individually but by the tribe, with their animals and chattels. There was one shot of the teeming crowds, seen from a high window in the palace, which recalled a famous shot in Sergei Eisenstein's *Ivan the Terrible*. The parting of the Red Sea (achieved by reversing shots of two miniature waterfalls) was described as the most spectacular scene ever filmed. It merely looked like two walls of water artificially piled up.

The cameras rolled on the very ground Moses had walked on the slopes of Mount Sinai, but the burning bush was not any the more effective for having been filmed in the actual location. It looked like a glowing Christmas tree. A major mistake was to give God a voice. "I am that I am," He boomed. It would have been better if He had remained silent. The camera tricks with a lighting bolt spelling out the ten commandments were crass.

DeMille, describing Moses as "one of the greatest human beings, human even to the point of sin" invited cinema-goers to notice the likeness between Michelangelo's Moses and Charlton Heston's Moses. When Moses ccame down from the mountain, Heston looked like somebody who had seen the face of God and he did not need DeMille's unnecessary and overwritten commentary. It was with this role that the 32-year-old actor became the public's ideal hero for the epics of the 1950s.

The drunken orgy, which had taken three weeks to film, was something of a disappointment, being just a lot of extras milling around and the voiceover commentary having to do all the hard work, talking about the adultery and lasciviousness, which nobody could see.

Yul Brynner, shaven-headed, bare-chested, bare-legged, straight from his success in *The King and I*, was easily the most exotic member of the cast and in his chariot

"Let my people go!" Yul Brynner as Rameses and Charlton Heston as Moses in The Ten Commandments.

he looked as if he has stepped off an Egyptian frieze. He looked better than he acted. The treacherous Nefretiri, described as "a sharp-clawed peacock," was played by Anne Baxter as a 1920s vamp, who said things to Moses like "You stubborn, splendid, adorable fool, I killed for you. I'll kill anybody who comes between us." She had just murdered her old nanny (Judith Anderson). All that was missing in Baxter's performance was a bath in asses's milk.

Cedric Hardwicke made a droll Pharaoh. Edward G Robinson leered away as the chief Hebrew overseer. Vincent Price was very camp as the master-builder, especially when he was whipping Joshua (John Derek), the pretty stone-cutter. The seven daughters of Jethro were played by a gaggle of giggling American high-school girls who put on a cabaret for Moses. The movie's big surprise was that Yvonne de Carlo (playing Moses's wife) didn't dance.

What DeMille has really done is to throw sex and sand into the moviegoers' eyes for almost twice as long as anyone else has ever dared to... In some respects, perhaps the most vulgar movie ever made.
Time

For all the millions that have been spent, the heroic is constantly transmuting itself into the commonplace.
Times Educational Supplement

A Biblical strip-cartoon inflated to super-Jumbo proportions, steeped in the usual mixture of Hollywood balloon talk, sexual titillation and milling hordes.
The Financial Times

Anyone with a nostalgic feeling for the DeMille badness of the past will be sorry that this film, which may be the last of its genre from the master, has to be such an utter catastrophe.
New Republic

1957 • The Bridge on the River Kwai

CREDITS

Shears	William Holden
Major Warden	Jack Hawkins
Colonel Nicholson	Alec Guinness
Colonel Saito	Sessue Hayakawa
Major Clipton	James Donald
Lieutenant Joyce	Geoffrey Horne
Studio	Columbia
Director	David Lean
Producer	Sam Spiegel
Screenplay	Pierre Boule*
Photography	Jack Hildyard
Music	Malcolm Arnold

AWARDS

ACADEMY AWARDS

Best Picture	Sam Spiegel
Best Direction	David Lean
Best Actor	Alec Guinness
Best Screenplay	Pierre Boule*
Best Cinematography	Jack Hildyard
Best Editing	Peter Taylor
Best Music Scoring	Malcolm Arnold

ACADEMY NOMINATIONS

Best Supporting Actor
Sessue Hayawaka

BAFTA AWARDS

Best Film	
Best British Film	
Best Actor	Alec Guinness
Best Screenplay	

*Though Pierre Boule got the credit for the screenplay, he did not write the screenplay, which was written by two blacklisted writers, Carl Foreman and Mihael Williams. They were awarded posthumous Oscars in 1985

BEST PICTURE

The Bridge on the River Kwai

STARS OF 1957

Rock Hudson • John Wayne
Pat Boone • Elvis Presley
Frank Sinatra

1957 Blockbusters

Peyton Place
Sayonara
Raintree Country
A Farewell to Arms
Gunfight at the OK Corral

THE WORLD

- Harold Macmillan becomes British Prime Minister
- USSR launch first satellite into outer space
- European Common Market established
- Race riot in Little Rock, Arkansas

THE BRIDGE ON THE RIVER KWAI was based on an actual incident during the Second World War: the building of the notorious Burma–Siam "Death Railway" by European prisoners of war.

In 1943, the British surrendered to the Japanese on the orders of military command. Colonel Nicholson and his regiment marched into the POW camp whistling "Colonel Bogey", which the soundtrack took up in a big patriotic way. Colonel Saito, the Japanese commander, thought the British were cowards for having surrendered and despised them for being defeated and having no shame. He was not the sort of man to obey the Geneva Convention and insisted that the officers should work on the bridge alongside the men. When Nicholson refused he was threatened with death and made to stand in the sun all day long and then put in a steel-sheet iron oven. "That man's the worst commanding officer I've ever come across," said Nicholson.

Nicholson, a ramrod disciplinarian and single-minded fanatic, a soldier of the old school, had the kind of guts that could get everybody killed. The story became a psychological battle of wills, an heroic battle of two men, each inflexible, according to his nation's code of honour. Nicholson, although flogged and starved in solitary confinement, finally won. It was a moving moment when he emerged from the iron-oven.

> " There has been a lot of argument about the film's attitude toward war. I think it is a painfully eloquent statement on the generally folly and waste of war. "
>
> *David Lean*

The scenes between the two commanders became more and more satirical as the film went on. Nicholson took over the building of the bridge, which he saw as a means of turning defeat into victory. He felt it would be good for morale and he was keen to show the Japanese the mettle and skill of the British soldier. In order to get the work finished on time he persuaded the sick and his brother officers (who, like him, had been incarcerated in a steel-sheet iron oven, for refusing to do manual labour) to volunteer. So blinkered was he in his obsession and racial arrogance, that he was unaware he was collaborating with the enemy. "Must we build a better bridge than they could build themselves?" asked the camp doctor.

There was a beautiful scene, played with Alec Guinness's characteristic understatement, when he was leaning over the railing of the completed bridge, wondering what the sum total of his 28 years of army life had meant and whether it had made any difference at all. So identified is Guinness with the role, that it comes as a surprise to learn he was not David Lean's first choice. Charles Laughton and Noel Coward were preferred. Guinness himself turned down the role three times, convinced he could not make it work. *The Bridge on the River Kwai* made him an international star.

The film spared the audience the atrocities that really happened in Japanese POW camps. Saito was not the incompetent, sadistic drunk of Pierre Boule's novel but a man afraid of losing face. Sessue Hayakawa, a famous Hollywood film star in the silent film era, captured the man's dignity and shame as well as his brutality. Had he not been killed, Saito would most certainly have committed suicide.

There were longueurs when the action shifted out of the camp. William Holden played a cynical American POW whose primary thought was self-preservation and to this end he had masqueraded as an officer for an easier life. Having escaped the

"Do not speak to me of rules. This is war! This is not a game of cricket." Alec Guinness in The Bridge on the River Kwai.

camp, he was then persuaded, much against his will, to go back and sabotage the bridge. "We'd like to have you with us," said the British major (Jack Hawkins, very British) who was in charge of the raid. The commandos were accompanied by beautiful Siamese girls, solely for box-office reasons.

The bridge, 90 feet high, 425 feet wide, a symbol of brutality and courage, was finally blown up in a nerve-wrecking finale in which it seemed as if Nicholson himself would sabotage the attempt. In the event, it was only blown up by accident when he fell mortally wounded on the detonator. It was a moment of triumph, tragedy and irony. The camp doctor (James Donald), who was always on hand to observe and to comment, but never to participate, had the final words: "Madness, madness." In the novel the bridge remained standing. The film, rightly, gave the public what they wanted to see.

David Lean was not the first choice for director. William Wyler, John Ford and Howard Hawks had all turned it down. Lean would go on to make *Lawrence of Arabia*, *Doctor Zhivago*, *Ryan's Daughter* and *A Passage to India*. He was no longer interested in making the sort of small movies – *Brief Encounter*, *Oliver Twist* and *Great Expectations* – which had made him famous.

It will be called a comedy; it is. It will be called a swell adventure story, a slickly calculated piece of commercial entertainment, an angry razz at the thing called war, a despairing salute to the men war makes, an ironic masterpiece; it is in some degree all of these things.
Time

A huge, expensive chocolate box of a war picture.
New Statesman

As thrilling an adventure film as was ever made.
The Evening News

1958 • South Pacific

CREDITS

Nellie Forbush	Mitzi Gaynor
Emile de Becque	Rossano Brazzi
Lt Cable	John Kerr
Luther Billis	Ray Walston
Bloody Mary	Juanita Hall
Liat	France Nuyen
Studio	Twentieth Century Fox
Director	Joshua Logan
Producer	Buddy Adler
Music	Richard Rodgers
Lyrics	Oscar Hammerstein
Screenplay	Paul Osborn
Photography	Leon Shamroy

AWARDS

ACADEMY AWARDS

Best Sound Recording Fred Hynes

ACADEMY NOMINATIONS

Best Colour Cinematography
Leon Shamroy
Best Score for a Musical
Alfred Newman, Ken Darby
Best Sound Fred Hynes

BEST PICTURE

Gigi

STARS OF 1958

Glenn Ford
Elizabeth Taylor
Jerry Lewis
Marlon Brando
Rock Hudson

1958 Blockbusters

Auntie Mame
Old Yeller
Cat on a Hot Tin Roof
Gigi
No Time For Sergeants

THE WORLD

- Manchester United Football team in Munich air crash
- Silicon chip invented in US
- Military coup in Iraq
- Introduction of stereo recordings

RICHARD RODGERS and Oscar Hammerstein's musical opened on Broadway in 1943 and ran for 1925 performances, winning many awards, including the Pulitzer Prize. The film, which was made with the full co-operation of the American navy, was extremely long, extremely slow and not a patch on the stage show.

South Pacific, set during Second World War and based on James Michener's *Tales of the South Pacific*, narrated two wartime romances. Nellie Forbush, a young US navy nurse, fell in love with Emile de Becque, a middle-aged French planter. Lt Cable, a young US marine, fell in love with Liat, a native girl. Nellie was an unsophisticated and uneducated woman from Kansas, who had never heard of Marcel Proust and Anatole France, let alone read them. So, she wasn't too keen to marry the cultured Emile and even less so when she learned he was a widower who had been married to a Polynesian woman, who had borne him two children. His marriage shocked her far more than his casual confession that he had killed a man in France. She was willing to accept the murder without any explanation. "I hardly know you," she said, "but I know it's all right."

Nellie was a knuckle-headed, cockeyed optimist, who couldn't make up her mind if she was going to wash Emile right out of her hair or marry a wonderful guy. Her dilemma made her so unhappy she wanted to walk out of the entertainment she has devised for the servicemen. "I can't go on!" she cried. "I'm sure you can," said a friend, who had seen umpteen backstage stories. "You're the whole show." And so, on she went to sing "A Hundred and One Pounds of Fun" and, predictably, knocked all the sailors for six.

Meanwhile, young Cable didn't mind going for a swim with Liat, and even having sex with her, but he, too, balked at the idea of marriage, especially when he thought what colour their children might be and what the folks back home might think. His dilemma was solved when he was killed in action. Nellie finally made up her mind to marry Emile when he was out of town on a mission, helping the Americans to lick the Japanese, and she was worried he might get killed, too.

The leading roles were poorly cast. They needed more dynamic personalities. The musical had been specially written for Mary Martin. The role of Emile had been created by the opera singer, Ezio Pinza. Joshua Logan, who had staged the original Broadway show, took Mitzi Gaynor and Rassano Brazzi to see Martin perform on stage just before they began filming; not, perhaps, the most tactful thing to do. Gaynor didn't have the emotional impact and Brazzi, a leading romantic actor of the Italian screen, dubbed by Giorgio Tazzi, merely looked earnest.

John Kerr, who had had a big success in *Tea and Sympathy* on stage and screen, was too self-effacing as Cable. He had two songs, "The Girl Back Home" (originally dropped from the Broadway show) and "You've Got To Be Carefully Taught", both dubbed by Bill Lee. The latter was a plea for racial tolerance, which argued that "You've got to be carefully taught to be afraid of people whose skin is of a different shade." The sentiment didn't go down too well in some Southern states in America.

> " I tried to forget whom I'd worked with before. We're trying to give *South Pacific* the same fresh treatment we gave it on stage. "
>
> *Joshua Logan*

Some Unenchanted Evening. Mitzi Gaynor and Rossano Brazzi in South Pacific.

Liat was played by France Nuyen, a model, who had never acted before and who couldn't speak English. She looked lovely miming her way through "Happy Talk". Juanita Hill repeated her stage role of Bloody Mary, the half-caste trader and virago, but her singing, despite the fact that she had sung the role in the theatre, was dubbed by Muriel Smith.

South Pacific was filmed in Hawaii. The location was underused and never anything more than travelogue background. Director, Joshua Logan was defeated by the sheer size of Todd-AO and its wide, steeply curving screen. His approach was stagey rather than cinematic. The camera remained in one position. The most distracting aspect of the production was the use of different colour filters to heighten the emotion. There was also no choreography and the chorus boys were left standing around doing nothing during "Nothing Like A Dame".

South Pacific is about as tastelessly impressive as a ten-ton marshmallow.
Time

The picture does not have the tempo and bounce it should have in some scenes. But let's not be too analytical, for it does have, by and large, a wonderful surge of charm and gusto that just keeps coming for hours and hours.
The New York Times

A big bore...
as lively as a hippopotamus.
New Statesman

1959 • Ben-Hur

CREDITS

Judah Ben-Hur	Charlton Heston
Quintus Arrius	Jack Hawkins
Messala	Stephen Boyd
Esther	Haya Harareet
Sheik Iderim	Hugh Griffith
Miriam	Martha Scott
Simonides	Sam Jaffe
Tirzah	Cathy O'Donnell
Balthasar	Finlay Currie
Pontius Pilate	Frank Thring
Studio	MGM
Director	William Wyler
Producer	Sam Zimbalist
Screenplay	Karl Tunberg
Photography	Robert Surtees
Music	Miklos Rozsa

AWARDS

ACADEMY AWARDS

Best Picture	Sam Zimbalist
Best Direction	William Wyler
Best Actor	Charlton Heston
Best Supporting Actor: Hugh Griffith	
Best Colour Cinematography	
	Robert Surtees
Best Colour Art Direction	William
A. Horning and Edward Carfagno	
Best Colour Set Direction	Hugh Hunt
Best Colour Costume Design:	
	Elizabeth Haffenden
Best Editing	Ralph E. Winters
and John D. Duning	
Best Sound	Franklin E. Milton
Best Sound Effects	
	A. Arnold Gillespie
Best Visual Effects	Robert MacDonald
Best Audible Effects	Milo Lory
Best Music Score of a Drama or a	
Comedy	Miklos Rozsa

ACADEMY NOMINATIONS

Best Adapted Screenplay Karl Tunberg

BEST PICTURE

Ben-Hur

STARS OF 1959

Rock Hudson • Cary Grant
James Stewart • Doris Day
Debbie Reynolds

1959 Blockbusters

*The Shaggy Dog • Some Like It Hot
Pillow Talk • North by Northwest
Imitation of Life*

THE WORLD

• Formation of European Free Trade
  Association
• Cuban revolution
• First photograph of the dark side
  of the moon

GENERAL LEW WALLACE, American Civil War hero and Nobel Prize winner, published *Ben-Hur, A Tale of Christ*, in 1880. Two million copies were sold. There were two silent film adaptations: the first, a one-reel version in 1907; the second in 1926, with Roman Navarro and Francis X Bushman, directed by Fred Niblo.

William Wyler's *Ben-Hur* was an epic to out DeMille DeMille. It told the story of the impact of Christ on a Jewish family. Charlton Heston, a ready-made glyph for moral and physical strength, was cast in the title role of an aristocratic, noble, rich and powerful Jew, who was converted to Christianity. "It's a fine part," he said, "but it could so easily dissolve in the scenery." Heston was his usual manly, blue-eyed, flinty-jawed, stolid and slightly wooden self. He was not the first choice. Marlon Brando and Rock Hudson had been preferred.

> Hated Hur. Loved Ben.
>
> *Anon*

Stephen Boyd was cast as Messala, a role turned down by Kirk Douglas, who had wanted to play Ben-Hur. Messala was a not very bright public schoolboy, who dreamed of restoring order in Judea. He and Ben-Hur were friends when they were boys. They were like brothers. They fell out when Ben-Hur wouldn't support him in his persecution of the Jews. Wrongfully arrested, Ben-Hur spent three years in chains, sweating and slaving away in the galleys with only his hate to keep him alive. He saved a sadistic Roman consul's life during a sea battle. The consul (Jack Hawkins) adopted him as his son and heir and he became the finest charioteer in Rome.

The climax comes shortly after the interval. For most people *Ben-Hur* means one thing and one thing only – the magnificent chariot race in the biggest arena ever built, one of the finest action scenes ever shot. (William Wyler had been one of the 30 assistant directors who had dealt with the crowds in the 1926 silent version.) Messala didn't race fairly, whipping not only his horses but the other competitors as well. He had attached lethal knives to his wheels in order to churn up the wheels of his rivals' vehicles. Chariots crashed and bodies were dragged under the screeching wheels. The race was directed by Andrew Marton and the stunt man, Yakima Canutt. Heston's double was Canutt's son, Joe, who was observed at one point being thrown out of the chariot, but, with clever editing, Heston was shown scrambling back on.

Ben-Hur's life was tenuously linked to Christ's. He came face to face with Him twice. The first time was when He gave Ben-Hur water on his way to the galleys. The second time was when he gave Christ water when Christ was on His way to Golgotha. The actual crucifixion with the hammering of nails and the cross thudding into its socket in the ground was dramatic. The religious content had restraint, except when Christ's blood poured down the hillside. A pre-credit sequence recorded the birth of Jesus in a manager and the arrival of the three wise men in a manner which would not have disgraced a primary school's nativity production.

The American actors (with the exception of Haya Harareeet) played the Jews. The Brits played the Romans. Hugh Griffith, as a Welsh Arab horse-dealer, provided a limited amount of bushy-eyebrowed light relief. The 81-year-old Finlay Currie was cast as a Magi. "I'm ready for sleep," he confessed half way through the film and cinema-goers knew exactly how he felt. *Ben-Hur* at 212 minutes was a slow marathon. The film took itself very seriously. Nobody was allowed to sell confectionery and ice cream during the actual screening.

Karl Tunberg got sole credit for the literate script, although Maxwell Anderson, Gore Vidal, SN Bernham, and especially Christopher Fry, had all had a hand in it.

"There is no law in the arena. Many are killed." Charlton Heston as Ben-Hur.

William Wyler has proved with *Ben-Hur* that taste and intelligence need not be lacking in a film spectacle.
Saturday Review

Stands as the superspectacular and most tasteful and intelligent Biblical-fiction film in Hollywood's history
The New York Herald Tribune

The most tasteful and visually exciting film spectacle yet produced by an American company.
Film Quarterly

I found *Ben-Hur* in every way bloody bloody and bloody boring. Watching it was like waiting at a railway road crossing while an interminable freight train lumbers past.
Esquire

1960 • Swiss Family Robinson

CREDITS

Father	John Mills
Mother	Dorothy McGuire
Fritz	James MacArthur
Roberta	Janet Munro
Pirate Chief	Sessue Hayakawa
Ernst	Tommy Kirk
Francis	Kevin Corcoran
Captain Moreland	Cecil Parker
Studio	Walt Disney
Director	Ken Annakin
Producer	Bill Anderson
Screenplay	Lowell S Hawley
Photography	Harry Waxman
Music	William Alwyn

AWARDS

ACADEMY AWARDS
None

ACADEMY NOMINATIONS
None

BEST PICTURE

The Apartment

STARS OF 1960

Doris Day
Rock Hudson
Cary Grant
Elizabeth Taylor
Debbie Reynolds

1960 Blockbusters

Psycho
Sparticus
Operation Petticoat
The Apartment
Exodus

THE WORLD

- Sharpeville Massacre in South Africa
- Trial of DH Lawrence's *Lady Chatterley's Lover*
- Brezhnev elected Soviet President

JOHNANN RUDOLF WYSS's classic story, published in 1813, was inspired by Daniel Defoe's *Robinson Crusoe* and was written to teach children "how blessed are the results of patient continuance in well-doing." It had been filmed in 1940 with Thomas Mitchell, Edna Best and Freddie Bartholomew. Walt Disney, who had no interest in Wyss's moral teaching, took the title and threw out the book. The production was filmed on the island of Tobago in the West Indies. The studio had to import all the animals: there were zebras, elephants and ostriches from Africa, tigers from India, turtles from the Galapagos and anacondas from the Amazon. The film did wonders for the island's tourist industry.

Mr and Mrs Robinson and their three children were shipwrecked on their way to a new life in New Guinea during the Napoleonic Wars. Mr Robinson (John Mills) wondered if life would have been better if they had stayed in Berne. Mrs Robinson (Dorothy McGuire) had no doubts that they had made the right decision and the longer they stayed on the island the more they liked it. When the opportunity finally came for them to leave, only their bookish son, Ernst, decided to return to Europe to complete his education.

> " *Don't you feel this is the kind of life we were meant to live on Earth?* "
>
> *Johnann Rudolf Wyss*

The Robinsons were a resourceful family and built the most luxurious penthouse in the trees, with every convenience, whose gadgets and contraptions looked as if they had been designed by Heath Robinson (no relation). The actual building was done entirely off-screen. The family battled with sharks and tigers, but there was never any dramatic tension, not even when their eldest son, Fritz (James MacArthur, doing his own stunt) fought with a 12-foot anaconda.

The screenplay introduced some teenage romance with a girl (Janet Munro), who had disguised herself as a cabin boy as a precaution against being raped by pirates. Neither Fritz nor Ernst realised she was a girl until they decided the best way to cross a river was to strip naked. The discovery led to a bit of sibling hormonal rivalry, which was never seriously developed. Life on an idyllic tropical island remained totally idyllic.

There were two sequences that give particular pleasure to the 12-year-old market. The first was the madcap point-to-point race in which the riders had no control over the direction in which the donkey, elephant, zebra and ostrich were going. The second was a fight against the pirates which was played entirely for farce to a circus music accompaniment on the soundtrack. The Robinsons used shot, spears arrows and bombarded their cutlass-waving attackers with home-made, powder-filled coconut grenades and cascading logs. Everybody was blown up. Nobody was hurt, not even those unlucky enough to fall into the tiger pit. The violence was slapstick. The pirates were no more dangerous than the pirates in James Barrie's *Peter Pan*.

Walt Disney, as always, provided simple and wholesome family entertainment. There wasn't anything Swiss about it except, possibly, for the singing of "O Tannenbaum". The script didn't offer any acting opportunities to the cast, who played a supporting role to the island and its improbable mixture of animals. The production, which was praised for its warmth, humanity, robust charm and extrovert humour, got a better press than it deserved.

The Swiss family Robinson (John Mills, Tommy Kirk, Dorothy McGuire and James MacArthur) give thanks to God for saving them from being drowned.

One of the best romantics stories that has been brought to the screen. It's fun, fun, fun all the way.
The Daily Express

Ken Annakin has dodged both the cloying sweetness and the bloody horrors of earlier Disney efforts in this field.
Saturday Review

I do wish Walt Disney would stop mucking about with the books we loved.
Time and Tide

1961 • 101 Dalmatians

CREDITS

Pongo	Rod Taylor
Anita	Lisa Davis
Perdita	Cate Bauer
Roger	Ben Wright
Horace	Frederic Worlock
Jasper	J Pat O'Malley
Cruella De Vil	Betty Lou Gerson
Studio	Walt Disney
Director	Wolgang Reitherman
	Hamilton S Luske
	Clyde Geronimi
Producer	Walt Disney
Screenplay	Bill Peet
Music	George Bruns

AWARDS

ACADEMY AWARDS
None

ACADEMY NOMINATIONS
None

BEST PICTURE

West Side Story

STARS OF 1961

Elizabeth Taylor
Rock Hudson
Doris Day
John Wayne
Cary Grant

1961 Blockbusters

West Side Story
The Guns of Navarone
The Parent Trap
The Absent-Minded Professor
El Cid

THE WORLD

- John F Kennedy becomes US President
- Yuri Gagarin is first man in space
- Berlin Wall erected
- South Africa becomes republic

WALT DISNEY's cartoon was based on the modern children's classic by Dodie Smith. The adaptation was spot on: 6,469,952 spots, to be exact. It told a rattling good adventure story. The animation was elegant, witty and lively. The colours were beautifully subdued.

Pongo, a male Dalmatian, fed up with being a bachelor, decided to get his human pet, a musician called Roger, to fall in love with Anita, a human pet of a pretty Dalmatian called Perdita. Pets and humans were soon married. Perdita gave birth to 15 puppies. Cruella De Vil, a relation of Roger and Anita, wanted to buy them and when she was refused, she hired two imbecile cockney burglars to dognap them and take them to her crumbling mansion in the country.

Cruella, a fairy tale witch in modern dress, was modelled on Tallulah Bankhead, Auntie Mame, Morticia Addams and Maudie Littlehampton. She was a chain-smoking, manic, Gothic bitch, with high cheekbones, bulging eyes and a fetish for fur. She was very camp, swirling in and out in a cloud of smoke from her long cigarette-holder. She talked ten to the dozen and was liable to stub out her cigarette in food, a vulgar trick she picked up from Jesse Royce Landis in Alfred Hitchcock's *To Catch a Spy*.

There was a delightful sequence after the humans had failed to trace the kidnappers. The dogs decided it was up to them and organise a Twilight Bark, a dog alert, which relayed the news from London to the home counties through a canine underground network. The sequence, carried out as a military operation, was a witty spoof of numerous British war films.

The puppies (and all the other stolen puppies) escaped from Cruella's mansion. At one point, trudging through the snow, they recalled Napoleon's blizzard retreat from Moscow and, at another, every POW film cinema-goers had ever seen when the dogs rolled about in soot to disguise themselves as Labradors. The cross-country chase with Cruella in full pursuit was a parody of a John Buchan adventure.

101 Dalmatians had considerable doggie charm. The animals were recognisable as animals and human types. The dogs were caricatured Brits. A shaggy sheepdog was cast in the role of a retired and deaf old Blimpish buffer and his Number 2, a sergeant, was played by a cockney cat. There were some good jokes at the expense of television serials, game shows and commercials. The story ended with Roger and Anita giving home to 101 Dalmatians, Roger presuming Pongo has fathered the whole lot.

The cartoon was remade in 1996 as a live-action movie with Glenn Close as Cruella De Vil.

" I live for fur. I adore fur. "

Cruella De Vil

The wittiest, most charming, least pretentious cartoon feature Walt Disney has ever made.
Time

Gone is the treacly realism; back have come charm and zest.
New Statesman

The new sureness of feeling is reflected in the draughtsmanship which is both benign and stylish.
The Observer

Warms the heart, amuses the mind and can be unreservedly recommended.
The Times

1962 • Lawrence of Arabia

CREDITS

TE Lawrence	Peter O'Toole
Prince Feisal	Alec Guinness
Auda Abu Tayi	Anthony Quinn
General Allenby	Jack Hawkins
Sherif Ali	Omar Sharif
Turkish Bey	Jose Ferrer
Col Brighton	Anthony Quayle
Mr Dryden	Claude Rains
Jackson Bentley	Arthur Kennedy
General Murray	Donald Wolfit
Studio	Columbia
Director	David Lean
Producer	Sam Spiegel
Screenplay	Robert Bolt
	Michael Wilson
Photography	Freddie Young
Music	Maurice Jarre

AWARDS

ACADEMY AWARDS

Best Picture	Sam Spiegel
Best Direction	David Lean
Best Colour Cinematography	
	Freddie A. Young
Best Colour Art Direction	
	John Box and John Stoll
Best Set Decoration	Dario Simoni
Best Editing	Anne Coates
Best Sounding Recording	John Cox
Best Original Music Score	
	Maurice Jarr

ACADEMY NOMINATIONS

Best Actor	Peter O'Toole
Best Supporting Actor	Omar Sharif
Best Adapted Screenplay	Robert Bolt

BEST PICTURE

Lawrence of Arabia

STARS OF 1962

Doris Day
Rock Hudson
Cary Grant
John Wayne
Elvis Presley

1962 Blockbusters

The Longest Day
In Search of the Castaways
Lover Come Back
That Touch of Mink
The Music Man

THE WORLD

• Cuban missile crisis
• Thalidomide drug issued
• Nelson Mandela jailed
• Death of Marilyn Monroe

LAWRENCE OF ARABIA, the best of David Lean's epics, was an account of TE Lawrence's efforts to unite the Arab tribes against the Ottoman Turks during First World War. The film was historically inaccurate but visually stunning.

Lawrence, poet, scholar, soldier, seconded to the Arab Bureau, was a larger-than-life, desert-loving, narcissistic, sadomasochistic fanatic and mystic, who identified with the Arabs. He dressed in flowing robes and danced a *pas de deux* with his shadow. A shameless exhibitionist, he was always willing to cavort for the benefit of the press photographers. Iron-willed, self-assured, a born leader, Lawrence didn't believe in destiny: he made his own. His insubordination ("I don't mean to be, it's just my manner") exasperated his superiors. He had an almost blasphemous conceit. "Do you think I'm just anybody?" he cried. "I'm different." The Turks put a £20,000 reward on his head. He was fearless. "The trick is ... not minding that it hurts," he explained after letting a match burn down to his fingers for a bet.

He traversed the uncrossable Nefud Desert for a land assault on Aqaba, which was impregnable from the sea, and then crossed the Sinai Desert ("Why not? Moses did") to report to the British military command in Cairo in person that Aqaba has been taken. There was a deeply moving scene when he insisted on bringing the Arab boy, who had accompanied him all the way, into the officers' mess and the officers tried to bar the boy's way.

The Arabs thought he was a prophet. "The man who gives victory," said Prince Feisal, leader of the Arab revolt, "is prized above all others." Lawrence wanted to stop the Arabs falling under British colonial rule; but the Arab Council failed, disintegrating into petty squabbles. The politics were not always easy to follow. Nobody came out of the story well. The Arabs were represented as greedy, barbarous and cruel, personified by Anthony Quinn's highly coloured portrait of Auda Abu Tayi, a violent old rogue, the self-styled "river of his people."

Robert Bolt's screenplay was accused of offering no insight into the complexities of Lawrence's character. Lawrence remained an enigmatic figure, introvert and extrovert, sensual yet aesthetic. Peter O'Toole, tall, handsome, blue-eyed, flaxen-haired, sand-flecked, rode the whirlwind with hypnotic grace, charm and authority and yet his performance was restrained, gentle and softly spoken. O'Toole, always aware of the flaws and contradictions, had not been the first choice and he landed the role only because Albert Finney (who was nearer to Lawrence's physical size) had turned it down it after four days' work and because Marlon Brando was not available.

Alec Guinness played the shrewd and sceptical Prince Feisal with authority and dry wit. "What I owe you is beyond evaluation," he admitted to Lawrence; but like his British counterparts, he was pleased to be rid of him. Guinness had played Lawrence with great success on the stage in Terence Rattigan's *Ross*, an adaptation of Rattigan's screenplay, which Anthony Asquith had been going to direct with Dirk Bogarde in the lead until David Lean announced his film.

Jack Hawkins was cast as an unscrupulous Allenby, an interpretation which gave

> " I deem him one of the greatest beings alive in our time… We shall never see his like again. His name will live in history. It will live in the annals of war… It will live in the legends of Arabia. "
>
> *Winston Churchill quoted on the posters*

"Do you think I am anybody?" Peter O'Toole as Lawrence of Arabia.

a lot of offence. His scenes with Lawrence had a theatrical thrust and parry. Claude Rains played an amalgam of political advisors with calculated cynicism. Arthur Kennedy was cast as the American journalist, who created the Lawrence legend. Anthony Quayle, in the dull role of a solid, honest, not-very-bright soldier, was not dull at all. Joseph Ferrer played the Turkish Bey who had Lawrence tortured and raped, the defining moment in Lawrence's life. Thereafter, he developed a blood-lust and revelled in the killing.

Omar Sharif was given what was and still is the longest entrance in cinematic history. Initially, he was seen as a tiny dot on the horizon, gradually advancing on a camel, as out of a mirage, towards the camera. Lean always said he wished he had made the entrance even longer. Freddie Young's panoramic photography of sand, landscape, rock formations, dust storms, is memorable.

Lawrence of Arabia, though perhaps the most literate and tasteful and exciting of the modern expensive spectaculars, fails to give an acceptable interpretation of Lawrence and fails to keep its action clear and intelligible.

The New Yorker

Impeccable academic direction and a genuine response to the setting, but the whole thing has rather the air of a blockbuster in search of a hero.

Sight and Sound

Sets a new standard for the spectacular, far beyond being an absorbing and exotic adventure story it provides a subtle exploration of the eternal enigma of one of the most intriguing of our century's heroes.

The New York Herald Tribune

1963 • Cleopatra

CREDITS

Cleopatra	Elizabeth Taylor
Marc Antony	Richard Burton
Julius Caesar	Rex Harrison
Rufio	Martin Landau
High Priestess	Pamela Brown
Flavius	George Cole
Sosigenes	Hume Cronyn
Apollodorus	Cesare Danova
Brutus	Kenneth Haigh
Octavius	Roddy McDowell
Studio	Twentieth Century Fox
Director	Joseph L Mankiewicz
Producer	Walter Wanger
Screenplay	Joseph L Mankiewicz
	Ranald MacDougall
	Sidney Buchman
Photography	Leon Shamroy
Music	Alex North

AWARDS

ACADEMY AWARDS

Best Colour Cinematography
Leon Shamroy
Best Colour Art Direction
John DeCuir, Jack, Martin Smith
and Hilyard Brown,
Herman Blumenthal, Elven Webb,
Maurice Pelling and Boris Jurago
Best Set Direction: Walter M. Scott,
Paul S. Fox and Ray Moyer
Best Colour Costume design
Irene Sharaff,
Victorio Nino Novarese and Rennie
Best Special Effects Emil Kosa, Jr

ACADEMY NOMINATIONS

Best Picture	Walter Wagner
Best Actor	Rex Harrison
Best Film Editing	Dorothy Spence
Best Original Score	Alex North
Best Sound	James P. Corcoran

BEST PICTURE

Tom Jones

STARS OF 1963

Doris Day • John Wayne
Rock Hudson • Jack Lemmon
Cary Grant

1963 Blockbusters

It's a Mad, Mad, Mad World
Tom Jones
How the West Was Won
Irma La Douce

THE WORLD

- Race riots in Alabama
- President Kennedy assassinated
- Great Train Robbery in UK
- The Beatles become internationally known

AGE CANNOT whither her nor custom stale her infinite variety. Shakespeare, Dryden, Shaw, DeMille had all been down the Nile. Cleopatra, who was not Egyptian but half-Macedonian, half-Greek, had a way of mixing politics and passion. Her sexual and political skills were considerable. She was a remarkable, brilliant and ruthless woman who very nearly became empress of the world. The film traced her life and career from her first meeting with Antony (when she was 22 and he was 52) to her death in 30 BC just before her 40th birthday.

When Tallulah Bankhead appeared in Shakespeare's *Antony and Cleopatra* on Broadway, it was said she barged down the Nile and sank. Twentieth Century Fox's *Cleopatra*, at the time the most costly film ever made, nearly sank before it ever reached the cinemas. Filming had begun in England with Elizabeth Taylor as Cleopatra, Peter Finch as Caesar and Stephen Boyd as Marc Antony. With only 11 minutes filmed, Taylor became so seriously ill that the production was closed down. When it recommenced, the director, Rouben Mamoulian and

> " The picture was conceived in a state of emergency, shot in confusion and wound up in blind panic. "
>
> *Joseph L. Mankiewicz*

the original actors were replaced by Joseph L Mankiewicz, Richard Burton and Rex Harrison. Mankiewicz rewrote the screenplay. The production moved to Rome and shooting began before the script was complete. Taylor and Burton's affair hit the headlines. When the film was released, audiences came to see Elizabeth and Richard rather than Cleopatra and Antony.

Cleopatra remained resolutely modern. "We've gotten off to a bad start. I've done nothing but rub you up the wrong way," she said. "I am not sure," replied Caesar, "that I want to be rubbed by you at all, young lady." Some of her best lines were calculated to make audiences laugh. "I have been reading your commentaries on Gaul," she announced. The Queen of Egypt had no difficulty in accepting rape, murder and pillage but she did draw the line (too late) at Caesar burning the great library at Alexandria.

There was a great deal of drollery and rude banter in Rex Harrison's light comedy performance. He played Caesar as if he were in Bernard Shaw's play or a play by Noel Coward. (Coward had been considered for the role.) Mankiewicz, no doubt feeling that he had already covered Caesar's assassination and Antony's great speech in the forum in his 1953 film version of Shakespeare's *Julius Caesar* (with Marlon Brando and John Gielgud), relegated both scenes to mime. They were played as part of Cleopatra's horrific premonition. Burton was reduced to waving his arms about.

Antony was portrayed as a man walking in Caesar's shadow, weak, besotted, unable to shake off Cleopatra's shackles. Full of wine and self-pity, he growled, scowled and ranted. Asked by her what had happened to him, he retorted she had happened to him. Half the time Antony did not know what he was doing. There was nothing in Burton's brooding, truculent, masochist performance to deserve Octavius's eulogy.

When Cleopatra learned that Antony had married Octavia, she behaved like any heroine in any 1940s Hollywood woman's picture would have. She tore up the scenery. Taylor, who lacked regality, was at her best with these suburban tantrums. Vocally, emotionally and intellectually she was underparted. The voice was strident

Richard Burton, Elizabeth Taylor and Joseph L Mankiewiez on the set of Cleopatra.

and all her effects were external. ("I have no technique," she admitted. "The one thing I know how to do is be.") She was more successful modelling the exotic clothes, head-dresses, eye-shadow and cleavage. The supreme irony was that Antony and Cleopatra's love affair on screen did not measure up to the reports of Burton and Taylor's love affair off-screen.

There were moments which suggested that, given half the chance, Burton could have played Shakespeare's Antony. He was at his best when Cleopatra was degrading him, asking for a third of the Roman Empire and insisting that he kneel before her throne. He was also impressive in a long speech expressing his disgust at what he had become. Best of all was the scene when he woke to find his whole army had deserted him and rode out to do battle single-handed with Octavius's soldiers, who refused to engage him in combat.

The most memorable scene was the spectacular parade, which heralded the arrival of Cleopatra in the Roman capital. She sat atop a huge black sphinx drawn by numerous slaves. The parade was a mixture of circus, Busby Berkeley, *Folies Bergere* and a New York ticker-tape parade. "Nothing like this has come to Rome since Romulus and Remus," quipped Antony, a joke that showed that Mankiewicz was well aware of the kitsch. And just in case cinemagoers missed the joke, Cleopatra gave Caesar a big wink.

The script, based on Plutarch, Appian, Suetonius, was literate, urbane, epigrammatic, but banal. Mankiewicz's direction was leaden, the pace snail-like. The camerawork and editing were dull. The film was overlong. A number of distinguished actors disappeared into the scenery. Mankiewicz had initially wanted to make three two-hour films. The picture was cut to 246 minutes and then cut again to 194 minutes. (The four-hour version is available on video.) There was talk of resurrecting the film to its original six-hour entirety but nothing came of it. Burton always said his best performance was in the discarded footage.

Surely the most bizarre piece of entertainment ever to be performed.
Elizabeth Taylor

Seldom can such a mountain of a film have given birth to such a mouse of a performance.
Time

I don't see how you can fail to find this a generally brilliant, moving and satisfying film.
The New York Times

Cleopatra Gets The Needle.
The Sunday Telegraph

1964 • Mary Poppins

CREDITS

Mary Poppins	Julie Andrews
Bertie	Dick Van Dyke
Mr Banks	David Tomlinson
Mrs Banks	Glynis Johns
Jane Banks	Karen Dotrice
Michael Banks	Matthew Garber
Ellen the maid	Hermione Baddeley
Mrs Brill, the cook	Reta Shaw
Katie Nanna	Elsa Lanchester
The Constable	Arthur Treacher
The Admiral	Reginald Owen
Uncle Albert	Ed Wynne
Mr Dawes Jr	Arthur Malet
Bird Woman	Jane Darwell

Studio	Walt Disney
Director	Robert Stevenson
Producer	Walt Disney, Bill Walsh
Screenplay	Bill Walsh, Don DaGardi
Songs	Richard M Sherman
	Robert B Sherman

AWARDS

ACADEMY AWARDS

Best Actress   Julie Andrews
Best Editing   Cotton Warburton
Best Visual Effects Peter Ellenshaw,
    Hamilton Luske and Eustace Lycett
Best Original Music score
    Richard M. and Robert B. Sherman
Best Song 'Chim Chim Cher-ee' by
    Richard M. and Robert B. Sherman

ACADEMY NOMINATIONS

Best Picture   Walt Disney
Best Director   Robert Stevenson
Best Adapted Screenplay
          Bill Walsh, Don DaGradi
Best Adapted Score   Irwon Kostal
Best Art/Set Decoration in Color
    Carroll Clark, William H. Tuntke
      Emil Kuri and Hal Gausman
Best Costume Design in Color
          Tony Walton
Best Sound   Robert O. Cook

BEST PICTURE

My Fair Lady

STARS OF 1964

Doris Day • John Wayne
Jack Lemmon • Cary Grant

1964 Blockbusters

Goldfinger
My Fair Lady
The Carpetbaggers
From Russia with Love

THE WORLD

- Civil Rights Bill in USA
- Nelson Mandela sentenced to life imprisonment
- Death penalty abolished in UK

L P TRAVERS had set her popular Mary Poppins books in her own time, the 1930s. The film put the story back to the Edwardian era and gave it the full whimsical Walt Disney treatment, mixing live action and animation.

Mr Banks, a city banker, and his wife, a twittering suffragette, were always so busy that they had no time for their children, who had already driven six nannies out of the house in four months. The children wanted a nanny of cheerful disposition, rosy cheeks, very sweet, fairly pretty and who sang songs. They got 27-year-old Julie Andrews, who was the same age as her fictional counterpart and, with her open umbrella, neat blue coat, carpetbag and splayed feet, she looked as if she could have stepped out of one of Mary Shepherd's drawings.

Andrews was charming. Some people wished she had been more astringent. Travers's Mary Poppins, part-witch, part-Good Fairy, was vain, officious, subversive and slightly scary. She was a brusque, no-nonsense, nanny-knows-best sort of nanny. "I want to make one thing quite clear," she said. "I never explain anything." Travers likened her to a wooden Dutch doll. Disney sweetened her and took out all the toughness. Andrews, with her upturned nose, sparkling eyes, peaches-and-cream complexion and beautiful voice, got the role because Disney was impressed by her whistling ability.

It's supercalifragilisticexialidocious

Mary Poppins, prim and proper, kind yet firm, was never cross. Eminently practical and confoundedly cheerful, she conversed with dogs and could do anything with "A Spoonful of Sugar", one of the better songs in an unmemorable selection. She took the children to the park where they jumped through a chalk pavement picture and had a jolly day in a Disneyfied countryside. They met singing farmyard animals, danced with a quartet of penguin waiters (in the Gene Kelly manner) and rode on merry-go-round horses, which broke loose from their carousel and cantered off.

Mary Poppins had a friend, Bert, a busker, a one-man band, a street artist and a chimney sweep. Dick Van Dyke's cheery, nimble, long-legged, wide-mouthed cockney had clearly never heard Bow Bells; his accent was terrible. Van Dyke worked far too hard. His more appealing performance was as the doddery old chairman of the bank.

The chairman and his board of governors tried to persuade Mr and Mrs Banks's son to invest his money instead of giving it to a Bird Woman. The boy's refusal ("Give me back my tuppence!") started a panic in the city and caused a run on the bank. Mr Banks was court martialled. His buttonhole was torn up, his umbrella was turned inside out and a hole was punched through his bowler. David Tomlinson (not nearly heavy enough as the stuffy father) was given pastiche Alan J Lerner and Frederick Loewe songs to sing and spoke them in the Rex Harrison/Professor Higgins manner of *My Fair Lady*.

There was a delightful sequence when the nursery magically tidied itself up. The chimneysweeps had an energetic knees-up on the roofs of London, but the choreography wasn't nearly inventive enough to sustain its length.

Mary Poppins was an innocent, jolly, wholesome, family entertainment, admirable for little children. There was to have been a stage version, but it never materialised. At the Academy Awards ceremony, Julie Andrews wittily thanked Jack Warner for making her success as Best Actress possible. Warner had turned her down for the role of Eliza Doolittle in his film production of *My Fair Lady*, the role she had created on the New York and London stages and which went to Audrey Hepburn, who had to be dubbed.

She [Julie Andrews] tries to affect the prim manner of a stern governess, but she is fooling no one. She is all of a dew. If she did nothing but stand there smiling for a few hours, she would cast her radiance everywhere. It would be enough.

Newsweek

Though overlong and sometimes over-cute *Mary Poppins* is the drollest Disney film in decades.

Time

A noisy medley of clashing colours, derivative songs, cartoonish animals and three-dimensional supporting actors.

The Observer

Does he [Walt Disney] really think children can sit still for two hours and nineteen minutes without an interval? Doesn't he remember that a narrative is essential to most children's enjoyment.

The Evening News

*Julie Andrews at the
Academy Award ceremony*

1965 • The Sound of Music

CREDITS

Maria	Julie Andrews
Captain Von Trapp	Christopher Plummer
The Baroness	Eleanor Parker
Max Detweiler	Richard Haydn
Mother Abbess	Peggy Wood
Liesl	Charmian Carr
Louisa	Heather Menzies
Friedrich	Nicholas Hammond
Studio	Twentieth Century Fox
Director	Robert Wise
Producer	Robert Wise
Music	Richard Rodgers
Lyrics	Oscar Hammerstein II
Book	Howard Lindsay, Russel Crouse
Screenplay	Ernest Lehman
Photography	Ted McCord

AWARDS

ACADEMY AWARDS

Best Picture	Robert Wise
Best Direction	Robert Wise
Best Editing	William Reynolds
Best Sound	James P. Corcoran and Fred Hynes
Best Music Score Adaptation	Irwin Kostal

ACADEMY NOMINATIONS

Best Actress	Julie Andrews
Best Supporting Actress	Peggy Wood
Best Colour Cinematography	Ted McCord
Best Art/Set Decoration in Color	Boris Leven, Walter M. Scott and Ruby Levitt
Best Costume Design in Color	Dorothy Jeakins

BEST PICTURE

The Sound of Music

STARS OF 1965

Sean Connery • John Wayne
Doris Day • Julie Andrews
Jack Lemmon

1965 Blockbusters

Doctor Zhivago
Thunderball
The Magnificent Men in Their Flying Machines
The Great Race
That Darn Cat

THE WORLD

- Winston Churchill dies
- Malcolm X shot dead
- War between India and Pakistan
- Unilateral declaration of independence by Rhodesia
- Myra Hindley charged with murder

RICHARD RODGERS and Oscar Hammerstein's musical, based on Maria Augusta Trapp's autobiography, *The Trapp Family Singers*, was highly calculated claptrap, a schmaltzy mixture of singing nuns, singing children and non-singing Nazis in a fairy tale Tyrolean Austria just before the First World War.

The Sound of Music was already a dated, old-fashioned operetta when it was first staged in New York in 1959. It has never been popular with critics but it has always been hugely popular with audiences. The original Broadway production ran for 1435 performances. The London production ran for 2385 performances. The secret of the success of Rodgers' less than memorable score was constant reprise.

Hammerstein once said a revival had to be twice as good at least since the original was always remembered as being twice as good as it really was. It is difficult these days for a stage revival to compete with the memory of the film, then the most successful celluloid version of a musical ever made. Audiences returned to it again and again. There was one 47-year-old Cardiff widow who saw the film twice a day every day and once on Sunday for over a year, a total of 940 times.

"How do you catch a cloud and pin it down? How do you hold a moon beam in your hand?" You may well ask. No one was allowed to sing in the abbey but that did not stop the twinkling, gossiping, cheery, wimpled nuns from singing "How do you solve a problem like Maria?" Nor did it stop the wise, benign and tolerant mother superior belting out the operatic "Climb Ev'ry Mountain".

Maria, a boisterous orphan, was packed off to be governess to seven motherless children. She fell in love with their father and rushed back to the abbey. The mother superior pointed out that the abbey was not a place to hide and advised her to abandon the religious life and acknowledge her feelings. Maria had a wedding, and a wedding train, fit for royalty. The soundtrack absurdly reprised "How do you solve a problem like Maria?" as she walked down the aisle.

What saved *The Sound of Music* from being mawkish was Julie Andrews, the only member of the cast who was not dubbed. Her voice was as clear as a bell. The opening aerial shot, zooming in on her, arms outstretched, in an Alpine meadow, was memorable. Later, she was observed striding down an avenue with her carpet bag and guitar case. Prim and puckish, pert and charming, always optimistic, she had a radiant, bossy, enthusiastic, head-girl quality. "Julie Andrews has a wonderful British strength," said Moss Hart, "that makes you wonder why they lost India."

The father was a retired naval officer, a strict disciplinarian, who ran his schloss with naval precision. Christopher Plummer's performance belonged to the Ivor Novello matinee idol school of acting. He underplayed the martinet with mock-severity and sang a wistful "Edelweiss" as an anti-Nazi protest. Eleanor Parker had the unrewarding role of his mistress, the ditched baroness, recast for the film as a Machiavellian, enamelled bitch. "Goodbye Maria," she said, "I am sure you will make a very fine nun."

> " There is a genuineness about her; an unphoninesss. She goes right through the camera, on to the film and out to the audience. Julie seems to have been born with the magic gene that comes through on the screen. "
>
> *Robert Wise on Julie Andrews*

Julie Andrews and the children "climb ev'ry mountain" while singing 'Do Re Mi' in The Sound of Music.

"Do Re Mi" always stopped the show in the theatre. In the film, the picnicking, frolicking, skipping, bicycle-riding, running, giggling children had the added advantage of being able to sing in a variety of picturesque Salzburg locations.

The Sound of Music was even more sentimental than the stage version but it was also more dramatic, although never believable in the final stretches. How did the Trapp family, for instance, get from the Festival to the Abbey without being stopped by the Storm Troopers? The romantic nonsense was occasionally unexpectedly moving. The maudlinism, however, proved too sweet and cloying for most critics.

It is a sweet mixture and you need a strong stomach to appreciate it to the full. But those with a sweet tooth will happily gobble it down.
The Times

I wish it well. As long, that is, I don't have to see it again.
The Sunday Times

Pure unadulterated kitsch, not a false note, not a whiff of reality.
Esquire

Calorie-counters, diabetics and grown-ups from eight to eighty had best beware.
The New York Herald Tribune

1966 • The Bible

CREDITS

Adam	Michael Parks
Eve	Ulla Bergryd
Cain	Richard Harris
Abel	Franco Nero
Noah	John Huston
Nimrod	Stephen Boyd
Abraham	George C Scott
Sarah	Ava Gardner
Three Angels	Peter O'Toole
Studio	Twentieth Century Fox
Director	John Huston
Producer	Dino De Laurentiis
Screenplay	Christopher Fry
Photographer	Giuseppe Rotunno
Music	Toshiro Mayuzumi

AWARDS

ACADEMY AWARDS
None

ACADEMY NOMINATIONS
None

BEST PICTURE

A Man for All Seasons

STARS OF 1966

Julie Andrews
Sean Connery
Elizabeth Taylor
Jack Lemmon
Richard Burton

1966 Blockbusters

Hawaii
Who's Afraid of Virginia Woolf?
A Man for All Seasons
The Sand Pebbles
The Russians Are Coming

THE WORLD

- Mrs Gandhi becomes Indian Prime Minister
- Cultural Revolution in China
- First lunar soft landing

THE BIBLE was a somewhat misleading title since the script covered only the first 22 chapters of Genesis. In the beginning, Dino De Laurentiis's intention had been to incorporate all *The Old Testament* with Robert Bresson, Frederico Fellini, Luchino Visconti, Orson Welles and John Huston directing different segments and the whole film lasting some 15 hours. The music was to have been by Igor Stravinsky and the cast to have included Maria Callas, Rudolf Nureyev and Laurence Olivier. There was talk of Richard Burton playing God. In the event John Huston alone directed and he played God.

The Bible was a lugubrious, self-indulgent, interminable epic; it was like watching a silent film. God came out of the story very badly, chucking Adam and Eve out of paradise, favouring Abel over Cain, flooding the earth, and forcing Abraham to sacrifice his son as proof of his obedience.

The creation of the world, filmed by Ernst Hass in different parts of the world, was accompanied by Huston reading from the Book of Genesis. Adam and Eve, who took ages to appear, were finally seen ambling though a murky and underlit Eden to the accompaniment of a heavenly choir. The camera took extra care not to show their full nudity, which was hidden by fern, tresses and even a cocked leg chastely raised when Adam first rose from the dust. The actors were generally filmed from either the back or from the waist upwards. It was all so discreet and coy as to be the worst sort of prudery, although it did seem as if Eve had an orgasm while eating of the forbidden fruit. She was played by a 19-year-old Swedish blonde, an anthropological student with no acting experience. Eve was blonde because market research had found the public didn't want a brunette Eve.

Huston had dismissed other Biblical films as "merely facades for whore houses." His version was that rare thing: Biblical spectacle without sex. He was no DeMille. There was no obscenity, so whatever iniquity was going on in Sodom and Gomorrah, it was kept carefully under wraps and left to giggles in the dark. The cities of the plain were destroyed by an atom bomb. When Lot's wife turned round to see what had happened, she saw a mushroom cloud, enough to turn anybody into a pillar of salt. Later, Abraham and Isaac, on their way to the sacrifice, walked through the charred remains of the cities.

The Bible couldn't be said to be either a religious or an uplifting experience. The high spot came with the animals going into the ark two by two. Huston had wanted either Charlie Chaplin or Alec Guinness to play Noah but when they turned him down, he played Noah himself. His funny old man performance owed something to the medieval miracle plays, something to André Obey's *Noah* and something to Doctor Doolittle. Noah was a kindly, gentle, slightly dotty uncle with big pouches under his eyes. He piped the animals aboard, patting them on their flanks and poured milk down a hippo's wide open jaws. The heathens, who stood around laughing in unison at the idea of building a boat on dry land, sounded as if they were a television studio audience watching a sit-com.

Christopher Fry's screenplay was lifted verbatim from the King James Version and the dialogue sounded very awkward in the actors' mouths. George C Scott was

> ❝ My function, I believe, will be to ensure that the film is made with delicacy and good taste. It must be sincere, with no adornment and interpolation. ❞
>
> *John Huston*

"Am I my brother's keeper?" Richard Harris as Cain.

a very hoarse Abraham. Richard Harris mimed Cain. Franco Nero looked suitably stunned when he was hit over the head with the jawbone of an ass. Stephen Boyd didn't have much to do as Nimrod, except climb the Tower of Babel and shoot an arrow at a cloud. The next thing he knew everybody was babbling away and he couldn't understand a word. Ava Gardner was somewhat too glamorous to be playing the barren Sara. Peter O'Toole played The Three Angels (and sometimes just The Two Angels) in a cowl.

This is probably as fine a version of the Old Testament as we shall ever see in movies.

Saturday Review

Huston conducts his ensemble rather like an old-fashioned Sunday school teacher who has put on a million dollar spring pageant and copped the best part for himself.

Time

His triumph is that despite the insanity of the attempt and the grandiosity of the project, the technology doesn't dominate the material.

The New Yorker

What partly saves *The Bible* from the pathos, awe, elephantiasis and sameness which seem automatically to strike any film costing more than $10,000 is really John Huston playing Noah.

Cinema

1967 • The Graduate

CREDITS

Mrs Robinson	Anne Bancroft
Ben Braddock	Dustin Hoffman
Elaine Robinson	Katharine Ross
Mr Braddock	William Daniels
Mr Robinson	Murray Hamilton
Studio	United Artists
Director	Mike Nichols
Producer	Lawrence Turman
Screenplay	Calder Willingham
	Buck Henry
Photography	Robert Surtees
Songs	Paul Simon

AWARDS

ACADEMY AWARDS

Best Direction	Mike Nichols

ACADEMY NOMINATIONS

Best Picture	Lawrence Turman
Best Actor	Dustin Hoffman
Best Actress	Anne Bancroft
Best Supporting Actress	
	Katharine Ross
Best Adapted Screenplay	
Calder Willingham, Buck Henry	
Best Cinematography	
	Robert Surtees

BEST PICTURE

In the Heat of the Night

STARS OF 1967

Julie Andrews
Lee Marvin
Paul Newman
Dean Martin
Sean Connery

1967 Blockbusters

The Jungle Book
Guess Who's Coming to Dinner?
Bonnie and Clyde
You Only Live Twice
The Dirty Dozen

THE WORLD

- Civil War in Nigeria
- Six Day War
- Che Guevara killed
- First human heart transplant
- First British colour TV broadcast

THE GRADUATE, a witty satire on American social and sexual mores, was the cult film for the 18–25 group, who identified with Ben Braddock's adolescent fears of an older woman. Ben was spokesperson for the 1960s generation in much the same way that James Dean in *Rebel Without a Cause* had spoken for the 1950s. Simon and Garfunkel's eloquent and lyrical song, "The Sound of Silence", set the theme of "people talking without speaking, people hearing without listening."

Ben, a conventional, conservative, hard-working student, returned home to proud parents, laden with honours, but dissatisfied and worried about the future. He questioned bourgeois values where all that mattered was financial success. He wanted to be different. Mrs Robinson, a self-confessed alcoholic and neurotic middle-aged woman, the wife of his dad's partner, barged into his bedroom and ordered him to drive her home and then, when they were in her house, she frightened the life out of him. "For God's sake, Mrs Robinson, you're trying to seduce me (uncertain pause), aren't you? I think I should be going." Mrs Robinson, not the sort of woman to accept a rebuff, set the agenda. "Would you like me to seduce you?" she inquired. "I want you to know I'm available." Ben was only galvanised into action when she accused him of being a virgin and inadequate.

> " Mrs Robinson, if you don't mind my saying so, this conversation is getting a little strange. "
>
> *Ben Braddock*

They started an affair. "Haven't you forgotten something?" she asked at their first tryst. "I want you to know how much I appreciate this," he began, thinking she wanted him to thank her for being willing to go to bed with him, when all she wanted was the keys to the hotel room. Ben was always studiously polite. He called her "Mrs Robinson" even when they were in bed. He longed to have a conversation, not just sex, but she had no small talk.

The affair was both farcical and sordid. "I am not proud to spend my time with a broken-down alcoholic," he told her during a row and went on to describe their relationship as "the sickest, most perverted thing" that had ever happened to him. Later, he assured Mr Robinson that the affair had been nothing and that they might just as well have been shaking hands and then added in the same breath that he didn't love his wife but his daughter, Elaine.

The second half of the film concentrated on Ben's compulsive pursuit of Elaine and their on–off romance. The ending was a characteristic screwball finale with Ben in the role of true lover arriving at the altar to whisk the bride away before she said "Yes" to the wrong man. But in Nichols's film they gave the 1930s romantic cliché a 1960s twist. Ben arrived after Elaine had said "Yes," a rewrite not approved of by Charles Webb, the author of the novel on which the screenplay had been based. "It's too late!" screamed Mrs Robinson transformed into a raging harpy. "Not for me!" rejoined Elaine. Ben warded off the congregation with a huge golden cross and the couple jumped on a passing municipal bus.

Dustin Hoffman's performance as the 20-year-old shallow, callow, apprehensive, frustrated graduate was a memorable screen debut. He was hailed as the best young actor since Jack Lemmon. He was 30, but looked much younger. His faux pas ("Mrs Robinson, you are the most attractive of all my parents' friends") were hilarious. The comedy timing in these earlier scenes was excellent. But Nichols had chosen Hoffman because his face could register suffering. The solemn, serious face was

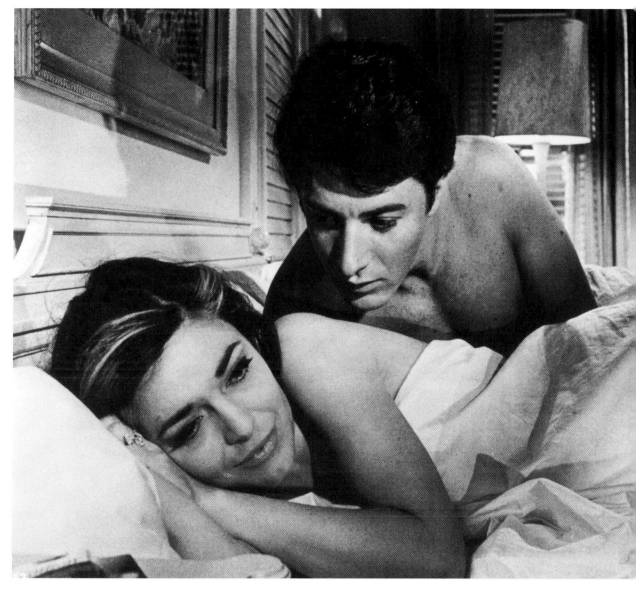

"This is Benjamin. He's a little worried about his future." Anne Bancroft and Dustin Hoffmann as the graduate.

often expressionless, blank, yet the inner life, guilt, dismay, confusion, was always there. Hoffman was less a figure of fun than of despair. Tears streaming down his face he let out a great cry of pain at the church window where he stood in a crucified position, bashing away at the glass.

Anne Bancroft, predatory, voracious, rapacious, always confident in her sexual prowess, cajoled, commanded and threatened Ben. She got very nasty when she realised she had lost him to her daughter. The major weakness of the script was that Mrs Robinson disappeared for too long. Bancroft only got the role after Doris Day and Jeanne Moreau had turned it down.

Funny, outrageous and touching, *The Graduate* is a sophisticated film that puts Mr Nichols and his associates on a level with any of the best satirists working abroad today.

The New York Times

[Mike Nichols] has made the freshest, funniest and most touching film of the year, and has filled it with delightful surprises, cheekiness, sex, satire, irreverence.

Saturday Review

A film for parents, then, reinforcing all their stuffiest received ideas about the rights and wrongs of youth.

The Times

The film somehow gets hoist with the petard of its own pretensions and Nichols ends up like his characters waiting to communicate something he can't quite get across.

Sight and Sound

1968 • Funny Girl

CREDITS

Fanny Brice	Barbra Streisand
Nick Arnstein	Omar Sharif
Rose Brice	Kay Medford
Florenz Ziegfield	Walter Pidgeon
Eddie Ryan	Lee Allen
Studio	Columbia
Director	William Wyler
Producer	Ray Stark
Book	Isobel Lennart
Music	Jule Styne
Lyric	Bob Merrill
Photography	Harry Stradling

AWARDS

ACADEMY AWARDS

Best Actress	Barbra Streisand*
Best Supporting Actress	Kay Melford

ACADEMY NOMINATIONS

Best Picture	Ray Stark
Best Cinematography	Harry Stradling
Best Film Editing	Robert Swink, Maury Winetrobe and William Sands
Best Score (musical)	Walter Scharf
Best Original Song	'Funny Girl'
Best Sound	Columbia Studio

*Streisand shared the Best Actress Award with Katherine Hepburn who won her Award for *The Lion in Winter*.

BEST PICTURE

Oliver!

STARS OF 1968

Sidney Poitier
Paul Newman
Julie Andrews
John Wayne
Clint Eastwood

1968 Blockbusters

Gone with the Wind (reissue)
2001: A Space Odyssey
Bullitt
Romeo and Juliet
Oliver!

THE WORLD

- Robert Kennedy assassinated
- Student protests throughout Europe
- Martin Luther King assassinated
- Russia invades Czechoslovakia

FUNNY GIRL, the musical, loosely based on the career and marriage of the great Jewish comedienne, Fanny Brice, opened on Broadway in 1964. The stage show ran for 1348 performances and created a new star, Barbra Streisand, who sang 11 out of the 16 numbers. The record album sold five million copies. Her face appeared on the covers of *Time*, *Vogue*, *Look* and *Life*. The musical came to London in 1966 and the run was curtailed only by her pregnancy. She then went on to make the film, produced by Ray Stark, husband to Fanny Brice's daughter.

Brice (1891–1951) was born on the Lower East Side of New York City and quickly graduated from chorus line to centre stage. She had a gift for mimicry and singing serious ballads. Gawky, skinny, angular, flat-chested, she used her Brooklyn accent and ugliness to comic effect. She first appeared in Ziegfield's *Follies* in 1910 and remained with the show through various editions until 1923. When her story was first filmed in *Rose of Washington Square* in 1939, with Alice Faye and Tyrone Power, she sued the studio for invasion of privacy. The case was settled out of court.

> " Barbra is the one reason for making *Funny Girl*. "
>
> *William Wyler*

Funny Girl was as much about Barbra Streisand as it was about Fanny Brice. William Wyler, directing his first musical, gave her a star entrance. He observed her arriving at the theatre, the camera behind her, as she walked through the stage door. The audience did not see Streisand's face until she paused to look in a mirror. "Hello, gorgeous," she said to her reflection. She then went into the empty auditorium and sat in the stalls and remembered how an ugly duckling became a star and lost a husband.

Brice's husband in real life was a gangster. In the film Nick Arnstein was turned into an inveterate gambler and played by the internationally famous bridge player, Omar Sharif, dark, slim, coal black eyes, everyone's idea of a glamorous ladies' man. Arnstein walked in and out of her life in a cavalier fashion. "You are woman. I am man," he sang. "Let's kiss." But she did the proposing. She tried to put up the money for him to run a gambling club but he rebuffed her. Arnstein finally went to prison for embezzlement.

Funny Girl, both the stage and film versions, were vehicles for Streisand's talent as a singer and comedienne. The strength of her performance was her vulnerability. The comedy was always in her self-deprecation. Her timing and off-hand, nasal delivery of the Jewish one-liners, was perfect, and especially so in the seduction scene in a private supper room.

The film (much better than the stage show) had three new production numbers: "The Roller Skater Rag", "The Swan" and "Funny Girl". The roller skating, in which Brice wrecked a chorus line, had been in the original stage show but it had been taken out when it proved too difficult to stage. The guying of *Swan Lake* and Anna Pavlova was not nearly as funny as the subversive debunking of a typical Ziegfield *Follies* production number with the chorus girls dressed as brides, all-in-white, and Brice massively pregnant. The number was a mixture of pastiche kitsch, a send-up of Busby Berkeley and also the genuine article. "I ought to fire you," said Ziegfield (Walter Pidgeon), "but I love talent."

The film ended with Streisand singing the Fanny Brice classic, "My Man," a torch song by Maurice Yvain, which she belted out in a black dress in a spot-lit close-up. Styne was not pleased about this interpolation, nor the sixties arrangement of a twenties song.

"I'm a bagel on a plate of onion rolls." Barbra Streisand as Fanny Brice.

Funny Girl was more of a play than a musical. The numbers were slipped in unobtrusively, except for "Don't Rain Over My Parade", which was given the full cinematic treatment in three separate locations: a station, a train and a tugboat crossing New York harbour. The last sequence, which had Streisand standing on deck like some figurehead, was shot from a helicopter. Wyler left the staging of the musical numbers to Herbert Ross, who had directed her in her Broadway debut in a small but effective role in the unsuccessful musical, *I Can Get It For You Wholesale*. Streisand would go on to film *Hello, Dolly!* in 1969 and *On A Clear Day You Can See Forever* in 1970. In 1975, Ross directed her in *Funny Lady*, the sequel to *Funny Girl*.

It is a movie full of old-fashioned emotion, fun, music and entertainment fit for anyone old enough to remember Miss Brice and young enough to be enchanted by Miss Streisand.
Newark Evening News

Not since Hans Christian Andersen has an ugly duckling done so well for itself.
The Guardian

There is something, too, about the poignance of a particular kind of ambition that is dated and almost nostalgic now.
The New York Times

When Streisand is around, she turns *Funny Girl* from disguised Hollywood hokum into something bordering on art.
Rex Read

1969 • Butch Cassidy and the Sundance Kid

CREDITS

Butch Cassidy	Paul Newman
Sundance Kid	Robert Redford
Etta Place	Katharine Ross
Percy Garris	Strother Martin
Sheriff Bledsoe	Jeff Corey
Bike Salesman	Henry Jones
Woodcock	George Furth
Studio	Twentieth Century Fox
Director	George Roy Hill
Producer	Paul Monash
	John Foreman
Screenplay	William Goldman
Photographer	Conrad Hall
Music	Burt Bacharach

AWARDS

ACADEMY AWARDS

Best Story & Screenplay
William Goldman
Best Cinematography   Conrad Hall
Best Original Score Burt Bacharach
Best Song   'Raindrops Keep Fallin"
by Burt Bacharach and Hal David

ACADEMY NOMINATIONS

Best Picture   Paul Monash
and John Foreman
Best Director   George Roy Hill
Best Sound   William Edmundson
and David Dockendorf

BEST PICTURE

Midnight Cowboy

STARS OF 1969

Paul Newman
John Wayne
Steve McQueen
Dustin Hoffman
Clint Eastwood

1969 Blockbusters

The Love Bug
Midnight Cowboy
Easy Rider
Hello, Dolly!
Paint Your Wagon

THE WORLD

- Richard Nixon becomes US President
- Maiden flight of Concorde
- Neil Armstrong, first man on the moon
- Woodstock pop festival

BUTCH CASSIDY and the Sundance Kid were bank and train robbers, members of the notorious "Hole in the Wall" gang, who lived at the turn of the 20th Century and were legends in their own life time. Their story surprisingly had been filmed only once before in a two-reel silent movie. Excerpts were used from it during the opening credits.

Butch was the thinker, who was always dreaming up new ways of getting rich. "I've got vision," he boasted. "The rest of the world's got bifocals." He was affable, optimistic, charming. The Kid was a man of few words but loads of sex appeal. With his droopy moustache, he tended to look morose. "He'll feel better after he's robbed a bank," said Butch. The film was about their relationship, casual, relaxed, yet deep.

Butch Cassidy and the Sundance Kid was the ultimate buddy movie. The robbers were, as played by Paul Newman and Robert Redford, a charismatic and immensely likeable pair. William Goldman's screenplay had a light, flippant touch. The banter was amusing. "Don't tell me how to rob a bank. I know how to rob a bank!" That was all they knew. They robbed ever so politely, with style and ineptitude, spectacularly so when they blew up a rail carriage and the safe inside it. Bank notes were flying all over the place, like confetti. There was a delightful performance by George Furth as the unfortunate train guard trying hard to do his duty by his employer.

The President of the Union Pacific Express railway company did not take kindly to the robberies and hired a posse to kill them. The boys couldn't shake them off. They were always on their heels. "I think we lost them. Do you think we've lost them?" asked Butch. "No," replied The Kid. "Nor do I," said Butch. There was a stunning image by photographer Conrad Hall of the robbers in the foreground and the posse miles away in the distance. Finally, they had to leap from a high promontory into the rapids far below. "I don't swim," said the Kid.

The boys emigrated to Bolivia, accompanied by Etta Place. She was the Kid's girl, smart, pretty, sweet, gentle, refined. The casual, non-romantic way he treated her was very romantic. Their relationship was wittily established in their first scene together when he was holding a gun and ordering her to undress and the cinemagoer was wrongfooted into expecting a rape. Etta gave a good reason for staying with them. "I'm 26, I'm single and I'm a teacher and that's the bottom of the pit."

When they were in Bolivia she taught them useful phrases, such as "This is a robbery. Hands up!" Since they weren't good linguists, they had to carry the phrases on bits of paper and refer to them during the raid. There was a neat sequence, played in mime, when a smiling bank manager escorted what he presumed was a respectable married couple to the vault, opened the safe for them personally and was then robbed and locked behind the iron bars he had just opened.

Etta finally left them. "I don't want to watch you die. I'll miss that one, if you don't mind." The lads were doomed; their days were numbered from the start. But what were they to do? The only thing they were good at was robbing trains and banks. "Why is everything we're good at illegal?" they asked themselves.

The pathos was underplayed. They remained nonchalant to the very last. "For a moment there I thought we were in trouble," said Butch. Surrounded by Bolivian cavalrymen and mortally wounded, they made plans to emigrate to Australia. They

> **" Not that it matters, but most of what follows is true. "**
>
> *Legend*

"They're taking trains. They're taking banks. And they're taking one piece of luggage!" Robert Redford and Paul Newman as Butch Cassidy and the Sundance Kid.

died with panache in a blaze of glory. The camera froze the frame just before the bullets reached them. The final frame was used for the poster.

Goldman's screenplay was action-led yet elegiac, fatalistic yet escapist. The violence paid homage to *Bonnie and Clyde* and *The Wild Bunch* and the lyricism to *Jules et Jim*. There was a charming interlude when Butch and Etta were riding on a bike and the soundtrack was playing Bacharach and David's "Raindrops Keep Fallin' on My Head".

Butch Cassidy and the Sundance Kid was stylishly directed by George Roy Hill and beautifully photographed by Conrad Hall. There was also a clever montage of 300 stills to recreate the gang's hectic three-day spree in New York. The film not only revived the Western, it also revived Newman's career and made Redford an international star. Newman, Redford and Hill would be reunited in 1973 in *The Sting*, an Academy award winner and blockbuster.

The charm eventually turns to whimsy. We learn to love the boys just a little too much for comfort.
The Guardian

Too cute for words and overrated to high hell; a soap bubble weighed down with praise from average minds.
Virgin

A mere exercise in smart-alecky device-mongering, chock-full of out of place out of period one-upmanship.
John Simon

Paul Newman and Robert Redford are wonderful to watch on the screen, even when the vehicle doesn't do them justice.
The New Yorker

1970 • Love Story

CREDITS

Jenny Cavilleri	Ali MacGraw
Oliver Barrett	Ryan O'Neal
Oliver's father	Ray Milland
Phil Cavilleri	John Marley
Studio	Paramount
Director	Arthur Hiller
Producer	Howard G Minsky
Writer	Erich Segal
Photographer	Dick Kratina
Music	Francis Lai

AWARDS

ACADEMY AWARDS

Best Original Music Score
Francis Lai

ACADEMY NOMINATIONS

Best Picture	Howard G. Minsky
Best Director	Arthur Hiller
Best Actor	Ryan O'Neal
Best Actress	Ali MacGraw
Best Supporting Actor	John Marley
Best Original Story and Screenplay	
	Erich Segal

BEST PICTURE

Patton

STARS OF 1970

Paul Newman
Clint Eastwood
Steve McQueen
John Wayne
Elliott Gould

1970 Blockbusters

Airport
MASH
Patton
The Aristocrats
Little Big Man

THE WORLD

- Edward Heath becomes British Prime Minister
- Boeing 747 Jumbo Jet introduced
- Gay Liberation Front holds first demonstration

ERICH SEGAL wrote *Love Story* as a screenplay and then recast it into a best-selling novel. The film, astonishingly popular, brought back romance to the cinema, reviving a kind of fiction that everybody thought was long dead. It was clean and wholesome. The nudity was tactful, so tactful that the boys wore their trunks in the showers. The coupling was covered by sheets and there was only the occasional swear word.

Love Story, tender and escapist, was a 1930s/1940s production for the 1970s. Audiences, who had been sated with sex, brutality and realism, wanted love. It was a weepie to end all weepies. In Portland, Oregon, they issued tissues with tickets. Those, who didn't like it, dismissed it as "a marzipan heartbreaker", "lachrymose pornography" and "Camille with bullshit."

The film opened on a snowy landscape with a young man sitting on a park bench in front of an empty ice rink with his back to the camera. His voice was heard on the soundtrack: "What can you say about a 25-year-old girl who died? That she was beautiful and brilliant, that she loved Mozart and Bach and the Beatles and me."

> **"** Love means never having to say you're sorry. **"**
>
> *Slogan*

Oliver and Jenny were two talented and beautiful people who came from the opposite ends of the social scale. He was at Harvard and he was rich. His father wanted him to go to Law School. She was at Radcliffe and she was a poor music student. His dad was a powerful lawyer and he always addressed him as Sir. Her dad was an Italian pastry cook and she called him by his Christian name. She had a good relationship with her father. He had a bad relationship with his. They had an idyllic affair. They studied in each other's arms and fooled about in the snow. Oliver was meant to be too rich for Jenny. She accused him of loving her "negative social status" but there was nothing in their behaviour to suggest any real difference in class.

Oliver was wistful, warm and vulnerable. Jenny was smug, literate and rasping. He described her as "a superior smart-arse." She called him "preppie." Verbal volleyball wasn't his idea of a relationship. When Jenny said she was going to Paris, Oliver immediately proposed. She gave up Paris and became a teacher and the breadearner so that he could continue studying at college. His father threatened to disinherit him if he married. Oliver was Protestant. Jenny was a lapsed Catholic. They refused to wed in church and had a do-it-yourself wedding with pretentious quotations from Elizabeth Barrett and Walt Whitman.

Oliver's contempt for his father was never concealed. "Father," he said, "you don't know the time of day." He behaved as if something terrible has happened to him; his rebellion was as unreasonable as it was adolescent. There was no reconciliation. When he asked his dad for $5000, he couldn't bring himself to tell him it was to pay for his wife's hospital bills.

Jenny had a terminal illness; presumably leukaemia, although it was never stated what the illness was. She likened death to falling off a cliff in slow motion. The schmaltzy piano tinkling did nothing for her superficial death scene. Music was provided by Bach, Mozart and Handel when it might have been better if Jenny had loved Verdi and Puccini.

Love Story was dismissed as turgid, contrived, banal, bland, trivial and sickly sweet. The acting was described as facile, unconvincing and wooden. The performances were underestimated. Ali MacGraw and Ryan O'Neal gave the characters an inner life. Oliver's role was modelled on Erich Segal's room mate at Harvard, Tommy Lee Jones, who had a small part as one of Oliver's room mates.

"She loved Mozart and Bach and the Beatles and me." Ryan O'Neal and Ali MacGraw as Oliver and Jenny in Love Story.

It's a lying, thoughtless and evasive piece of nonsense, of nausea which aims at reassuring everyone that everything's rosy – or almost.

New Statesman and Nation

The corn is reaped with great deftness and discretion.

The Sunday Telegraph

A story that bypasses the brain and assaults the tear ducts.

Newsweek

No doubt sociologists will ponder over *Love Story* wondering why on earth this little mouse of a film (the best-selling novel was adapted from its script) should have caused such a stampede at the box office. Presumably an affirmation of romance – even one as lushly absurd as this – is manna to a society sated with the realities of Vietnam, Black Power, student protest and hippie extravagances.

Monthly Film Bulletin

1971 • Fiddler on the Roof

CREDITS

Tevye	Topol
Golde	Norma Crane
Tzeitel	Rosalind Harris
Hodel	Michele Marsh
Motel	Leonard Frey
Yente	Molly Picon
Lazar Wolf	Paul Mann
Studio	United Artists
Director	Norman Jewison
Producer	Norman Jewison
Music	Jerry Block
Lyrics	Sheldon Harnick
Screenplay	Joseph Stein
Photography	Oswald Morris

AWARDS

ACADEMY AWARDS

Best Cinematography Oswald Morris
Best Sound   Gordon K. McCallum
              and David Hildyard
Best Scoring Adaptation and Original
   Song Score   John Williams

ACADEMY NOMINATIONS

Best Picture   Norman Jewison
Best Director   Norman Jewison
Best Actor   Topol
Best Supporting Actor Leonard Frey
Best Art/Set Direction
       Robert Boyle, Michael Stringer
              and Peter Lamont

BEST PICTURE

The French Connection

STARS OF 1971

John Wayne
Clint Eastwood
Paul Newman
Steve McQueen
George C Scott

1971 Blockbusters

Bill Jack
The French Connection
Diamonds Are Forever
Dirty Harry
The Summer of '42

THE WORLD

• War between Pakistan and India
• British Industrial Relations Act
• Rolls Royce declared bankrupt
• Joe Frazier beat Muhammad Ali

THE REPRESSION and harassment of Jews in Tsarist Russia must have seemed an unlikely subject for a Broadway musical, but *Fiddler on the Roof*, premiered in New York in 1964, was an international success, playing in 20 countries. The book, based on the stories of the Yiddish author, Sholom Aleichem, was Jewish almost to the point of parody, offering buckets of cosy sentiment, whimsical humour and homespun philosophy.

The action was set in 1905 in Anatevka, an impoverished, ramshackle shetl in the Ukraine, during the pogrom, when Jewish settlements were all being abolished. The dire poverty and the violence of the pogrom were muted. The story centred on one family and was told against a background of the breaking down of Jewish traditions, observances and customs. Tevye, a poor milkman and father of five daughters, wanted to marry off the eldest to a rich, old widower, a butcher; but she wanted to marry a poor tailor. His second daughter married a revolutionary, who was arrested, and she joined him in exile in Siberia. The third married a Christian and was disowned.

> " Without our traditions our life would be as shaky as a fiddler on the roof. "
>
> *Sholom Aleichem*

Tevye was forced to accept the world was changing. But he found it hard. He talked a great deal to God. "Am I bothering you too much?" he asked. "We know we are the Chosen People but can't You once in a while choose somebody else?" The most telling dialogue came in the form of a compliment from the well-meaning policeman: "You are," he said, without a trace of irony, "an honest, decent person, even though you are a Jew."

In order to persuade his wife to accept their daughter's rejection of the butcher, Tevye invented a nightmare in which the butcher's first wife rose from the grave to threaten murder if her husband remarried. The nightmare was staged as a jolly cemetery number, a ghoulish, exuberant mixture of Marc Chagal and Hammer Horror, the restless spirits of the dead and the living side by side. The scene was a striking, theatrical evocation of Jewish superstition.

Tevye had been created by Zero Mostel in New York and played in London by Topol. The 35-year-old Israeli actor, a burly presence, acted the heavy peasant father and narrator with bombastic vitality and shrugging good humour. "They are so happy," he said of the villagers, "they don't know how miserable they are."

Fiddler on the Roof was far too long and made longer by Norman Jewison's leisurely and ponderous direction. Jewison had made it clear that he didn't like musicals before he began. The songs made little impact; even a potential show-stopper, such as Jerome Robbins's choreography for the wedding celebrations, was presented in blurred bits and pieces, which did not allow cinema-goers to see the choreography. The most interesting part of the sequence was a traditional Russian dance by bearded Jews with bottles perched on their homburgs, a fine balancing act.

Jerry Block's score mixed traditional harmonies with the musical idiom of Broadway. Topol sang "If I Were a Rich Man", as if he were still in the theatre, hamming it up, waggling his hips, stomping his feet and waving his outstretched arms. Issac Stern played the music for the symbolic fiddler, mimed by Tutte Lemkow, who scraped away on roof and dusty road.

Fiddler on the Roof ended on a down-beat note with the villagers forced out of

"If I were a rich man..." Topol as Tevye in Fiddler on the Roof.

their homes at three days' notice and taking to the roads with their handcarts and emigrating to Palestine, Poland and America. The whole production, filmed on location in Yugoslavia, was shot through a nylon stockinged lens to achieve an authentic and sombre period look.

If you liked the show I doubt if this revamping will prove as artistically satisfying.
The Daily Telegraph

The whole thing is buried up to its neck in a quagmire of cute national traditions.
The Times

Topol has succeeded in transmuting what could have been mere schmalz into theatrical gold.
The Observer

Topol labours under the handicap of having to project a great amount of charm and personality when he has none to spare.
Time

1972 • The Godfather

CREDITS

Don Vito Corleone	Marlon Brando
Michael Corleone	Al Pacino
Sonny Corleone	James Caan
Clemenza	Richard ellano
Tom Hagen	Robert Duvall
McCluskey	Sterling Hayden
Jack Woltz	John Marley
Barzini	Richard Conte
Kay Adams	Diane Keaton
Studio	Paramount
Director	Francis Ford Coppola
Producer	Albert S Ruddy
Screenplay	Mario Puzo
	Francis Ford Coppola
Photography	Gordon Willis
Music	Nino Rota

AWARDS

ACADEMY AWARDS

Best Picture	Albert S. Ruddy
Best Actor	Marlon Brando
Best Screenplay	Mario Puzo
	and Francis Ford Coppola

ACADEMY NOMINATIONS

Best Supporting Actor
James Caan, Robert Duvall
and Al Pacino
Best Director Francis Ford Coppola
Best Adapted Screenplay Mario Puzo
and Francis Ford Coppola
Best Film Editing William Reynolds
and Peter Zinner
Best Costume Design
Anna Hill Johnstone
Best Sound Bud Grenzbach,
Richard Portman
and Christopher Newman

BEST PICTURE

The Godfather

STARS OF 1972

Clint Eastwood
George C Scott
Gene Hackman
John Wayne
Barbra Streisand

1972 Blockbusters

The Poseidon Adventure
What's Up Doc?
Deliverance
Jeremiah Johnson
Cabaret

THE WORLD

- Bloody Sunday in Northern Ireland
- Massacre at Munich Olympics
- Israel storm hijacked plane at Entebbe
- Watergate scandal begins

MARIO PUZO's novel, based on legend, fact, rumour and fantasy, remained on the best-selling list for 67 weeks. Its real subject matter was a demonstration of how the American Mafia organisation worked. Crime was big business.

The Godfather, the gangster movie of the 1970s, acknowledged its debt to the classic gangster movies of the 1930s – *Public Enemy No 1*, *Scarface*, *St Valentine's Day* – but unlike them, it took no moral stance. Francis Ford Coppola's ambivalence was much criticised. Many people felt that the movie not only humanised the Mafia but that it also glorified and romanticised their power, wealth, brutality, corruption and political influence. So ambiguous was the film's attitude that it was widely believed that it had been made with the Mafia's approval. It was reported that some of them had actually appeared as extras in the wedding sequence.

> " I always wanted to use the Mafia as a metaphor for America. "
>
> *Francis Ford Coppola*

Brando was cast as Don Vito Corleone, the head of one of the five Mafia families; although out of deference to the Italian–American Civil Rights League (who didn't like Italians being portrayed as gangsters and gangsters being portrayed as Italians) words like "Mafia" and "Cosa Nostra" were never used. Corleone didn't see himself as a criminal but as a law-giver, a protector and benefactor, who preferred negotiation to violence. Everybody was on his payroll: politicians, judges, cops, newspapermen. He helped a popular singer to advance his film career. "I'll make him an offer he can't refuse," he said, referring to the movie producer who woke up one morning to find his sheets covered in blood and the head of his $600,000 horse at the bottom of the bed.

The first sight of Brando was a shock. The face was crusty, craggy, dried-up; the complexion was sallow; the temples and moustache were grey; the skin was pock-marked; the cheeks were puffed out (he wore an elaborate mouth-plate to make his jowls heavy); the eyes were sad, weary, dead. The voice was husky, rasping yet strangely quiet. He looked so old and, as the film progressed, he got even older. In real life Brando was only 47, but up there on the screen he was well into his seventies. His sentimental death scene, played out with his grandson in the garden, was as unexpected as it was moving and given an added irony and poignancy when the little boy pretended to gun him down with a hand pesticide spray. The scene looked as if it was being improvised, especially when Corleone stuffed his mouth full of orange peel to amuse the little boy, who, suddenly, frightened by the monster face, burst into tears.

Brando, portly, paternal, bourgeois, underplayed, tempering Corleone with a listless shrug and flick of the hand. His performance, deceptively gentle, showed a great deal of respect for Corleone. He gave him humanity, even nobility. It was a small role yet it dominated the film. Brando (who was not the first choice for the Don and had to audition) got all the attention, but there were fine performances throughout. James Caan played the volatile eldest son, who died in an ambush on the highway, which was as bullet-ridden as the machine-gunning finale in *Bonnie and Clyde*. Robert Duvall was beautifully understated as the Don's adopted son and consilier. Al Pacino played Corleone's favourite son, Michael, a college boy and war hero, who, initially, didn't want to get involved in his father's business.

"We're not murderers despite what the undertaker says." James Caan, Marlon Brando, Al Pacino and John Cazale in The Godfather.

The special strength of Pacino's admirably controlled and eminently plausible transition from innocence to ruthlessness was that when he finally became the Godfather, Marlon Brando's presence was unmistakably there in his performance.

There were many memorable sequences. Most memorable of all were the two baptisms that ended the film, two rituals, one sacred, the other profane. At the very moment that Michael was renouncing Satan and all his works in the Cathedral at the baptism of his son, so were his henchmen massacring his rivals all over the city. Men were being gunned down in bed, massage parlours, in hotel swing doors and on cathedral steps. The camerawork, the lighting, the editing, the constant cross-cutting from font to bloodbath, was electrifying.

The Godfather was the first part of a trilogy. The first two parts were combined in 1978 and re-edited in chronological order for a four-part television mini-series.

One of the most brutal and moving chronicles of American life ever designed within the limits of popular entertainment.
The New York Times

What you will see is a piece of gangster entertainment that glosses over and glamorises a pretty squalid era of American history.
The Daily Mirror

Overblown, pretentious, slow and ultimately tedious three-hour quasi-epic.
Vogue

The greatest gangster picture ever made.
The New Yorker

1973 • The Exorcist

CREDITS

Mrs MacNeil	Ellen Burstyn
Father Merrin	Max von Sydow
Father Karras	Jason Miller
Lt Kinderman	Lee J Cobb
Burke	Jack MacGowran
Sharon	Kitty Win
Regan	Linda Blair
Studio	Warner
Director	William Friedkin
Producer	William Peter Blatty
Screenplay	William Peter Blatty
Photography	Owen Roizman
	Billy Williams
Music	Jack Nitzsche

AWARDS

ACADEMY AWARDS

Best Screenplay	William Peter Blatty
Best Sound	Robert Knudson
	and Chris Newman

ACADEMY NOMINATIONS

Best Picture	William Peter Blatty
Best Actress	Ellen Burstyn
Best Supporting Actor	Jason Miller
Best Supporting Actress	Linda Blair
Best Cinematography	Owen Roizman
Best Film Editing	
Jordan Leondopoulos, Bud Smith,	
Evan Lottman and Norman Gay	
Best Art/Set Direction	Bill Malley
	and Jerry Wunderlich

BEST PICTURE

The Sting

STARS OF 1973

Clint Eastwood
Ryan O'Neal
Steve McQueen
Burt Reynolds
Robert Redford

1973 Blockbusters

The Sting
American Graffiti
The Way We Were
Papillon
Magnum Force

THE WORLD

- US withdraw from Vietnam
- Watergate inquiry continues
- Yom Kippur war
- Widespread industrial unrest in UK
- Death of Pablo Picasso

THE EXORCIST, a study of paranoia and schizophrenia, was a supernatural horror story about a 12-year-old girl, who was diabolically possessed and caused three deaths. William Peter Blatty based his novel on a reported case of possession and exorcism of a 14-year-old Canadian boy in 1942. The film, raw and violent, luridly sensational, full of cheap shocks and crude novelty, played on the audience's fears. Lights flickered on and off. There were strange noises in the attic. Furniture moved and drawers opened of their own volition. A Virgin Mary statue in a local church was desecrated. A dead body was found with its head turned backwards.

The Exorcist produced hysteria worldwide. Audiences groaned, screamed, fainted and were sick. The St John's Ambulance Brigade was on permanent stand-by. The film was strongly criticised for exploiting the subject matter and merely taking the audience for a harrowing ride without leaving them any the wiser. Many people found it obscene. Some audiences attended *The Exorcist* as they might attend a porn film, waiting impatiently for the juicy bits. Its release on video in the UK was delayed by 25 years.

> " People get out of *The Exorcist* what they bring to it... I think a great many people approached the film negatively and saw only the devil. I saw the presence of God in the film – or I believed I did. "
>
> *William Friedkin*

William Friedkin, an agnostic, gave the mixture of fact and fantasy, knowledge and superstition, a documentary reality. The film had a low-key, over-extended beginning to establish a normal suburban home. Regan MacNeil's disorder might well have been hysterical rather than supernatural. She might, in fact, have needed a doctor more than she needed an exorcist, but the doctors could do nothing for her and she became more and more vicious and destructive. She masturbated with a crucifix. Her language was blasphemous and obscene. She vomited and spewed green bile over anybody who came near her. She had the punch of a heavy-weight boxer and the kick of a horse. She put up an enormous fight during the 20-minute exorcism. The bed-shaking, the growling, the screaming, the levitating and the terrible convulsions were painful to watch. The extended scene was shot in sub-zero temperatures so that the breath of the actors could be seen.

Linda Blair's features and voice were transformed. She took on a demoniac appearance: matted hair, twisted mouth, blistering wounds, bloated body, scarred face and a bloody, rotating head. She looked like a ravaged doll. The sound effects were achieved by recording the screams of pigs being slaughtered. The rasping voice was dubbed by Mercedes McCambridge, whose contribution was not, initially, on the credits. Similarly, Eileen Dietz would claim that her body had been used and she brought an action against the company.

The leading male character was a young Catholic priest, counsellor to the Jesuits, who had lost his faith and wanted to get out of the priesthood. He felt guilty about putting his mother in a geriatric hospital. The fight between Regan and the priest was a fight for the tormented priest's soul. He regained his faith only at the expense of his life.

Max Von Sydow (memorable as Death in Ingmar Bergman's *The Seventh Seal*) played the archeologist/exorcist who inadvertently released the demon during one of

"Something almost beyond comprehension is happening." Max von Sydow and Jason Miller in The Exorcist.

his digs in Iraq, which gave the prelude an unnecessary clichéd 'Curse of the Pharaohs' stamp. His arrival at the MacNeil house caught in a shaft of light looked as if it might have been inspired by René Magritte and was used memorably in the poster.

Many critics felt that *The Exorcist* should have been banned. The censors were worried about the effect it might have on a psychologically sick child. The film, however, was supported by the Jesuits. Three of its members acted as technical advisors and took small roles. Some people saw *The Exorcist* as Catholic propaganda to scare Catholics back into the church. Certainly, churches noted an increase in attendance.

The film inspired two sequels, *Exorcist II: The Heretic* (1977) and *The Exorcist III* (1990), numerous imitations, and *Repossessed* (1990), a parody in which Linda Blair appeared

Designed to arouse our prurient and morbid curiosity and pander to superstitions.
The Spectator

The Exorcist succeeds at one level as an effectively excruciating entertainment, but, at another, deeper level, it is a thoroughly evil film.
Village Voice

An insult to the intelligence and a disgrace to the cinema.
The Evening News

A crude slice of Grand Guignol, seriously deficient in both artistic imagination and spiritual feeling.
The Times

Make no mistake this is rubbish and its popularity makes me fear for the entire future of the cinema.
The Daily Express

1974 • The Towering Inferno

CREDITS

Michael O'Halloran	Steve McQueen
Doug Roberts	Paul Newman
James Duncan	William Holden
Susan Franklin	Faye Dunaway
Harlee Claiborne	Fred Astaire
Patsy Simmons	Susan Blakely
Roger Simmons	Richard Chamberlain
Lisolette Mueller	Jennifer Jones
Jernigan	OJ Simpson
Senator Gary Parker	Robert Vaughn
Dan Bigelow	Robert Wagner

Studio	Twentieth Century Fox
	Warner Bros
Director	John Guillermin
Producer	Irwin Allen
Screenplay	Stirling Silliphant
Photography	Fred Koenekamp
	Joseph Biroc
Music	John Williams

AWARDS

ACADEMY AWARDS

Best Cinematography
  Fred Koenekamp and Joseph Biroc
Best Editing   Harold F. Kress
            and Carl Kress
Best Song   'We May Never Love
      Like This Again' by Al Kasha
            and Joel Hirschhorn

ACADEMY NOMINATIONS

Best Picture   Irwin Allen
Best Supporting Actor Fred Astaire
Best Original Dramatic Score
            John Williams
Best Art/Set Decoration
      William Creber, Ward Preston
          and Ralph Bretton
Best Sound: Theodore Soderberg
          and Herman Lewis

BEST PICTURE

The Godfather Part II

STARS OF 1974

Robert Redford • Clint Eastwood
Paul Newman • Barbra Streisand
Steve McQueen

1974 Blockbusters

Blazing Saddles
Young Frankenstein
Earthquake
The Godfather Part II
The Trial of Billy Jack

THE WORLD

• Alexander Solzhenitsyn deprived
  of Soviet citizenship
• President Nixon resigns
• Turkey invades Cyprus
• First test-tube baby born

INITIALLY, there had been two separate books, but they had a similar story. Warner Bros was going to film *The Tower* by Richard Martin Stern. Twentieth Century Fox was going to film *The Glass Inferno* by Thomas M Scortia and Frank M Robinson. The two studios decided it would better to co-operate and make one film.

The Glass Tower was a glamorous glass-fronted skyscraper, 138 storeys high. There were 83 floors of offices; the top 50 are residential. It was the tallest building in the world. The gala inauguration, attended by leading members of society, government and stars of stage and screen, took place before the management had finished installing the safety equipment.

A short circuit caused a fire on the 81st floor, trapping the guests on the top floors. There was no way down. Doors burst open, ceilings fell, stairwells crumbled, floors exploded, windows shattered, elevators turned into crematoriums. There was flame and smoke everywhere. The sprinklers didn't work. Characters were burned, choked, drowned, crushed and swept out of windows. The Navy sent in a helicopter but it blew up. The characters drew lots to see who would be first to take the scenic elevator and the breeches buoy, both potential death traps. An executive and his secretary had decided to have sex, instead of attending the party. The wages of sin were death. The man, his head covered by a wet towel, staggered through a burning room and caught fire. The sequence looked like something out of Hades.

An elderly tenant emerged from the building complaining that they had never had any fire-drills. The builder pointed out there was nothing any of them could do to bring back the dead but he personally was going to pray to God that something like this would never happen again. The architect thought they should leave the shell of the building as "a shrine to all the bullshit in the world." The fire chief thought it would be a good idea if in the future architects and firemen worked together.

In a disaster film of this kind, where there are only cardboard characters playing a supporting role to the spectacular stunts, there is only one thing a casting director can do and that is to cast as many stars as possible. The first part of the story belonged to Paul Newman, who played the architect and he had to do all sorts of heroic and gymnastic things, such as climbing and crawling all over the inside of the building and saving children. The second part belonged to Steve McQueen, who played the fire chief and he had to do all sorts of heroic and gymnastic things on the outside of the building. The two stars came together in the final reel when they blew up the water tanks, unleashing gallons of water to kill the flames. There was nothing either actor could do with his role, except look as if he was in charge.

It was a reasonable certainty that the stars will come out of the disaster alive and that the supporting players would have to die. Jennifer Jones plunged to her death out of the scenic elevator. Richard Chamberlain fell out of the breeches buoy. This was fair since he was playing the electrical contractor, who was responsible for putting in the faulty wiring in the first place. Chamberlain behaved like a dastardly, cowardly, drunken villain should, fighting to get on the buoy and kicking other people off.

> " I am a limited actor. My range isn't that great and I don't have that much scope. I'm pretty much myself most of the time in my movies. "
>
> *Steve McQueen*

"One tiny spark becomes a night of blazing suspence."
Steve McQueen and Paul Newman prepare to do battle with the flames in The Towering Inferno

William Holden, realising he had third billing and a rotten role into the bargain, did nothing for the builder, except wear a pair of spectacles with heavy frames. Faye Dunaway wore a dress, which allowed her to let it all hang out. OJ Simpson, as a security guard, saved a cat. Fred Astaire played a dapper, penniless conman who found true love and a fortune, only to see it go out of the scenic elevator; he got the cat instead. The real stars were the firemen, stuntmen, technicians and photographers. The film was dedicated to the firefighters of the world.

The Towering Inferno was a typical example of a number of 1970s disaster movies, which had begun with *Airport*, *The Poseidon Adventure*, *Juggernaut*, *Earthquake*, and which would continue through the decade with *The Hindenberg*, *The Avalanche* and *The Meteor*.

The glass tower becomes a combustible symbol of American affluence, built precariously on rotten foundations.
Newsweek

One of the few examples of an epic which dwarfs its advance publicity. Its impact is truly colossal.
The Sunday Express

Just another disaster film, more ridiculous than disastrous.
The Daily Telegraph

It seems you can get away with any amount of gloating, voyeuristic horror if you convince everyone it's a prestige epic.
The Listener

1975 • Jaws

CREDITS

Brody	Roy Scheider
Quint	Robert Shaw
Hooper	Richard Dreyfuss
Ellen Brody	Lorraine Gray
Vaughn	Murray Hamilton
Studio	Universal
Director	Steven Spielberg
Producers	Richard D Zanuck
	David Brown
Screenplay	Peter Benchley
	Carl Gottlieb
Photography	Bill Butler
Music	John Williams

AWARDS

ACADEMY AWARDS

Best Editing	Verna Fields
Best Sound	Robert Hoyt,
Roger Heman, Earl Madery	
and John Carter	
Best Original Score	John Williams

ACADEMY NOMINATIONS

Best Picture	Richard D. Zanuck
	and David Brown

BEST PICTURE

One Flew Over the Cuckoo Nest

STARS OF 1975

Robert Redford
Barbra Streisand
Al Pacino
Charles Bronson
Paul Newman

1975 Blockbusters

One Flew Over the Cuckoo Nest
Return of the Pink Panther
Shampoo
Dog Day Afternoon
Funny Lady

THE WORLD

- Vietnam War ends
- 37 countries sign Human Rights pact
- First domestic video cassette introduced

JAWS was everywhere: on billboards, bath towels, sweaters, jeans, socks, T-shirts, tumblers, even underwear. A media phenomena, it inspired 35 political posters. *Jaws* was a monster success, the ultimate castration complex, and nobody wanted to go swimming. The screenplay, based on the best selling book by Peter Benchley, lived up to its advance reputation. It was first-rate hokum, efficient, gripping entertainment and it established Steven Spielberg at 27-years-old.

A killer shark came to a tourist beach town for lunch and decided the food was so good that he would stay. The great white shark, with its massive, ferocious jaws, has no bones, only muscle. He is an eating machine and he eats anything and everything. All he does is swim and eat and make little sharks. He is condemned to a life without sleep or rest. He has to swim or he will drown.

Jaws was a symbolic reflection of post-Watergate cover-up. The mayor (Murray Hamilton) didn't want to frighten the tourists away during the 4th of July celebrations. The town needed the dollars. The mayor was a bit of a shark himself, greedy and devious, exerting undue pressure on the police chief.

> ❝ The film feeds on the paranoia of not knowing what's below the waterline. ❞
>
> *Steven Spielberg*

There was a skilful, realistic, Hitchcockian opening with a beautiful young woman (Susan Backlinie) going for a naked swim in the moonlight and suddenly, horrifically, thrashing about in the water and being tugged down and devoured, the price she paid for having had casual sex on the beach. The scene was used on the phallic poster.

The best parts of *Jaws* were the early sequences when the shark wasn't seen, his presence established only by John Williams's four-note cello theme tune. The music raised the stakes every time it was heard. The suspense was brilliantly sustained. Firstly, there was the false alarm – bathing caps mistaken for fins, screams from couples who were just enjoying themselves – and then there was the real thing and all the panic, which turned out to be a hoax. It becomes nerve-racking just watching the swimmers. There was clever filming when bathers kept walking in front of the camera, stopping Police Chief Brody (and cinema-goers) from seeing what was going on in the water. The tension was increased by filming the swimmers from the shark's viewpoint under the water. A dog disappeared and then a little boy disappeared. All that was left was a floating, empty air-mattress.

The shark was a mechanical monster, operated by hydraulic pistons and known to the film crew as Bruce. There were in fact three Bruces designed by Robert A Mattey, who had designed the giant squid in Walt Disney's 1954 blockbuster, *20,000 Leagues Under The Sea*. Bruce gave the production a hard time, initially sinking, then exploding and, if that weren't enough, his jaws refused to shut. Bruce, the weather and the tourists at Martha's Vineyard (the film's location), caused Spielberg endless delays.

Three men went after Bruce. Brody, a marine biologist and a professional shark-hunter tried to slow him down with bullets, poison and yellow barrels, which they harpooned into his back. But what made Bruce really mad was their raucous singing. Unable to stand it any longer, he came after them and destroyed the boat. The shark-hunter was swallowed whole, sliding into the gaping jaws. It was the policeman, the least likely of the trio, who blew up boat and shark with a compressed oxygen tank.

The truck in Spielberg's first movie, the excellent *Duel*, was precursor to the shark. Spielberg never showed the face of the driver. Similarly, the shark was not seen for a long

"Just when you thought it was safe to back into the sea." Roy Scheider and Robert Shaw in Jaws.

time. When he finally reared his enormous head, the whole cinema jumped, not just Brody, who had casually tossed a bit of bait over his shoulder. Brody's response – "I think we need a bigger boat" – remains one of the cinema's great classic understatements and provided the audience with the necessary cathartic release.

Roy Scheider's police chief, wrestling with his conscience, worrying for the safety of the tourists, was almost too recessive. Richard Dreyfuss played the marine biologist, who was dropped in a cage in the ocean, ostensibly so that he could give the shark an injection, but in reality so that the shark could attack him and give the audience some more thrills. Robert Shaw was cast as the shark-hunter, a dangerous, sly-eyed, grizzled, sneering, old soak, who thought only of the bounty. The role was part Ancient Mariner, part Robert Newton, part Ernest Hemingway's *The Old Man and the Sea*, part Captain Hook, part Long John Silver (without the parrot) and a great deal of Captain Ahab. "*Jaws* was not a novel," said Shaw. "It was a story written by a committee, a piece of shit." The observation no doubt, in part, explained his megalomaniac acting.

James Ferman, Secretary of the British Board of Censors, awarded Jaws an "A" certificate, which meant that those under 14 did not need to be accompanied by an adult and that children as young as five years old could see it. He made this observation to justify his classification: "It is generally assumed by the media that all frightening experiences are harmful but this is not so. They are part of growing up and maturing. Life is full of experiences, some good, some bad, but they all teach us things."

There were three sequels: *Jaws 2* in 1978, *Jaws 3* in 1983 and *Jaws: The Revenge* in 1987. It wouldn't be safe to go back into the sea for some time.

Jaws deserves the rewards that come from giving sheer value for money.
The Times

Dumb, mechanical, purely malignant and without the redeeming features of grace or beauty to make villainy attractive, they are as one dimensional as nature's characters go. It doesn't help that this particular facsimile looks like a foam rubber pillow with the zipper open.
Village Voice

You need a strong stomach to sit through the film. It clenches you in its ferocious teeth from the second it opens and never lets up.
The Daily Express

The ads show a gaping shark's mouth. If sharks can yawn, that's presumably what this one is doing. It's certainly what I was doing all through this picture.
New Republic

1976 • Rocky

CREDITS

Rocky Balboa	Sylvester Stallone
Adrain	Talia Shire
Paulie	Burt Young
Apollo Creed	Carl Weathers
Mickey	Burgess Meredith
Studio	United Artists
Director	John G Avildsen
Producer	Irwin Winkler
	Robert Chartoff
Screenplay	Sylvester Stallone
Photography	James Crabe
Music	Bill Conti

AWARDS

ACADEMY AWARDS

Best Picture	Irwin Winkler
	and Robert Chartoff
Best Director	John G. Avildsen
Best Editing	Richard Halsy
	and Scott Conrad

ACADEMY NOMINATIONS

Best Director	John G. Avildsen
Best Actor	Sylvester Stallone
Best Actress	Talia Shire
Best Supporting Actor	
Burgess Meredith and Burt Young	
Best Original Screenplay	
	Sylvester Stallone
Best Original Song	'Gonna Fly
Now' by Bill Conti, Carol Connors	
	and Ayn Robbins
Best Sound	Harry Warren Tetrick,
	William McCaughey,
Lyle Burbridge and Bud Alper	

BEST PICTURE

Rocky

STARS OF 1976

Robert Redford
Jack Nicholson
Dustin Hoffman
Clint Eastwood
Mel Brooks

1976 Blockbusters

A Star is Born
Kong Kong
Silver Streak
All the President's Men
The Omen

THE WORLD

- Soweto massacre
- Death of Mao Tse-tung
- Concorde begins transatlantic flights

ROCKY was a typical 1930s boxing film, small-scale, low-budget and quickly shot. Mixing harsh reality and fantasy, Sylvester Stallone's screenplay, written when he, his wife and child were on the breadline, belonged to the school of American playwright Clifford Odets and *Golden Boy*. The characters were drawn from stock. The story was corny and clichéd. It had worked for John Garfield in *Body and Soul*. It had worked for Kirk Douglas in *The Champion*. It had worked for *David and Goliath*. It worked again. The audience was emotionally involved.

Rocky was a small-time club boxer, no longer a contender, a has-been, one of life's losers. "I'm nobody," he said. "I'm yesterday. I never had any luck." Rocky was a nice, simple guy, 30-years-old, a gentle, clumsy giant, whom nobody took seriously, least of all a teenage girl he lectured on morality. Battered and bruised, without and within, he should have retired and forgotten about the boxing ring. "You had the talent to become a good fighter. Instead of that you became a leg-breaker (a debt-collector)," said the manager of the club where he trained. "It's a living," he retorted. "It's a waste of a life," snapped the manager.

> " You've got to be a moron to want to be a fighter. It's a racket where you're almost guaranteed to end up a bum. "
>
> *Rocky*

The black boxer, Apollo Creed, was the undisputed world heavy-weight champion, but he couldn't find anybody to fight with him. The promoters came up with a gimmick to celebrate the American Bicentennial: Creed would take on an unknown challenger. Rocky (the self-styled "Italian Stallion") saw it as a chance in a million and went into training immediately, using a side of beef in the freezing room of a meat packaging company as a punch bag.

Creed (an amusing self-regarding, self-mocking performance by Carl Weathers) arrived dressed as George Washington. The farcical razzmatazz continued when he discarded his cloak to reveal another costume, which transformed him into Uncle Sam. Creed climbed into the ring, thinking the fight would be over in three rounds, and was knocked down in the first round. Rocky himself expected to go only three rounds, but despite the relentless pummelling, the broken nose, the thudding pain and being blinded with blood, he refused to give in and went the full 15 rounds. The fight was inspired by Muhammed Ali and Chuck Wepner.

Stallone wrote the screenplay for himself and he was willing to work for nothing (and a large slice of the profits) if he could have the leading role. He identified with Rocky: local boy makes good, small-part actor rockets to fame. It was a role Marlon Brando and Robert Mitchum might have played. It was obvious that Stallone had observed Brando's vocal and physical mannerisms in *On the Waterfront* and that Rocky and Terry Molloy were kin. His performance, sincere, tender, inarticulate, was the turning point in his career and it established him as a superstar. Apart from Charlie Chaplin and Orson Welles, he was the only person to get an Academy award nomination for best actor and best screenplay.

Talia Shire played the plain, shy, repressed girl, who worked in a pet shop and fell in love with Rocky. She was not comfortable in his apartment until he took off her woolly hat and her spectacles and started kissing her. They sank to the floor. There was no "fooling around" while he was training, though. "Women," he explained "weaken knees". Burgess Meredith played the craggy manager of the gym,

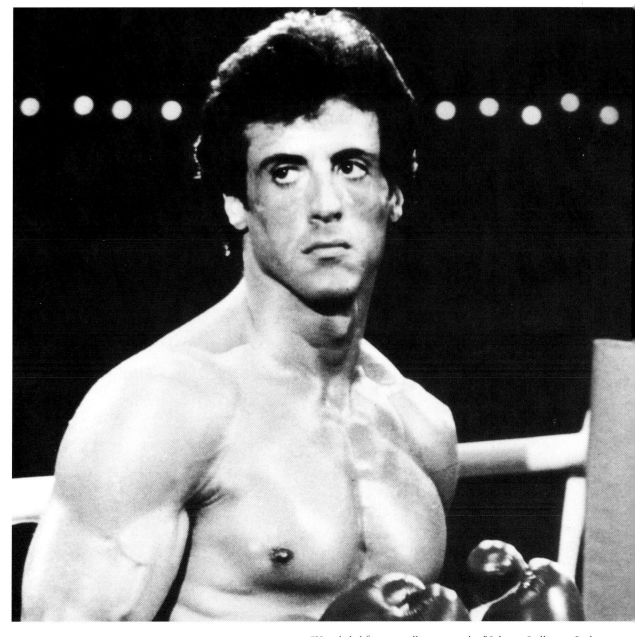

"His whole life was a million-to-one shot." Sylvester Stallone as Rocky.

a one-time fighter, now 76 years old. "You've got heart," he said to Rocky, "but you fight like a dog." He had a sad scene when he begged Rocky for a job.

Rocky was excellent publicity for America and the American Dream. There was no cynicism, no disillusionment, only optimism. Even the loan-shark wasn't a real villain. The satire was reserved for TV journalism, big business and the hangers-on. There were four sequels, spread over the next nine years, all directed by Stallone himself.

Here is a new star with the exciting aura of someone like Gary Cooper, physically strong, outwardly tough, yet somehow vulnerable and lonely within.

The Sunday Express

The power of *Rocky* lies in its audacity in breaking free of currently fashionable despair and paranoia to shout from the rooftop, 'The American Dream' works.

The Spectator

Rocky is a textbook example of an overly grandiose script, performed with relentless grandiloquence.

Washington Star

The picture is poorly made, yet its naive, emotional shamelessness is funny and engaging.

The New Yorker

1977 • Star Wars

MAY THE FORCE BE WITH YOU. A long time ago in a galaxy far, far away, a princess was kidnapped by the forces of the evil. The forces of good were represented by a local farm boy and a strange old hermit with mystical powers. They hired a cynical mercenary air pilot to rescue her. The co-pilot was a seven-foot hairy gorilla-like creature, who looked like a walking carpet made out of angora wool and yak hair.

Star Wars started bang in the middle of a saga with Episode IV. George Lucas parodied old movies, Saturday matinee serials and pulp fiction, with particular reference to Flash Gordon and Edgar Rice Burroughs's *John Carter of Mars* series of books. There were also many allusions to medieval fairy tale romance, gangster showdowns, swash-buckling adventures, war movies and aerial combats.

Here was a director who had obviously seen and studied the DW Griffith epics and such films as *Metropolis*, *Forbidden Planet*, *The Wizard of Oz*, *Gulliver on Mars*, *Gunfight at the OK Corral* and Akira Kurosawa's *The Hidden Fortress*.

> " One of the reasons I started doing the film was that I was interested in creating a new kind of myth and using space to do it because that's the new frontier. "
>
> *George Lucas*

George Lucas was in the same line of business as Homer, Malory and Tolkein, but without their literacy and poetry. His heroes stood alongside Dan Dare, Buck Rogers, Captain Blood, Dr Who and Tarzan. There was a climax every 15 minutes. "It's mindless comic-strip junk," was The *Daily Mail* headline.

The desert planet recalled David Lean's *Lawrence of Arabia*. The burning homestead paid specific homage to John Ford's *The Searchers*. The saloon bar could have been out of any Western you cared to mention. That scene, with the heroes trapped in a garbage mixer with the walls closing in on them, was Saturday matinee time. The battle along the canyon trench was inspired by dog-fight footage from the Second World War. The finale, with the heroes getting medals for their heroism, was a mixture of Hollywood medieval epic and the Olympic Games at Nuremberg as filmed by Leni Riefenstahl in *Triumph of the Will*.

Star Wars, technically overwhelming, was amusement arcade entertainment, a robotic caper, pure escapism, strangely uninvolving with shootings in corridors and battles in the skies with torpedoes, bullets, swords and lasers. The human drama played a secondary role to the battles, enhanced by visual effects, produced with models and animation. Lucas, who was more interested in the technology than the actors, would go on to form the special effects company, Industrial Light and Magic.

Han Solo, the mercenary, launched Harrison Ford's career in the adventure genre and which he consolidated in the *Indiana* films. Luke Skywalker, the farm boy, did nothing for Mark Hamill's career. Princess Leia, the only girl, was a dull role and Carrie Fisher had little to do and was not helped by an awful wig.

Alec Guinness, hooded and bearded, played Obi-Wan Kenobi, a wise old hermit, wise enough to have $2\frac{1}{4}$% of the film profits. Kenobi, who had once been a Jedi knight, wielded a glowing light sabre. To everybody's surprise, he died in a laser duel with a former pupil, Darth Vader, the evil leader of the Empire. Darth, who had been seduced by the dark side of the Force, wore a black cloak, a helmet with a gridded mask and had the stature of a medieval warrior.

"A long time ago in a galaxy far, far away..."Alec Guinness and George Lucas on the set of Star Wars.

There were also two droids. C3P0 was a golden mechanical robot, who looked like something out of a De Chirico painting. He had the voice of an English butler and was always chattering away, always moaning and always in a flap. R2-D2 (known as Ar-too) was a cute, rotund mobile computer, who beeped, bleeped and whimpered and looked like an industrial vacuum cleaner. The two droids had a Laurel and Hardy relationship along the lines of "How did we get into this mess?"

Star Wars, a stunning exercise in merchandising, put science fiction back on the map. Sci-Fi hadn't been on the map in such a big way since Stanley Kubrick's *2001: A Space Odyssey* in 1968. It made spectacle fashionable again. The film became the stuff of legend. There were queues round the block eight and nine deep. The Force (the mystical power that bound the universe together) was destined to be with audiences for a long time to come.

Star Wars will undoubtedly emerge as one of the true classics in the genre of science fiction/fantasy film.
Hollywood Reporter

There's no breather in the picture, no lyricism… it's an epic without dream. But it's probably the lack of wonder that accounts for the film's special huge success.
The New Yorker

Lucas's film is so ingeniously staged and so ebulliently performed that it is the kind of film to give plastic movies a good name.
The Financial Times

You can't call it the height of originality. The entirely mindless could go and see it with pleasure. But it plays enough games to satisfy the most sophisticated.
The Guardian

Star Wars will do very nicely for those lucky enough to be children or unlucky enough never to have grown up.
New York

1978 • Grease

CREDITS

Danny Zucco	John Travolta
Sandy Olsson	Olivia Newton-John
Betty Rizzo	Stockard Channing
Kenickie	Jeff Conaway
Deedy	Barry Pearl
Sonny	Michael Tucci
Putzie	Kelly Ward
Frenchie	Didi Conn
Studio	Paramount
Director	Randal Kleiser
Producer	Robert Stigwood
	Allan Carr
Screenplay	Bronte Woodard
	Allan Carr
Photography	Phil Butler
Music	Jim Jacobs
	Warren Casey

AWARDS

ACADEMY AWARDS

None

ACADEMY NOMINATIONS

Best Original Song
'Hopelessly Devoted to You''
by John Farrar

BEST PICTURE

The Deer Hunter

STARS OF 1978

Burt Reynolds
John Travolta
Richard Dreyfuss
Warren Beatty
Clint Eastwood

1978 Blockbusters

Superman
In Lampoon's Animal House
Every Which Way But Loose
Heaven Can Wait
Jaws 2

THE WORLD

- Camp David Treaty between Egypt and Israel
- First test tube baby born
- PW Botha becomes South African Prime Minister

GREASE, the Jim Jacobs and Warren Casey pastiche of a 1950s rock and roll musical, made its stage debut in Chicago in 1971, arrived off-Broadway in 1972, and went on, following a very long run in the theatre, to become the most successful movie musical of all time.

Grease was an adolescent, swaggering high-school romp, which took a nostalgic, cliché-ridden, stridently sexist look at the 1950s, the age of leather jackets, balloon skirts, rigid quiffs and bobbed hair, an era when kids had to decide who their role model was going to be (Sandra Dee? Elvis Presley?) and whether they were going to be square or cool, prim or macho.

The kids looked like drop-outs. Their horseplay was mindless. Highlights of the school year included mooning on television and the possibility of a gang-bang. Everybody had seen James Dean in *Rebel without a Cause* and they had their own watered-down version of "the chicken run." There was no evidence that anybody did any schoolwork. Everybody was horny. The condoms were damaged. Nobody cared if the condoms were damaged. The combs were out, but the boys were slobs. The girls were for one thing and one thing only and that was 15 minutes in the back of a car.

> " If I'm androgynous, I'd say I lean towards macho-androgynous. "
>
> *John Travolta*

John Travolta played Danny Zucco, the narcisstic gang-leader and heart-throb, a preening, Brylcreamed stud, who strutted his way through "Grease Lightening" with the gang while servicing a car. His pelvic-thrusting body language in tight-fitting trousers had plenty of energy, but the role wasn't anything like as good as the one he had in *Saturday Night Fever*. Olivia John-Newton played Sandy Olsson, a prim and proper goody two shoes, who was always nice, who was always respectful to her parents, who didn't smoke, who didn't drink and who didn't have sex in cars, or anywhere else for that matter.

There was a pre-credit sequence in which Sandy and Danny frolicked on a moonlit beach in the Sandra Dee/Bobby Darren romantic manner. However, once Sandy arrived at high school, she discovered Danny was a completely different person. It wasn't cool to be sentimental and Danny didn't want to lose face in front of his mates. So he rejected her. Sandy sat around moping, until she decided to change her image and arrived in full leather gear to sing "You're The One I Want". Her transformation was as glib as it was unbelievable.

As is usual in Hollywood high-school films, everybody looked far too old. Travolta was 24. Newton-John was 29. Jeff Conaway was 27. Stockard Channing was 32. Channing played the bad girl who got pregnant. ("I feel like a defective typewriter," she confided. "I skipped a period.") Her boyfriend and her girlfriends immediately ditch her. She sang a defiant "There Are Worse Things That I Can Do", only to find she wasn't pregnant after all.

A number of stars made guest appearances. Frankie Avalon appeared in a tacky sub-Busby Berkeley dream sequence. Sid Caesar got a custard pie in his face. Best of all was Eve Arden as the headmistress, who would willingly have murdered her pupils. "Anybody doing tasteless and vulgar movement will be disqualified," she announced at the annual dance. "Let's keep it clean." Nobody paid the slightest attention.

"Grease is the word." John Travolta dances.

It has no book to speak of. To put it another way, the book is unspeakable. The music goes in one ear and out the same ear.
New Republic

As a piece of cinema, it is shamefully unreal, inadequate and vulgarised, with square, lumpen choreography and only a rare, pulse-quickening song.
The Sunday Times

Tarted-up with in-jokes for those who remember the real thing, it has a spurious nostalgic appeal but little life of its own except as a vehicle for John Travolta and Olivia Newton-John.
Screen International

Travolta turns in much the same performance as that in *Saturday Night Fever* but displays some signs that he may be more, one day, than a pair of gyrating hips.
The Morning Star

1979 • Kramer vs Kramer

CREDITS

Ted Kramer	Dustin Hoffmann
Joanna Kramer	Meryl Streep
Margaret Phelps	Jane Alexander
Billy Kramer	Justin Henry
John Shaunessy	Howard Duff
Jim O'Connor	George Coe
Phyllis Bernard	Judith Williams
Studio	Columbia
Director	Robert Benton
Producer	Stanley R Jaffe
Screenplay	Robert Benton
Photography	Nestor Almendros
Music	Henry Purcell
	Vivaldi

AWARDS

ACADEMY AWARDS

Best Picture	Stanley R. Jaffe
Best Direction	Robert Benton
Best Actor	Dustin Hoffman
Best Supporting Actress	
	Meryl Streep
Best Screenplay	Robert Benton

ACADEMY NOMINATIONS

Best Supporting Actress	
	Jane Alexander
Best Supporting Actor	Justin Henry
Best Cinematography	
	Nestor Almendros
Best Film Editing	Jerry Grenberg

BEST PICTURE

Kramer vs Kramer

STARS OF 1979

Burt Reynolds
Clint Eastwood
Jane Fonda
Woody Allen
Barbra Streisand

1979 Blockbusters

Star Trek, The Movie
Rocky 2
The Jerk
Alien
10

THE WORLD

- Idi Amin expelled from Uganda
- Russians invade Afghanistan
- Ayatollah Khomeini declares Iran an Islamic republic

KRAMER VS KRAMER was an old-fashioned tearjerker, at least as old, and probably even older than Charlie Chaplin's 1921 silent movie, *The Kid*, with Jackie Coogan. Skilfully written, directed and acted, it knew how to manipulate an audience's emotions. There were two separate themes: the traumas of families torn apart by separation and the joys, responsibilities and guilt of parenting. The film was chosen for the Royal Command Performance. "Fit for a Queen!" was one prophetic headline.

Ted and Joanna Kramer had been married for eight years. Ted was a very ambitious young advertising executive in New York and was obsessed with his career at the expense of his wife and his seven-year-old son, Billy. One day he came home to find Joanna walking out on him, leaving him to bring up the boy. Normally too busy, too wrapped up in himself, he was forced to learn his way round the kitchen. His son knew more about shopping than he did. He didn't even know which grade Billy was in at school. The strain of coping with the demands of single parenthood and his job proved too high. He lost a major account for the firm and was fired on the 22 December. "Shame on you," he told the boss he thought was his friend.

Fifteen months later Joanna came back, asking for custody of Billy. They went to court. Ted's character was assassinated. The good things he

> " I wanted to avoid making a preachy, polemical film… If there are any villains in this film they are the lawyers. I don't want audiences to condemn Joanna or rush to judgement over Ted, but to see them both as victims of a peculiar social pressure that cannot be relieved by courts and legal processes. "
>
> *Robert Benton*

had done and which lost him his job were used against him. He lost the case. The final scene was open-ended. Joanna told Ted she renounced her claim. But the last shot was of her going up in the elevator to see Billy. The chances that she would change her mind were high. There was no pat, happy ending.

Dustin Hoffman and Meryl Streep gave a demonstration in contrasting acting styles. Hoffman (he was going through a divorce in real life while he was filming) was extrovert, ingratiating, expansive. Streep was introvert, pale, hesitant. He was in a Hollywood film. She might have been acting in a film by Bergman, Truffaut or Rhomer. Truffaut had in fact been going to direct the film at one stage. Nestor Almendros, his photographer, stayed on board.

The emphasis was on father and son. So Streep was off the screen for most of the time. Joanna, frustrated in her lack of fulfilment, wanted to find herself and to do something with her life. In the courtroom, she explained she had always been a daughter, a wife, a mother, never herself, and her self-esteem was low. Much of the dialogue was improvised. Accused of failing in the most important relationship of her life, she nodded her head in agreement. There were many close-ups of Streep's pale face suffering. She looked so deeply disturbed that it seemed highly unlikely that the judge would have given her custody.

"What law was it that said a woman was a better parent simply by virtue of her sex." Dustin Hoffman and Meryl Streep as the Kramers.

Justin Henry, a snub nose seven-year-old, who had never acted before, was a natural performer. The growing relationship between father and son was nicely developed; it had the spontaneity of improvisation. The domestic scenes had pathos when daddy explained it was daddy's fault that mummy had left and when Billy had an accident in the park and had to be rushed to hospital. There was humour, too, when he defied daddy and went to get some ice cream from the fridge and when he met a strange, nude woman in the corridor of his home and the woman explained she was "a business associate" of his father.

There was good support from Jane Alexander as friend to Ted and Joanna, divided in her loyalties, and by Howard Duff as Ted's lawyer, cynically tramping all over Joanna, so that his client would win. In the battle for custody of the child, the screenplay championed the father. "I'm his mother," Joanna argued in court. "What law was it that said a woman was a better parent simply by virtue of her sex?" Ted asked. Some saw the film as a subtle backlash against women's lib. *Kramer vs Kramer* was not a film for feminists.

Kramer vs Kramer is a perceptive, touching intelligent film about one of the raw sores of contemporary America.
Variety

What this Stanley R Jaffe production does have is wisdom, insight, compassion, and an extraordinary sensitivity to present-day problems and pains.
Hollywood Reporter

At every point in the film where we might be given insights into a messy human situation we are given instead a wrenching tug at the heart-strings.
New Society

It is the most proficient, least sentimental study of love on the rocks to have emerged in years.
The Scotsman

1980 • The Empire Strikes Back

CREDITS

Luke Skywalker	Mark Hamill
Han Solo	Harrison Ford
Princess Leia	Carrie Fisher
Ben Obi-Wan Kenobi	Alec Guinness
Lando Cairissian	Billy Dee Williams
C-3PO	Anthony Daniels
Darth Vader	David Prowse
R2-D2	Kenny Baker
Chewbacca	Peter Mayhew
Yoda	Frank Oz
Studio	Twentieth Century Fox
Director	Irvin Kershner
Producer	Gary Kurtz
Screenplay	Leigh Brackett
	Lawrence Kasdan
Photography	Peter Suschitzky
Music	John Williams

AWARDS

ACADEMY AWARDS

Best Sound — Bill Varney, Steve Maslow, Gregg Landaker and Peter Sutton
Best Visual Effects — Brian Johnson, Richard Edlund, Dennis Muren and Bruce Nicholson

ACADEMY NOMINATIONS

Best Score — John Williams
Best Art/Set Direction — Norman Reynolds, Leslie Dilley, Harry Lange, Alan Tomkins and Michael Ford

BEST PICTURE

Ordinary People

STARS OF 1980

Burt Reynolds
Robert Redford
Clint Eastwood
Jane Fonda
Dustin Hoffman

1980 Blockbusters

Nine to Five
Stir Crazy
Any Which Way You Can
Airplane!
Smokey and the Bandit 2

THE WORLD

- Iran–Iraq war
- Black majority rule in Zimbabwe
- US funds Contras in Nicaragua
- John Lennon murdered in New York

A LONG TIME ago in a galaxy far, far away, the *Star Wars* saga continued. On the frozen planet Hoth (a freezing location in Norway) populated with strange anthropomorphised creatures, Luke Skywalker was visited by the spirit of Ben Obi-Wan Kenobi, who told him to go the planet Dagobah and learn the secrets of the Force from Yoda, who had been training the Jedi knights for 800 years. Yoda (a realistic puppet creation voiced by Frank Oz) was an elf-like wizard, dressed in rags and he lived in a misty, creepy swamp of giant banyan trees. He had long ears, Peter Lorre eyes and a green face.

Yoda lectured Luke ("You've got to believe"), gave him a crash course in mysticism and had him hanging upside down. He tried to teach him to control his emotions. Luke had a dreamlike duel with Darth Vader, which turned out to be a duel with himself. Having defeated the dark (Darth?) side of his nature in a quick light sabre fight, he abandoned his training in mid-course to save his mates. The question was could Luke, who wasn't a fully qualified Jedi knight, be corrupted and become a force for evil? Later, while he was fighting with Darth Vader he discovered Darth Vader was his father, which gave the saga an unexpected Freudian twist.

> " I want the second one to be even better than the first one, otherwise I won't be able to make the third, fourth and fifth. "
>
> *George Lucas*

Once again the story and characters played a secondary role to the hyperactive special effects. The interplanetary designs were awesome. The flight through the asteroid field was particularly effective. So, too, was the occasion when the heroes thought they were inside a cave and found they were inside a giant prehistoric monster from *The Lost World*. There was also a great shot of Luke plunging down an endless shaft into an abyss.

The militarism was shallow. The rebel forces looked and behaved like American pilots. The enemy were as plastic as their uniforms. The high spot was the slowly advancing imperial walkers (four-legged, gigantic, metallic, dromedary-like machines) equipped with laser weapons and heavy metal feet crushing everything in their path.

Harrison Ford, as scruffy Han Solo (described as "a gorgeous guy with a laser brain") flirted with the Princess and was fractionally more interesting than Carrie Fisher. Mark Hamill, as an actor, seemed incapable of suggesting any emotion to make Luke's rite of passage meaningful. Darth Vader had his personal Wagnerian theme tune. Alec Guinness made an occasional misty appearance and provided a voiceover. Chewbacca, the hairy gorilla, was even more soppy and sentimental than he had been first time round.

The Empire Strikes Back ended in mid-galaxy with Han Solo freezingly encased in a carbonic slab and carted off to Jabba the Hutt. Would he be able to escape? In another era, cinema-goers would have been able to find out the following Saturday. This time they had to wait two years.

Luke Skywalker and Darth Vader fight it out. Mark Hamill and David Prowse in The Empire Strikes Back.

Here we have the American imagination at its most grandiose, and the deliberate shallowness of the film – the way in which human feelings are systematically devalued, in which human beings are turned into supporting roles for technological fantasies – left me uneasy.

The Spectator

But it is hard to place one's affections anywhere in a world which is ruled by buttons and dials, computers and blips and people whose conversation is so technical, inaudible and dull that it might be better if the film gave up the idea of dialogue and settled for subtitles where necessary.

The Daily Telegraph

The Empire Strikes Back is malodorous offal... everything is stale, limp, desperately stretched out, and pretentious.

National Review

I cannot help thinking that kids got something eminently richer out of Errol Flynn, Disney and *The Wizard of Oz.* The older entertainments had soul as well as spectacle.

New Yorker

1981 • Raiders of the Lost Ark

CREDITS

Indiana Jones	Harrison Ford
Marion Ravenwood	Karen Allen
Belloq	Paul Freeman
Toht	Ronald Lacey
Sallah	John Rhys-Davies
Marcus Brody	Denholm Elliott
Studio	Paramount
Director	Steven Spielberg
Producer	Frank Marshall
Screenplay	Lawrence Kasdan
Photographer	Douglas Slocombe
Music	John Williams

AWARDS

ACADEMY AWARDS

Best Editing	Michael Kahn
Best Art Direction	Norman Reynolds and Leslie Dilley
Best Set Direction	Michael Ford
Best Sound	Bill Varney, Steve Maslow, Gregg Landaker and Robert Charman
Best Visual Effects	Richard Edlund, Kit West, Bruce Nicholson and Joe Johnston
Best Sound Editing	Ben Burtt and Richard L. Anderson

ACADEMY NOMINATIONS

Best Picture	Frank Marshall
Best Director	Steven Spielberg
Best Cinematography	Douglas Slocombe
Best Original Score	John Williams

BEST PICTURE

Chariots of Fire

STARS OF 1981

Burt Reynolds
Clint Eastwood
Dudley Moore
Dolly Parton
Jane Fonda

1981 Blockbusters

Superman 2
On Golden Pond
Arthur
Stripes
The Cannonball Run

THE WORLD

- Ronald Reagan becomes US President
- First report of AIDS
- Prince Charles marries Lady Diana Spencer

RAIDERS OF THE LOST ARK, a first collaboration between George Lucas and Steven Spielberg, was a very enjoyable and very expensive comic strip. It marked a return to the high-spirited, rip-roaring, thrill-a-minute fantasy-adventures of Saturday cinema matinees of the 1930s and 1940s. The screenplay, totally familiar, yet totally fresh, had a genuine affection for the "Perils of Pauline", hair-breadth escape genre. There were no pauses: one action-filled cliffhanger followed another.

For 3000 years man had been looking for the Ark of the Covenant, the sacred cabinet holding the broken stone tablets of the Ten Commandments. Indiana Jones was enlisted by the FBI to get hold of the cabinet before the Nazis did, for the contents would give, who ever had them, invincible power.

The excitement began immediately with an excellently edited trailer with Indiana attempting to rob an Indian tribe of its golden idol, which was housed in a Peruvian temple in a booby-trapped cave. ("Nobody has come out of there alive," observed somebody helpfully.) Indiana evaded collapsing floors, rotting corpses, descending portcullises, impaling lances, falling masonry and a great, big rolling boulder, only to be robbed of his prize at the very last minute by a French rival archaeologist, who was in league with the Nazis.

> " He is a remarkable combination of Errol Flynn in *The Adventures of Don Juan* and Bogart as Fred C Dobbs in *The Treasure of Sierra Madre.* "
>
> *Steven Spielberg on Harrison Ford*

As with Superman and Batman, Indiana also had two separate characters: on the one hand, there was the mild-mannered, shy academic, protector of rare antiquities, and, on the other, there was the brawny, intrepid man of action. Indiana wore a leather jacket, a battered fedora and carried a bullwhip. In his travels, he faced poison arrows, swordsmen in masks, bald wrestlers, tarantulas, snakes and a monkey given to saluting Hitler. Whatever the trauma, his rugged face, unshaven and weary, always remained deadpan. His bravura set-piece came when he commandeered a truck and beat off a convoy of stuntmen. Pushed through the windscreen, he still managed to cling on to the radiator, slip under the moving vehicle and climb back on. As the adverts put it, "Indiana is the ultimate hero in the ultimate adventure."

"I'm making it up as I go along," he explained. Flash Gordon, Blackhawk, Don Winslow, Commando Cody, Bulldog Drummond, Rider Haggard and John Buchan would all have recognised a kindred spirit. Faced with a prodigious Arab brandishing a scimitar he didn't waste time and, in the best-remembered (although not original) gag, he shot him. The violence was never serious.

Karen Allen played the hard-drinking, tough tomboy girlfriend Indiana had ditched and who now ran a dive in Nepal and could drink any man under the table. She wanted to be his partner because she knew he knew how to give a girl a good time. At one point she was carried off, Ali-Baba fashion, in a basket. "You can't do this to me!" she screamed, "I'm an American!" She faced death by the Nazis and a fate worse than death by a French archeologist with the same fortitude.

In the final sequence the Nazis discovered God in a gruesome, supernatural blaze which engulfed and liquefied them. Caricatured Nazis are always a useful stand-by when filmmakers are looking for villains, who will offend nobody. Ronald Lacey,

"I'm making it up as I go along." Harrison Ford and Karen Allen in Raiders of the Lost Ark.

dressed in a typical German leather greatcoat and wearing spectacles, was a comic cartoon Gestapo.

The scenario, shot at a spanking pace, only ran out of steam in its last stretches. The final curtain, which paid homage to *Citizen Kane*, was neat. Harrison Ford was perfect as the reluctant hero.

Two hugely successful sequels followed: *Indiana Jones and The Temple of Doom* in 1984 and *Indiana Jones and The Last Crusade* in 1989.

This is textbook film-making, a charmed collaboration between two of the brightest talents of the new Hollywood to put intelligence into escapism and make a popular entertainment of the highest possible calibre.
The Sunday Telegraph

It's pure delight at 24 frames a second.
The Financial Times

Never mind the plausibility, the film-makers seem to be saying, just feel the bumps.
The Guardian

Children may well enjoy its simple-mindedness, untroubled by the fact that it looks so shoddy and so uninventive.
The Observer

1982 • E.T. – THE EXTRA TERRESTRIAL

CREDITS

Elliott	Henry Thomas
Mary	Dee Wallace Stone
Keys	Peter Coyote
Michael	Robert MacNaughton
Gertie	Drew Barrymore
Studio	Universal
Director	Steven Spielberg
Producer	Steven Spielberg
	Kathleen Kennedy
Screenplay	Melissa Mathison
Photography	Allen Daviau
Music	John Williams

AWARDS

ACADEMY AWARDS

Best Sound   Robert Knudson, Robert Glass, Don Digirolamo and Gene Cantamessa
Best Visual Effects Carlo Rambaldi, Dennis Murren and Kenneth F. Smith
Best Sound Effects Editing
     Charles L. Campbell and Ben Burtt
Best Original Score   John Williams

ACADEMY NOMINATIONS

Best Picture   Steven Spielberg
Best Director   Steven Spielberg
Best Original Screenplay
          Melissa Matheson
Best Cinematography   Allen Daviau
Best Film Editing   Carol Littleton

BEST PICTURE

Gandhi

STARS OF 1982

Burt Reynolds
Clint Eastwood
Sylvester Stallone
Dustin Hoffman
Richard Pryor

1982 Blockbusters

Tootsie
Rocky 3
An Officer and a Gentleman
Porky's
The Best Whorehouse in Town

THE WORLD

- UK unemployment reaches 3 million
- Falklands War
- Israel withdraws from Sinai Peninsula
- First compact disc on sale

E.T. THE EXTRA-TERRESTRIAL, a close encounter between HG Welles and JM Barrie, was a small-scale movie, sensitive, warm, loving and full of childlike wonder and childlike innocence.

A young alien (ET) was stranded on earth 3 million light years from home. He had been accidentally left behind, when his spaceship was forced to make an unexpectedly abrupt departure. He was offered sanctuary and friendship by Elliott and his older brother, Michael, and his younger sister, Gertie, who hid, consoled, pet, fed and protected him from the adult world. The children were being brought up by their mother; their father was away in Mexico with some woman. ET filled a gap in their lives.

ET was disguised autobiography. Spielberg has described his fantasy as a very personal story about the divorce of his parents and how he felt when they broke up. He identified with Elliott, a serious, practical, mature little boy.

ET was squat and ugly. He had a shrivelled, leathery, tortoise-like body, a

> " A childhood fantasy of mine to make me feel less lonely in my life. "
>
> *Steven Spielberg*

huge head, a sad frog-like face with large round eyes, an elongating neck, protruding ears, long thin arms, expressive hand movements and the voice of an 82-year-old woman. His heart glowed. ET, created by Carlo Rambaldi and his team, was made out of aluminium and steel and he was capable of 150 movements; the skin was made of fibreglass, foam rubber and polyurethane. He looked like a vulnerable, wobbly toy. There was a delightful moment when he was hiding in a cupboard jam-packed with toys and the children's mother didn't even notice him. He spent the day, while the children were at school, shuffling around in an old dressing-gown, watching television, reading SF comics, raiding the larder, guzzling beer and getting drunk. There was some amusing slapstick when the distracted mother, totally unaware of his presence in the kitchen, swung open the fridge door and knocked him over.

ET, benevolent and tender, had supernatural attributes. He could hypnotise and make flowers grow. The story was, in part, a religious myth. He was discovered in a shed (the next best thing to a manger). He healed the sick, performed miracles, died, was resurrected and ascended. His glowing finger recalled Michelangelo's *God creating Adam* in the Sistine Chapel. The children's mother was called Mary. (The film was popular with born-again Christians.) The opening scene in a dark forest was in the timeless fairytale tradition, yet this forest was a friendly place. The NASA men with their torches searching the undergrowth were faceless and always seen from the waist down. (The whole film was shot from a child's point of view.) The faces of the doctors, who invaded the house through a milky-white, translucent tunnel, were hidden behind spaceship travel gear. The humans were almost as alien as ET.

Henry Thomas's Elliott was a real little boy living in a real Californian suburb. Wide-eyed with fear, he was unable to cry out when ET walked towards him for the first time. Elliott (E…T) identified with ET. Nothing could have been more natural than the scene when he was showing the alien his toys. They had an affinity. They shared the same symptoms, actions and thoughts. When ET got drunk, Elliott suddenly felt drunk at school. When ET was watching John Wayne and Maureen O'Hara in a love scene on television Elliott wanted to kiss a schoolgirl. There was a death scene in the hospital when they both nearly died; the emotional power of the film was quite exceptional.

"A million light years from home." ET and Henry Thomas.

How long could ET continue to survive in an alien atmosphere? Would he suffer the same fate as the frogs in the biology lesson at school and be seized for laboratory experiments and dissected? There was an exciting chase when alien and children were making a dash for freedom on their bikes and being pursued by adults in their cars. Just when it looked as if they were trapped, the bikes took off and soared into the air. It was a magical moment to recall Peter Pan and the children flying out through the window of the nursery or, even, perhaps, Steve McQueen and his motorbike leaping over the barbed wire in the POW film, *The Great Escape*. The bicycle flying in mid-air over the trees against the moon remains one of cinema's most memorable images. John Williams's symphonic score, soothing and benign, yet scary and suspenseful when it needed to be, moved to an operatic finale. "Stay!" pleaded Elliott. "Come!" pleaded ET. They hugged each other and Williams' music ensured there wasn't a dry eye in the cinema.

The most moving science fiction ever made on earth.
The New Yorker

A miracle movie and one that confirms Spielberg as a master storyteller of his medium.
Life

In reducing the unknowable to the easily loveable, the film sacrifices a little too much truth in favour of its huge emotional punch.
Time Out

The best Disney film Disney never made.
Variety

1983 • Return of the Jedi

CREDITS

Luke Skywalker	Mark Hamill
Han Solo	Harrison Ford
Princess Leia	Carrie Fisher
Ben Obi-Wan Kenobi	Alec Guinness
Grand Moff Tarkin	Peter Cushing
C-3PO	Anthony Daniels
R2-D2	Kenny Baker
Chewbacca	Peter Mayhew
Darth Vader	David Prowse
Anakin Skywalker	Sebastian Shaw
Emperor	Ian McDiarmid
Studio	Twentieth Century Fox
Director	Richard Marquand
Producer	Howard Kazanjian
Screenplay	Lawrence Kasdan
	George Lucas
Photography	Alan Hume
Music	John Williams

AWARDS

ACADEMY AWARDS

Best Visual Effects Richard Edlund,
Dennis Muren, Ken Ralston
and Phil Tippett

ACADEMY NOMINATIONS

Best Original Score   John Williams
Best Art/Set Decoration
Norman Reynolds, Fred Hole,
James Schoppe and Michael Ford
Best Sound   Ben Burtt,
Gary Summers, Randy Thom
and Tony Dawe
Best Sound Effects Editing Ben Burtt

BEST PICTURE

Terms of Endearment

STARS OF 1983

Clint Eastwood
Eddie Murphy
Sylvester Stallone
Burt Reynolds
John Travolta

1983 Blockbusters

Terms of Endearment
Trading Places
Superman 3
Flashdance
War Games

THE WORLD

- Anti-nuclear rallies in Europe
- Reagan proposes Star Wars missile shield in space
- Global Warming effect demonstrated

THE STAR WARS saga continued. Luke Skywalker returned home to rescue Han Solo, who was still encased in a carbonic slab, the prisoner of Jabba the Hutt, the gangster slug. Princess Leia woke Han from his "sleeping beauty" sleep with a fairytale kiss. "Who are you?" he asked. "Someone you love," she replied, helpfully. They were immediately arrested and Jabba dropped Luke into a pit as food for the revolting Rancour Beast, which he killed with ridiculous ease, much to the tearful distress of Rancour's keeper. Luke was then forced to walk the plank and fell into a pit which was inhabited by a sand-dwelling omnivore monster, which took 1000 years to digest its victims. Luke, wielding his light sabre in the swashbuckling manner of Errol Flynn, once again escaped without any difficulty and any drama.

Yoda, on his deathbed, told Luke he had to confront Darth Vader before he could become a Jedi knight. Luke discovered Leia was his twin sister. The big question was whether Luke would be

> ❝ My films are closer to amusement park rides than plays or novels. ❞
>
> *George Lucas*

able to kill his dad? It didn't look promising. "I can't kill my dad," he said, hoping against hope that he would be able to turn him back to his good side. Darth cut off Luke's right hand, a symbolic castration. Darth had a last-minute conversion and killed the Emperor. "Help me take off this mask," he pleaded with his son. (He wanted to see the son's face.) "But you'll die," said Luke and it wasn't long before he was giving dad a Viking's funeral.

Once again the sheer scale of the operation and the hardware (including the stalking war-machines) was often impressive. The Ewoks, who came to the aid of the Rebels, were cuddly bears, little furry balls, pretending to be Robin Hood and his merry men. They treated C-3PO as if he were a god. They decided to roast Han over a spit and serve him up as the main course at a banquet in C-3PO's honour. They defeated the stormtroopers with rocks (an unlikely success against sophisticated high-tech weaponery) and celebrated their victory with a teddy bears' picnic, which was watched over by the spirits of Yoda, Darth Vader and Ben Kenobi.

Harrison Ford had little to do. Mark Hamill and Carrie Fisher zipped through the forest on the air-motorbikes which hovered just above the ground. Alec Guinness put in another transparent appearance. C-3PO was his usually hand-flapping, camp self. R2D2 was still blinking, whistling and chirping. Much the most interesting character was Jabba the Hutt, a big, vile, slobbery, debauched, gluttonous, gap-toothed, hookah-smoking toad, who lusted in a nightclub. This "slimy piece of worm-ridden filth" was made from articulated foam latex and modelled on Sydney Greenstreet. He was strangled by Leia with the chain which had bound her to him when she was his prisoner.

Return of the Jedi (Episode VI) ended in victory for the Rebels. But this was not the end of *Star Wars*. George Lucas still had the prequels to write and film.

Lucas and his associates deserve their huge success because they genuinely respect and understand the children in the audience, in themselves, and in all of us.
Voice

One felt, after watching Jedi that there is no obvious way forward, that the vein is exhausted, the gold mine played out after three successive films.
The Scotsman

The film remains a cunning and prodigal synthesis of every kind of popular myth.
The Times
Let's face it – the magic has gone.
The New York Times

"Return to a Galaxy...far, far away." Carrie Fisher, Anthony Daniles, Mark Hamill and Harrison Ford in Return of the Jedi.

1984 • Ghostbusters

CREDITS

Dr Peter Venkman	Bill Murray
Dr Raymond Stantz	Dan Aykroyd
Dr Egon Spengler	Harold Ramis
Dana Barrett	Sigourney Weaver
Louis Tully	Rick Moranis
Janine Melinitz	Annie Potts
Walter Peck	William Atherton
Wintson Zeddmore	Ernie Hudson
Mayor	David Margulies
Studio	Columbia
Director	Ivan Reitman
Producer	Ivan Reitman
Screenplay	Dan Aykroyd
	Harold Ramis
Photography	Laszlo Kovacs
Music	Elmer Bernstein

AWARDS

ACADEMY AWARDS

None

ACADEMY NOMINATIONS

Best Original Song 'Ghostbusters'' by Ray Parker, Jr
Best Visual Effects Richard Edlund, John Bruno, Mark Vargo and Chuck Gaspar

BEST PICTURE

Amadeus

STARS OF 1984

Clint Eastwood
Bill Murray
Harrison Ford
Eddie Murphy
Sally Field

1984 Blockbusters

Indiana Jones and the Temple of Doom
Beverley Hills Cop
Gremlins
The Karate Kid
Star Trek 3

THE WORLD

- Miners' strike
- Indira Gandhi assassinated
- IRA bomb attack on Conservative Conference in Brighton
- Famine in Ethiopia

GHOSTBUSTERS was a spoof ghost horror movie, which was never frightening nor funny enough. Three sacked scientists, university researchers, became professional paranormal investigators in elimination and saved New York from a disaster of Biblical proportions. In their uniforms they looked like astronauts and behaved like firemen, brandishing flame throwers, laser beams and vacuum cleaners.

The scientists were played by three comics, graduates of the *National Lampoon* stage show and the *Saturday Night Live* television programme. Only Bill Murray had a fair deal and this was strange, since the script had been written by his two co-stars. Dan Aykroyd and Harold Ramis forgot to give themselves any characters to play. Murray (who took over from John Belushi who had died of a drug overdose) projected a bland exterior

" They're here to save the world. "

Slogan

and delivered what few good lines he had in a deadpan manner. "I worked in the private sector," he observed, "and they expected results." He was totally unfazed in the face of the Apocalypse: "We'll show this prehistoric bitch how we do things downtown."

The "prehistoric bitch" (Sigourney Weaver) was a cellist, who lived on the 12th floor of an Art Deco apartment block. Her next-door neighbour was a creepy nerd (Rick Moranis), who was always trying to waylay her in the corridor. Cellist and nerd were possessed and transformed into snarling hell-hounds. Since *Ghostbusters* was aimed at the family market, their bonding (it didn't bear thinking about) took place off-screen.

William Atherton, in his role of Environmental Protection Officer, was set up as the villain but his role was never developed. The most amusing cameo was by a disgusting green blob guzzling food on room service trolleys in hotel corridors. The best visual gag was the "no ghosts" sign, which was used in the highly successful advertising campaign.

The comedy played a secondary role to the special effects. The horrors were few: a skeleton taxi-driver, a fiendish attack on Sigourney Weaver and a leaping hell-hound. The final horror was a joke: a 50-foot Marshmallow Man, with a jaunty sailor hat, trampling all over New York, as if he were a latter-day King Kong.

The enormous success of *Ghostbusters* bore no relation to its negligible merits. The mixture of horror and laughs had been done infinitely better in Bob Hope films such as *The Cat and The Canary* and *Ghost Breakers*. Five years later Ivan Reitman and practically the whole cast would be reunited in another blockbuster, *Ghostbusters 2*.

Praise is due to everyone connected with *Ghostbusters* for thinking on a grandly comic scale and delivering the goofy goods, neatly timed and perfectly packaged.
Time

Despite the expensive special effects, *Ghostbusters* is a lumbering affair that lacks the finesse of good farce. The characters are constantly tripping over their own loose ends.
The Observer

Its jokes, characters and story lines are as wispy as the ghosts themselves and a good deal less substantial.
The New York Times

[*Ghostbusters*] is a great goofy, gorgeous treat that deserves to be savoured for a long, long time.
Films and Filming

"Who ya gonna call? Ghostbusters!" Harold Ramis, Bill Murray and Dan Aykroyd as ghostbusters.

1985 • Back to the Future

CREDITS

Martin McFly	Michael J Fox
Dr Emmett Brown	Christopher Lloyd
Lorraine Baines	Lea Thompson
George McFly	Crispin Glover
Biff Tannen	Thompson F Wilson
Studio	Universal
Director	Robert Zemeckis
Producer	Bob Gale
	Neil Canton
Screenplay	Robert Zemeckis
	Bob Gale
Photographer	Dean Cundey
Music	Alan Silvestri

AWARDS

ACADEMY AWARDS

Best Sound Effects Editing
Charles L. Campbell
and Robert Rutledge

ACADEMY NOMINATIONS

Best Original Screenplay
Robert Zemeckis and Bob Gale
Best Original Song 'Power of Love''
by Chris Hayes, Johnny Cola
and Huey Lewis
Best Sound Bill Varney,
Tennyson Sebastian II,
Robert Thirlwell
and William B. Kaplin

BEST PICTURE

Out of Africa

STARS OF 1985

Sylvester Stallone
Eddie Murphy
Clint Eastwood
Michael J Fox
Chevy Chase

1985 Blockbusters

Rambo
Rocky 4
The Color Purple
Out of Africa
Cocoon

THE WORLD

- Gorbachev succeeds as Party Leader in USSR
- First Live Aid concert
- *Rainbow Warrior* sabotaged
- Death of Rock Hudson

BACK TO THE FUTURE, a comic travel fantasy, was a cross between HG Wells and Frank Capra. The result was a nostalgic, teenage romance plus science fiction.

Martin McFly was a skateboarding, guitar-playing teenager, who was horribly embarrassed by his alcoholic mother and nerdish father. The person he hung out with most was a nutty professor, who had built a time machine out of a DeLorean, which he had stolen from some terrorists. The machine, fuelled by nuclear power, took Martin back to 1955 when his parents were teenagers.

Most children have wondered what their parents were like when they were kids. Martin had an opportunity not only to meet his parents' younger selves but to change their characters and make them cool, successful and loved. But first he had to play Cupid. He had to get Lorraine and George to interact and fall in love, but instead Lorraine got a crush on him and tried to seduce him. The Oedipal side was not underplayed. Martin recoiled in horror and terror. He had to make her switch her affections, otherwise he would not be born; but there was a major problem. Lorraine was unlikely to fall in love with a slack-jawed, cowardly, humiliated Peeping Tom, the sad butt of everybody's jokes. The satirical happy ending, with Martin coming back to the future and finding a successful, happy and affluent home with lovely parents, played like a caricature of a yuppie advertisement.

> **My mother has got the hots for me. That's heavy.**
>
> *Teenager Martin McFly*

Back to the Future was directed by Robert Zemeckis, who had a keen eye for so-called American progress and the disappearing pastoral scene. There were some good jokes about the contrasts in dress, cars, music, diet and courtship in 1955 and 1985. Lorraine presumed Martin's name must be Calvin Klein since he had Calvin Klein's name written all over his underwear. Martin introduced the school to rock 'n' roll and gave them a heavy metal, guitar-slamming rendering of Chuck Berry's "Johnny Be Goode". The students were shocked by the music and his ultra-physical performance. "I guess you guys ain't ready for this yet. But your kids are gonna to love it."

The aerobic gym in 1955 was a nice old drug store. The local cinema, a porn movie house in 1985, was screening *Cattle Queen of Montana* starring Barbara Stanwyck and Ronald Reagan in 1955. (In 1955, the idea that Reagan would become the President of the USA was as absurd as Jerry Lewis becoming Vice President.)

Michael J Fox, who was having a big success on television in *Family Ties*, took over the role of Matin McFly from Eric Stoltz, who had been sacked after five weeks of shooting. Fox, the 24-year-old eternal teenager, was likeable, if a bit bland. A 24-year-old Lea Thompson and a 21-year-old Crispin Glover played the McFlys as teenagers and parents, a remarkable double act by them both. Christopher Lloyd was cast as the mad-eyed, nutty professor, a latter-day Frankenstein, surrounded by clocks and gadgets, shot at by terrorists in one decade and harnessing lightning in another.

Back to the Future had a strong teen appeal and the formula was so successful that there were two sequels, *Part II* in 1989 and *Part III* in 1990, when Fox was touching 30.

"I guess you guys ain't ready for this yet. But your kids are gonna love it." Michael J Fox in Back to the Future.

Back to the Future is clever, funny, and, surprise, emotionally involving. It's by far the best pop movie of the season — by far the best of the year.
The New York Times

What could so easily have turned into juvenile whimsy becomes a tale of warmth, imagination and wit under the direction of Robert Zemeckis.
The Sunday Express

Back to the Future is also a rather moving film, but its whole tone is celebratory rather than mournful, comic rather than speculative, and that is no doubt why it remains so enjoyable.
The Spectator

1986 • Top Gun

CREDITS

Maverick	Tom Cruise
Charlie	Kelly McGillis
Ice	Val Kilmer
Goose	Anthony Edwards
Piper	Tom Skerritt
Carol	Meg Ryan
Studio	Paramount
Director	Tony Scott
Producer	Don Simpson
Screenplay	Jim Cash
	Jack Epps Jr
Photography	Jeffey Kimball
Music	Harold Faltermeyer

AWARDS

ACADEMY AWARDS

Best Song   'Take My Breath Away'
by Girgio Moroder
and Tom Whitlock

ACADEMY NOMINATIONS

Best Film Editing   Billy Weber,
Chris Lebenzon

BEST PICTURE

Platoon

STARS OF 1986

Tom Cruise
Eddie Murphy
Paul Hogan
Rodney Dangerfield
Bette Midler

1986 Blockbusters

Crocodile Dundee
Platoon
Star Trek 4
The Karate Kid
Aliens

THE WORLD

- 3.5 million unemployed in UK
- Chernobyl nuclear power disaster
- US space shuttle *Challenger* explodes
- Gorbachev introduces *Glasnost* and *Perestroika*

ON 3 MARCH 1969, The United States established an elite school for the top 1% of its pilots. The purpose was to teach them the lost art of aerial combat and to ensure that the handful of men who graduated were the best fighter pilots in the world. The Navy called the school Fighter Weapons School. The flyers called it Top Gun.

The American Navy gave the production their full co-operation, providing the hardware and the pilots, but only on the strict understanding that the film would be in good taste. They had refused to co-operate on *An Officer and a Gentleman*, finding the violence, sex and profanity totally unacceptable.

> " Up there with the Best of the Best "
>
> *Slogan*

Top Gun was a two-hour navy recruiting advertisement, to a rock 'n' roll score, aimed at teenagers. One of the trainee pilots admitted he gets a hard-on every time he flew. Recruitment soared the moment the teenagers learned there were two air combat missions a day.

The Top Gun trophy was up for grabs and Maverick, a high flier, who bucked authority, wanted it badly. He was an aggressive, arrogant, dangerous fool, a cocksure Narcissus on an ego trip. "Your ego is writing cheques your body can't cash," said his girlfriend.

Maverick walked into a ladies' room, looking for a girl who talked dirty and picked up his instructor, a sultry older woman, a civilian expert in the physics of high-speed jet performance, which sounded pretty sexual. "I don't normally invite my students to my place," she confessed, but it wasn't long before she was saying encouraging things like, "You big stud, take me to bed and lose me for ever." An unlikely affair started.

Tom Cruise, clean cut, sleek, assured, had a pretty face, good teeth, a grin, a fixated stare and sun-glasses. He bared his chest and appeared in his underpants. He also looked good in his uniform. Maverick was Cruise's first adult role but he still resembled an adolescent. His acting was limited and he was unequal to the emotional content. There was no chemistry between him and Kelly McGillis.

Val Kilmer, his hair erect, was cast as Ice Man, Maverick's smug ice-cold rival, who grinned, snarled, played with his pencil and strutted around the locker-room with just a towel round his loins. Kilmer always moved in close to Crusie's face for an eyeball to eyeball confrontation. Ice-Man flirted outrageously. "You can be my wing-man any time." He offered him a helping hand. "I can hold my own," said Maverick.

Top Gun exploited the male body. The pilots were likened to Olympic athletes, rock 'n' roll stars and gunslingers of the Wild West. The locker-room homo-erotic innuendo was explicit. Quentin Tarantino developed the gay interpretation in his cameo role at a party in Rory Kelly's *Sleep With Me* in 1994.

Top Gun was high tech, trigger-happy, patriotic jingoism (the ideal movie for Ronald Reagan's presidency) and appealed to youngsters who played video dog-fight games. The screenplay was a bit vague about which war the United States was fighting and this was not surprising since the USA was not at war. The enemy was an unidentified Eastern block adversary. The real stars were the planes and the 20 pilots who flew them.

"You big stud, take me to bed and lose me forever." Tom Cruise and Kelly McGillis in Top Gun.

Top Gun may well be the most brazenly eroticized poster in the history of warfare.

The New York Magazine

[Tom Cruise] absolutely no star quality, no charisma, no presence whatsoever, but whose every move demonstrates that he himself believes quite the opposite to be the case.

American Spectator

It's trite, it's hokey, it's manipulative, but *Top Gun* is perfect for unchallenging, exhilarating entertainment.

Video Review

1987 • Three Men and a Baby

CREDITS

Peter	Tom Selleck
Michael	Steve Guttenberg
Jack	Ted Danson
Sylvia	Nancy Travis
Rebecca	Margaret Colin
Jack's mother	Celeste Holm
Detective	Philip Bosco
Studio	Touchstone
Director	Leonard Nimoy
Producers	Ted Field
	Robert W Cort
Screenplay	James Orr
	Jim Cruickshank
Photography	Adam Greenberg
Music	Marvin Hamlisch

AWARDS

ACADEMY AWARDS
None

ACADEMY NOMINATIONS
None

BEST PICTURE

The Last Emperor

STARS OF 1987

Eddie Murphy
Michael Douglas
Michael J Fox
Arnold Schwarzenegger
Paul Hogan

1987 Blockbusters

Beverley Hills Cop 2
Fatal Attraction
Good Morning Vietnam
The Untouchables
Moonstruck

THE WORLD

- World population passes 5 billion
- Stock Exchange collapses in UK (Black Monday)
- IRA bomb Enniskillen

THREE MEN AND A BABY was an instant remake of the 1985 French hit, *Trois Hommes et un Couffin* (*Three Men and a Cradle*), which had been written and directed by Coline Serreau.

Three guys, an architect (Tom Selleck), an actor (Ted Danson) and a cartoonist (Steve Guttenberg), shared a luxury Manhattan apartment. They were philandering, sexually insatiable bachelors. One day, a six-month-old baby girl was left at their front door in a carry-cot. The script was never anything more than an inflated, glossy, television sitcom episode with one joke at the expense of fatherhood and male ineptitude. The American trio, three bland, good-looking cyphers, were handsome, successful, career men. The film would have been truer to the French original if they had been less glamorous, less ingratiating and not so rich.

The trio's lives were disrupted. They had sleepless nights. They spent their days feeding, bathing, changing nappies, buying baby food. They put their lives on hold, cancelled dates and didn't go to work. They knew nothing at all about babies. "I'll give you 10 bucks if you stop crying," was one approach. Another was to read to the baby the sports pages covering a prize fight. The actor, initially, was the most confident. "I'm an actor," he said, "I can do a father." The architect took the baby to the building site. The baby wore a cute pink hard hat. The actor's mum (Celeste Holm) refused to bail them out. Why on earth didn't the guys hire a nanny? They could afford to do so.

The screenplay, unlikely, soft-centred and lethargic, continued long after the story had finished. There was also a stupid drug-smuggling sub-plot and a sloppy finish. The real mum turned up to claim the baby. "I hope I didn't cause too much trouble," she said. The trio found they had no idea what to do with their lives when there was no baby to look after, so they invited the mother to come and live with them.

Three Men and a Baby, a perfect promotion for diapers, was not nearly as much fun as the Coen Brothers' anarchic *Raising Arizona*, but the baby boom, which had started with *Baby Boom* (the 1994 film with Diane Keaton),would continue gurgling well into the 1990s with the John Travolta *Look Who's Talking* trilogy of comedies.

> " They changed her diapers — she changes their lives! "
>
> *Slogan*

Three Men and a Baby has been given a new lease of life and an enjoyable new lease at that. Whether it deserved or required any such thing is another matter.
The New York Times

It is all carried out with indisputable charm, probably the major reason for the film's American success, that and the fact that it reminds men of just what a mum has to go through — disturbed sleep, midnight feed, smelly bottom and the inability to combine a career with bringing up a child.
The Sunday Times

They have the look of gays who've groomed themselves like guys. The movie has a kind of closet appeal that must have helped at the box office.
The Evening Standard

It is shamelessly sentimental and could send the hard boiled home to kick the cat.
Time Out

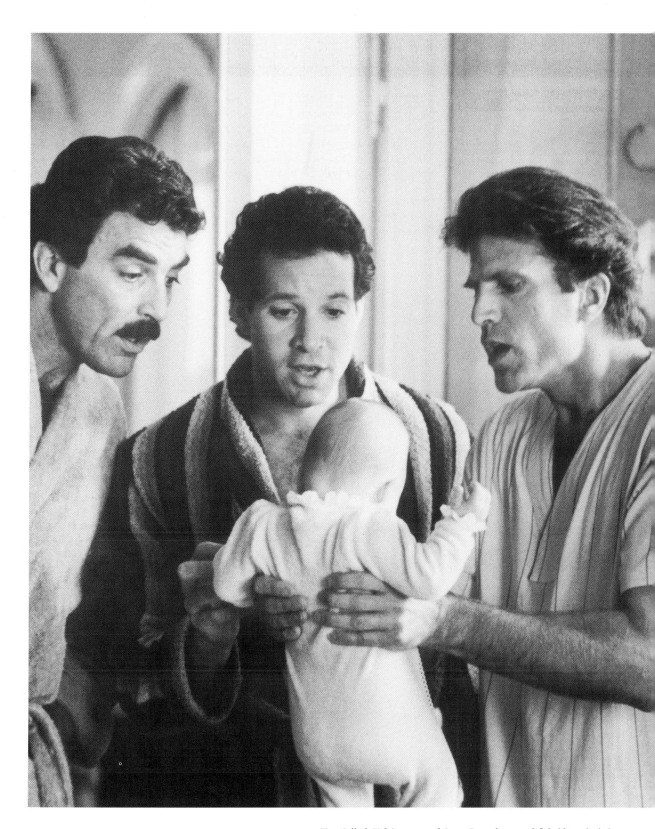

Tom Selleck, Ted Danson and Steve Guttenberg are left holding the baby.

1988 • Rain Man

CREDITS

Raymond Babbitt	Dustin Hoffman
Charlie Babbitt	Tom Cruise
Susanna	Valerie Golino
Dr Bruner	Jerry Molen
Studio	United Artists
Director	Barry Levinson
Producer	Mark Johnson
Screenplay	Ronald Bass
	Barry Morrow
Photography	John Seale
Music	Hans Zimmer

AWARDS

ACADEMY AWARDS

Best Picture	Mark Johnson
Best Direction	Barry Levinson
Best Actor	Dustin Hoffman
Best Original Screenplay	
Ronald Bass and Barry Morrow	

ACADEMY NOMINATIONS

Best Cinematography	John Searle
Best Film Editing	Stu Linder
Best Original Score	Hans Zimmer
Best Art/Set Direction	
Ida Random and Linda DeScenna	

BEST PICTURE

Rain Man

STARS OF 1988

Tom Cruise
Eddie Murphy
Tom Hanks
Arnold Schwarzenegger
Paul Hogan

1988 Blockbusters

Who Framed Peter Rabbit?
Going to America
Crocodile Dundee 2
Twins
Big

THE WORLD

- George Bush elected US President
- Gorbachev becomes Russian President
- Iran–Iraq war ends
- Lockerbie disaster

CHARLIE BABBITT's father died, leaving his fortune (3 million dollars) to Raymond Babbitt, the autistic savant elder brother he never knew he had. Feeling cheated of his birthright and wanting his share of the money, Charlie arrived at the institution where Raymond was held and kidnapped him. They hit the road.

Rain Man was the story of their journey across America in a '49 Buick and their changing relationship. Charlie was a brash, fast-talking yuppie car salesman, a self-centred hustler, a crass, cynical materialist, financially deeply in trouble. He hated his dad and he treated his girlfriend appallingly. He was spiritually autistic.

There was a splendid moment when Charlie, having been driven up the wall by Raymond's insistence on buying boxer shorts in Cincinnati and nowhere else, got out of his car and had hysterics. Gradually, Charlie was transformed from repellent con-man and fortune-hunter to likeable guy. He developed a conscience and was humanised. (There is a popular belief that mental illness can be a form of saintliness and that the affliction can heal others.) Charlie ended up thinking Raymond would be better off with him rather than in the asylum.

Raymond was extremely limited, yet extremely gifted. He didn't understand money, yet he was brilliant with numbers and could work out complicated sums in his head. He could tell, just from looking, how many toothpicks were lying spilled on the floor. He could memorise the telephone book. His memory came in useful when the brothers were gambling at Caesar's Palace in Las Vegas.

Rain Man was a buddy movie but a buddy movie with one major difference in that the relationship was one-sided. Institutionalised, self-absorbed, obstinate, child-like, Raymond had a problem communicating and understanding emotions. He was easily frightened (he had a panic attack at Cincinnati Airport) and kept reality and affection at bay with obsessive rituals relating to meals and television. He drifted into the Abbott and Costello "Who's on first?" routine without appreciating it was a comic routine.

Rain Man, a well-written road movie, touching and bleakly funny, was saved from being maudlin by Barry Levinson's direction and the acting. Dustin Hoffman's performance, passive, low-key, was notable for its meticulous observation of ill-coordinated physical detail: the lolling head, the trotting feet and the face void of all expression. Hoffman, true to Raymond's character, acted with himself, giving nothing to Cruise, no eye contact.

Hoffman had the more showy role, the sort of disabled role that wins Oscars, which Hoffman duly did. His performance was probably the most convincing of its kind since Peter Sellers' simpleton in *Being There*. Cruise was underestimated because he was thought of as a film star (as opposed to Hoffman who was thought of as an actor.) Cruise and Hoffman were a team and Cruise should, at the very least, have been nominated. It was his first serious role and he brought a new depth and maturity to his acting. He then went on to make *Born on the Fourth of July* in which he played a paraplegic and was nominated for an Oscar.

> " We were improvising all the time… I like danger. "
>
> *Barry Levinson*

"Chance, sometimes, makes us meet people who turn our lives upside down." Tom Cruise and Dustin Hoffman in Rain Man.

The film is touching without sentimentality and funny – very funny – without derision and condescension.
The Financial Times

His [Barry Levinson] sense of irony and paradox saves us from a lot of potential nonsense.
The Guardian

The script is so blah that it seems almost paint-by-numbers.
The New York Post

It's a piece of wet kitsch.
The New Yorker

1989 • Batman

AWARDS

ACADEMY AWARDS

Best Art direction   Anton Furst
Best Set direction   Peter Young

BEST PICTURE

Driving Miss Daisy

STARS OF 1989

Jack Nicholson
Tom Cruise
Robin Williams
Michael Douglas
Tom Hanks

1989 Blockbusters

Indiana Jones and the Last Crusade
Lethal Weapon 2
Honey, I Shrunk the Kids
Ghostbusters 2
Back to the Future 2

THE WORLD

• Death of Ayatollah Khomeini
• Demolition of Berlin Wall
• Tiananmen Square demonstration and massacre
• Hillsborough Stadium disaster

BATMAN, created by 18-year-old Bob Kane, first appeared in *Detective Comic* issue No 29 in 1939. When it was announced that Michael Keaton was to play the Caped Crusader, the Batman fans were outraged and bombarded the studio with letters. They feared Batman would be sent up. In the event, Keaton, who had worked with Tim Burton in the ghoulish *Beetlejuice*, was not his usual comic self.

In the role of Bruce Wayne, the millionaire philanthropist, who had been traumatised by the murder of his parents when he was a nine-year-old, Keaton was subdued, dark, brooding and lifeless. In the role of Batman, the night-time vigilante, acrobat, racing driver, fighter pilot and martial arts expert, he was lost inside a black rubber suit. (The black suit was a radical departure from the familiar tights and underwear.)

The hero was weak and the

" Wait till they get a load of me!

The Joker

villain was strong. Since the battle was unequal, there was no match. Faced with Jack Nicholson's bravura performance as The Joker, Keaton underplayed and remained enigmatic to the point of self-deletion. The film was dominated by Nicholson's psychotic hoodlum, an avant garde homicidal artist on an ego trip, terrorising the city with poisons and whose ambition was to have his face on the one dollar bill. The Joker's face was horribly disfigured as a result of his having fallen into a vat of acid. His hair was green, his lips were scarlet, his cheeks were rubbery, his face chalky white. He had a fixed smile. "You look fine," said his moll (Jerry Hall) when she caught him looking in a mirror. "I didn't ask," he retorted; his voice was lethal and genuinely chilling. He wore garish suits. "Let's broaden our mind," he said as he danced and cavorted his way into an art gallery to desecrate famous works.

Nicholson was ribald and lascivious, a cackling Joker. "Never," he said, "rub another man's rhubarb." He danced with death in the pale moonlight. The final scene took place in the belfry of a cathedral, always a good place for bats. The Joker was the first to admit he was theatrical and a bit rough. ("I always try to see how far I can go.") Nicholson was even more nutty than he had been in *The Shining* and *The Witches of Eastwick*. It was his malevolent performance which gave the production its energy. He was in a different film to Keaton.

Tim Burton developed the comic book's idea that Bruce Wayne and Jack Napier were two sides of the same coin, mirroring each other's psychosis. Keaton and Nicholson had the same sort of eyes and eyebrows. But who was the more crazy? The Joker was the more piqued: "Can somebody tell me what kind of world we live in where a man dressed up as a mouse gets all my press?" Bruce looked as if he could murder him with a handy poker.

There was no Robin. Batman without Robin is like David without Jonathan. Instead, Wayne was provided with a girlfriend (Kim Bassinger), a photojournalist. He tried to tell her who he was. "My life is complex," he began. He got no further and she never did find out. Her role was unimportant and it seemed to many that Bruce only slept with her so that the audience didn't think Bruce was gay.

Burton's vision was so nihilistic, children under 12 were banned from seeing the film. Gotham City, corrupt, greedy and violent, was a garbage-

"I always try to see how far I can go." Jack Nicholson as The Joker in Batman.

ridden, smoky purgatory of high-rise buildings and narrow canyon-like streets. The film was visually striking, echoing the visual style of the original Bob Kane comics. The ornate and cantilevered architecture drew on a number of different art styles, a Dada-esque mixture of art nouveau and Gothic. The lighting was film noir, dark and stylish, the world of the gangster movie. There were references to Raymond Chandler, Fritz Lang and *The Godfather*. Anton Furst said his satanic designs were based on the worst aspects of New York.

It has a funky, nihilistic charge and an eerie poetic intensity... It's mean and anarchic and blissful.
The New Yorker

It has the personality not of a particular movie but of a product, of something arrived at by corporate decisions.
The New York Times

The film, however, is a brave failure. Or, possibly, a flawed success.
The Scotsman

1990 • Ghost

CREDITS

Sam Wheat	Patrick Swayze
Molly Jensen	Demi Moore
Oda Mae Brown	Whoopi Goldberg
Carl Brunner	Tony Goldwyn
Willie Lopez	Rick Aviles
Subway ghost	Vincent Schiavelli
Studio	Paramount
Director	Jerry Zucker
Producer	Lisa Weinstein
Screenplay	Bruce Joel Rubin
Photography	Adam Greenberg
Music	Maurice Jarre

AWARDS

ACADEMY AWARDS

Best Supporting Actress
Whoopi Goldberg
Best Original Screenplay
Bruce Joel Rubin

ACADEMY NOMINATIONS

Best Picture	Lisa Weinstein
Best Film Editing	Walter Murch
Best Original Score	Maurice Jarre

BEST PICTURE

Dances with Wolves

STARS OF 1990

Arnold Schwarzenegger
Julia Roberts
Bruce Willis
Tom Cruise
Mel Gibson

1990 Blockbusters

Home Alone
Pretty Woman
Dances with Wolves
Teenage Mutant Ninja Turtles
Die Hard 2

THE WORLD

- PM Margaret Thatcher resigns
- Iraq invades Kuwait
- Nelson Mandela released from prison
- Reunification of Germany

GHOST was Jerry Zucker's first solo directorial effort. Up until then he had worked with his two brothers, memorably on *Airplane!* Ghost stories are always popular, but *Ghost* wasn't spooky at all. It was a lightweight murder story, alternating comedy and suspense, with just a hint of pain and anguish. "It's amazing," said the dead hero, "the love inside you, you can take it with you." Audiences found the message that there was life after death and that love lasted forever comforting. For those who didn't believe in life after death, *Ghost* was still an entertaining romantic fantasy thriller.

" Believe. "

Slogan

Sam and Molly, a yuppie New York couple, shared a loft. She said she loved him. He said "Ditto." He never actually told her he loved her in so many words until the last moments of the last reel, just when he was off to heaven. "I love you, Molly. I've always loved you." It seemed a bit late.

Sam was attacked by a Puerto Rican mugger, who was in league with Sam's best friend, a colleague at the bank where he worked, who was using the firm to launder money. Sam observed himself dying in Molly's arms and then went along to the hospital to watch the doctors failing to save his life. Here he met another ghost who told him, "We are all travellers on the same road that leads to the same end." It took Sam quite some while to grasp that he was actually dead and that he had a spiritual existence. He attended his own funeral. "Let us remember that love is eternal," intoned the priest.

Sam, finding himself stuck between two worlds, did all those things ghosts usually do in films: he went through walls, doors and turnstiles. He was attacked by a wild-haired phantom on the subway. "Stay out!" yelled the phantom. "This is my train!" Sam went into training with this spook (a manic performance by Vincent Schiavelli), who taught him how to concentrate and get things moving.

Sam pursued his killer and stayed around to save Molly from being murdered. What he couldn't do was communicate with the living and warn her that her life was in danger. He needed a medium. He found a fortune-teller in Brooklyn.

Patrick Swayze, who had made his name in *Dirty Dancing*, had romantic good looks, athletic grace and he moved like a dancer. He was macho yet sensitive: "I don't want the bubble to burst," said Sam. "Whenever anything good in my life happens, I'm afraid I'm going to lose it." Demi Moore, with her boyish haircut, looked very vulnerable and was so subdued that she seemed more dead than Swayze. "I'd give anything if I could touch you," sang the soundtrack. The most erotic scene was when he was alive and he and she were at the pottery wheel together, teasing a phallic object into shape with their slippery hands. Pottery classes soared wherever the film was shown. Many people were surprised that the film received only a 12 certificate.

Whoopi Goldberg brought a musical comedy vitality to the fake medium, who suddenly found she had the gift and didn't like it one bit. Dressed to the nines, she behaved like a caricature of a black woman when she arrived at the bank to collect some money. "I'd like to make a transfusion," she said.

The mugger (Rick Aviles) was killed in a car accident and was carted off by some blurred, monk-like figures in woolly costumes pretending to be hell-hounds. They turned up again to cart off Sam's ex-best friend (Tony Goldwyn) after he had been killed by a broken window-pane, which had gone straight through his body. The feel-good message could not have been clearer. Heaven was for yuppies. Hell was for muggers.

"I'd give anything if I could touch you." Demi Moore and Patrick Swayze in Ghost.

It is hard to escape the feeling that the huge success of *Ghost* in the United States owes much to the religious fundamentalism in American life, with its hunger for the assurance of personal immortality.
The Daily Telegraph

This creamy-toned fantasy certainly pushes the audience's emotional buttons; watching it you feel like a VCR that's being programmed by experts.
New Yorker

The whole thing left me with the gradually enveloping sense that I was crossing the River Styx without a paddle.
The Guardian

This far-fetched effort is purely for escapists, as demanding filmgoers won't buy it.
Variety

1991 • Terminator 2: JUDGMENT DAY

CREDITS

The Terminator	Arnold Schwarzenegger
Sarah Connor	Linda Hamilton
T-1000	Robert Patrick
John Connor	Edward Furlong
Dr Silberman	Earl Boen
Studio	Carolco Pacific Western
Director	James Cameron
Producer	James Cameron
Screenplay	James Cameron William Wisher
Photographer	Adam Greenberg
Music	Brad Fiedel

AWARDS

ACADEMY AWARDS

Best Make-up	Stan Winston and Jeff Dawn
Best Sound	Tom Johnson, Gary Rydstrom, Gary Summers and Lee Orloff
Best Sound Editing Effects Editing	Gary Rydstrom and Gloria S. Borders
Best Visual Effects	Dennis Muren, Stan Winston, Gene Warren, Jr and Robert Skotak

ACADEMY NOMINATIONS

Best Cinematography	Adam Greenberg
Best Film Editing	Conrad Buff, Mark Goldblatt and Richard A. Harris

BEST PICTURE

The Silence of the Lambs

STARS OF 1991

Kevin Costner
Arnold Schwarzenegger
Robin Williams
Julia Roberts
Macaulay Culkin

1991 Blockbusters

Robin Hood: Prince of Thieves
City Slickers
Beauty and the Beast
The Silence of the Lambs
The Addams Family

THE WORLD

- Civil War starts in Yugoslavia
- Yeltsin becomes Russian President
- Disintegration of Soviet Union

THE TERMINATOR (1984), a stylish, slick and violent movie, which owed something to television's *The Outer Limits*, cost $6 million and did more than $80 million business. It made James Cameron the leading science fiction special effects director and it made Arnold Schwarzenegger an international star.

Terminator 2 was the most expensive movie ever made at the time. Schwarzenegger in the title role arrived totally naked from nowhere during an electrical storm, just as he had done in *Terminator*. Part-human, part-machine, he enterd a cafe whose inmates were amazed at his size. They had never seen anything that big. Schwarzenegger, body-builder, pumper of iron, had not been Mr Europe, Mr World, Mr Universe and Mr Olympia for nothing. He ordered one of the inmates to give him his clothes, boots and motor cycle. Once he was dressed in black leather and wearing dark glasses, he was ready for business. All that remained for him to do was to reload his rifle with one hand (without looking) and he was on his way.

Schwarzenegger might have looked the same symbol of destruction as he did in *Terminator,* but in the intervening years

> " It's man's nature to destroy himself, but if a Terminator can learn the value of human life, then maybe we can, too. "
>
> *James Cameron*

he had changed his ruthless and amoral cinematic image for something kinder and gentler. He had made *Twins* and *Kindergarten Cop*, two comedies, both jokes at his expense, and was intent on projecting a more humane persona, more in keeping with his new role as Head of President Bush's Council on Physical Fitness. This did not mean, however, that he did not throw guys out of windows and smash payphones. There was one scene which recalled Clint Eastwood in *The Enforcer* when Dirty Harry was denied entry to a building. "I'll be back!" said the Terminator and, true to his word, he returned immediately in an armoured jeep and drove right through the plate glass.

The Terminator was the most compelling monster since Frankenstein's and as popular as Batman and Superman. At six foot and three inches, Schwarzenegger was perfect casting for a cyborg (living tissue over a metal skeleton). He looked like a machine. He had good looks, an impassive face, a strong jaw, a mean mouth, slanted eyes, a muscular body, a powerful stride and a thick Austrian accent. He was arrogant machismo personified: tough with a nice touch of self-mockery. In *Terminator*, his role was to kill the mother of the future saviour of mankind. In *Judgement Day*, he was reprogrammed as the good guy and his function was to save her son. He took on the role of guardian angel, father-figure, big brother and buddy to the boy. At one stage Schwarzenegger was going to play both the good and the bad Terminator.

T-1000, the latest Terminator, a relentless and tenacious killing machine, was a formidable adversary, far more advanced and deadly than the 1984 model. T-1000 couldn't be bargained with, he couldn't be reasoned with and he didn't feel either pity, remorse, pain or fear. Grim, determined, unstoppable and as fast as Hermes, he took on the shape of a young Los Angeles cop; but he could, in fact, take on the exact shape, sex, voice of anybody he wanted. He walked through solid walls, traversed iron bars and rose through the floor. His hands sprouted metal shafts to skewer eyes and impale bodies; he behaved like some malevolent relation of *Scissorhands*. He was constructed from metal liquid and could melt, crumble and decompose into blobs. If his body was blown full of holes and his head split apart, T-1000 could reconstruct himself immediately. He was indestructible.

Robert Patrick's villainous cop, clean-cut, crew-cut, snake-hipped, sleek as a cat, had

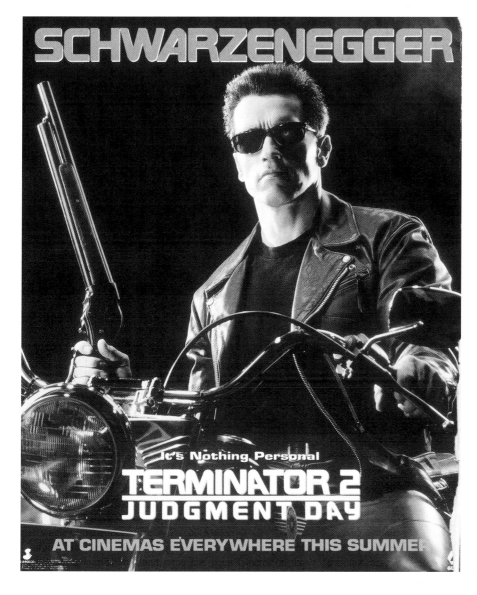

Poster

chilling blue eyes. He looked lethal in T-1000's human form. It was the best performance of its kind since Yul Brynner's robotic cowboy in Michael Crichton's *Westworld*. The special make-up and terminator effects were by Stan Winston. The Industrial Light and Magic visual effects were by Dennis Muren.

Linda Hamilton reprised her role of Sarah Connor, mother of the future saviour of mankind, who had been fathered in the earlier film by the good rebel (Michael Biehn). She had been locked up inside a psychiatric hospital as a result of having horrific visions of a nuclear holocaust with 3 billion dead. Shrill and paranoid, it wasn't long before she was out of hospital, blazing away. Sarah was dehumanised and turned into a violent, commando-like activist, a Terminator in all but name.

John, her 12-year-old son, a street-smart kid, taught the Terminator catch phrases, such as "No problemo" and "Hasta la

vista, baby". John was shocked by his attitude. ("You were going to kill those guys?" "Of course, I'm a terminator.") He got him to promise never to kill again. The Terminator more or less kept his word, concentrating on destroying machines and only mutilating, burning, maiming and shooting people in the legs.

Brad Fiedel provided a pounding metallic score. There were thrilling chase sequences on the road, involving cars, a juggernaut and helicopters. The first part of the action was better than the second part. The climax was not nearly as frightening as the hair-raising horrors of the first *Terminator film*.

The production censured and glorified technological violence at one and the same time; it was the perfect movie for the post-Gulf War years. James Cameron described *Terminator 2* as a violent movie about peace. "It's a very moral picture," he claimed.

1992 • Home Alone 2: LOST IN NEW YORK

CREDITS

Kevin	Macaulay Culkin
Harry	Joe Pesci
Marv	Daniel Stern
Kate	Catherine O'Hara
Peter	John Heard
Concierge	Tim Curry
Pigeon Lady	Brenda Fricker
Mr Duncan	Eddie Bracken
Desk Clerk	Dana Ivey
Bellman	Rob Schneider
Studio	Twentieth Century Fox
Director	Chris Columbus
Producer	John Hughes
Writer	John Hughes
Photographer	Julio Macat
Music	John Williams

AWARDS

ACADEMY AWARDS
None

ACADEMY NOMINATIONS
None

BEST PICTURE

Unforgiven

STARS OF 1992

Tom Cruise
Mel Gibson
Kevin Costner
Macaulay Culkin
Whoopi Goldberg

1992 Blockbusters

Batman Returns
Lethal Weapon 3
Sister Act
Aladdin
Wayne's World

THE WORLD

- Independence of Bosnia and Herzegovina
- Los Angeles court clears four policemen of beating Rodney King
- Prince and Princess of Wales agree to separate

MACAULAY CULKIN made his stage debut at the age of four and studied at The School of American Ballet. At 10, he became one of the highest paid actors in Hollywood and the biggest child star since Shirley Temple. Twentieth Century Fox, surprised, like everybody else, by the success of *Home Alone*, decided to make a carbon copy of the original, recycling scenes and gags, only this time making them more violent and more unpleasant. *Home Alone 2* was a winning box-office mixture of schmaltz and sadism.

In *Home Alone*, Kevin's parents went to Paris and inadvertently left Kevin at home. In *Home Alone 2*, Kevin managed to get to the airport but took the wrong plane and ended up in New York where he stayed at the Plaza Hotel and enjoyed the wish-fulfilment of every pre-pubescent, who had uncontrolled access to his dad's wallet and credit cards. He ate junk food, watched television and spent $967 dollars on room service. He was the sort of kid with whom children could easily identify.

> " He's up past his bedtime in the city that never sleeps. "
>
> *Slogan*

Kevin was vulnerable in the big city but never in any real danger, not even when he was all alone in Central Park late at night. He was a resourceful, mischievous lad and a dab hand with paint, glue, beads, nails and kerosene. He took over a conveniently empty house and waged battle single-handed with a whole new set of booby traps.

The villains were once again Harry and Marv, two comically inept, prat-falling housebreakers, who had escaped prison and were gluttons for more punishment in the Tom and Jerry vein. Joe Pesci and Daniel Stern were a classic double act, one small and fat, the other tall and thin, perfect casting. Harry and Marv were constantly outwitted, snared, clobbered, tarred, burned, blowtorched, electrocuted, nailed, stapled and smashed in the face by irons, doors, pots and bricks. The message was spelled out: "You can mess with a lot of things but you can't mess with kids at Christmas." They never had a chance against Kevin. Much of the slapstick was painful and painfully unfunny. The most macabre scene was the one when the pigeons attacked them, a scene which could have gone straight into Alfred Hitchcock's *The Birds*.

Kevin was given an extra set of cartoon villains: the hotel staff at The Plaza. They included Tim Curry's concierge (a podgy, smirking pervert), Iva Davey's hatchet-faced Front Desk Clerk and Rob Schneider's bellman. Kevin easily fooled them with a trick he employed in his first film, using a dummy silhouette and pocket voice-recorder with pre-recorded dialogue from an old gangster movie.

Kevin befriended a homeless, friendless Pigeon Lady in Central Park, a character who played much the same role as the Snow-Shoveller did in *Home Alone*. On Christmas Eve, she advised him to follow the star in his own heart and Kevin, sweet little boy that he was, did just that and gave all his money to charity.

Macaulay Culkin, wide-eyed, open-mouthed, blue-eyed, jug-eared, delivered his smug one-liners and dollops of folksy wisdom with precocious self-awareness.

Lost in NewYork. Joe Pesci, Macaulay Culkin and Daniel Stern in Home Alone 2.

The filmmakers pump up the volume on the schmalz and the sadism, hoping to attain a hyperbolic balance. What they achieve is double overkill.
The New Yorker

Macaulay Culkin is an infant prodigy to bring out the Herod in me.
The Mail on Sunday

This nice little movie may be the nastiest you've seen all year.
The Independent on Sunday

As for Macaulay Culkin the sooner his testicles descend and he becomes unemployable the better.
The Evening Standard

1993 • Jurassic Park

CREDITS

Dr Alan Grant	Sam Neil
Dr Ellie Sattler	Laura Dern
Ian Malcolm	Jeff Goldblum
Dr John Hammond	Richard Attenborough
Robert Muldoon	Bob Peck
Donald Gennaro	Martin Ferrero
Dr Wu	BD Wong
Arnold	Samuel L Jackson
Dennis Nedry	Wayne Knight
Tim	Joseph Mazello
Lex	Ariana Richards
Studio	Universal
Director	Steven Spielberg
Producer	Kathleen Kennedy
	Gerald R Molen
Screenplay	Michael Crichton
	David Koepp
Photography	Dean Cundey
Music	John Williams

AWARDS

ACADEMY AWARDS

Best Sound   Ron Judkins,
   Shawn Murphy, Gary Rydstrom
   and Gary Summers
Best Sound Effects Editing
   Richard Hymns, Gary Rydstrom
Best Visual Effects
   Michael Lantieri, Dennis Muren,
   Phil Tippett and Stan Winston

BEST PICTURE

Schindler's List

STARS OF 1993

Clint Eastwood
Tom Cruise
Robin Williams
Kevin Costner
Harrison Ford

1993 Blockbusters

The Fugitive
Mrs Doubtfire
The Firm
Sleepless in Seattle
Indecent Proposal

THE WORLD

- Bill Clinton becomes US President
- Single market in Europe
- Peace agreement between Israel and PLO

EVERYBODY likes dinosaurs but only so long as they are in a child's picture book and/or in a film by Stephen Spielberg. *Jurassic Park*, based on Michael Crichton's novel, was a monster success, offering enough terror and wonder to thrill and frighten any child or adult. Spielberg jettisoned much of the novel's scientific detail and inquiry into the morality of genetic engineering and concentrated on the action. The film opened with a man disappearing into a crate to be eaten by an unseen monster, an opening, which recalled Spielberg's *Jaws*.

Dr John Hammond, a billionaire entrepreneur, had built a prehistoric theme park on an island off the coast of Costa Rico. The theme park was filled with dinosaurs, which had been cloned from the blood found in a prehistoric insect trapped in amber. All the clones were female but nature had quickly found a way out of this impasse and the dinosaurs were breeding fast.

An adventure 65 millio[n] years in the making.

Slogan

Hammond invited some experts and his grandchildren to a preview on the very day that one of his employees, unbeknown to him, had decided to turn off the safety system. Crichton had been down this road before in *Westworld*, another theme park in which the system broke down and an animated cowboy gunman (played by Yul Brynner) went on the rampage. The experts here included two palaeontologists (Sam Neil and Laura Dern), a mathematician (Jeff Goldblum) and an attorney. Jeff Goldblum articulated the Chaos theory (what can go wrong will go wrong). Sam Neil was immediately established as a child-hater. He particularly didn't like babies, saying they were "noisy, messy, expensive and smelly." Later, when they were all stranded in the middle of the park, he turned surrogate father to the grandchildren, who were liable to be eaten by dinosaurs one minute and electrocuted on high wire fences the next.

The entrepreneur, described as a cross between Ross Perot and a dark Walt Disney, was not the capitalist villain of the novel. The role had been watered down; Hammond was just a misguided Scottish dreamer. There was no menace in Richard Attenborough's twinkling performance and he didn't get eaten. The fat employee (Wayne Knight), who was stealing embryo eggs for a rival organisation, however, did get his just deserts when he was spat on by a deadly, venomous, wing-spreading dilophosaurus. The weedy, greedy lawyer also got his just deserts when he was gobbled up while sitting on a lavatory, a scene played for laughs rather than horror. Audiences were much more likely to identify with the huge ox dropped into a plant-filled cage to be devoured by an unseen, noisy monster.

What the script might have lacked in subtlety and characterisation, it more than made up for in excitement. The first sight of the brachiosaurus was awesome and magical. The effects were sometimes beautifully simple, relying, for instance, just on a shaking cup of water and a ripple in a pool to herald the approach of a dinosaur. There was a nasty moment when the huge, roaring, tail-thrashing *Tyrannosaurus rex* broke through the wire to attack the children in the car. The chase down the road, with *T. rex* in full pursuit, was observed (nice touch, this) in the driver's rear mirror.

One of the high spots took place in a stainless steel kitchen with the children playing hide and seek with two increasingly impatient, claw-tapping, kangaroo-springing, door-opening velociraptors, who had brains as well as bite. The dinosaurs were the real stars. The actors played a supporting role to the life-size action models and computer-generated stampeding gallimimuses. The final scene in the museum, with the slowly collapsing skeleton, brought back memories of Ann Miller in the New York museum in the 1949 Gene Kelly-Stanley Donen musical film, *On the Town*. A sequel quickly followed.

"Ooohs and aaahs — that's how it starts. Later, it's running and screaming." Joseph Mazzello, Laura Dern, Ariana Richards and Sam Neil in Jurassic Park.

Doesn't have the imagination
– or the courage – to take us
anywhere we haven't been a
thousand times before.
The New Yorker

Sadism for the family.
The Evening Standard

It's a movie in love with
technology (as Spielberg is),
yet afraid of being carried
away by it (as he is).
Time

The real problem with
Spielberg is that for all the
technical cleverness, he
keeps falling back on the
same tricks.
New Yorker

1994 • Forrest Gump

CREDITS

Forrest Gump	Tom Hanks
Lt Dan Taylor	Gary Sinise
Jenny Curran	Robin Wright
Mrs Gump	Sally Field
Bubba	Mykelti Williamson
Studio	Paramount
Director	Robert Zemeckis
Producer	Wendy Finerman
	Steve Tisch, Steve Strakey
Screenplay	Eric Roth
Photography	Don Burgess
Music	Alan Silvestri

AWARDS

ACADEMY AWARDS

Best Picture	Wendy Finerman,
	Steve Tisch and Steve Strakey
Best Director	Robert Zemeckis
Best Actor	Tom Hanks
Best Screenplay	Eric Roth
Best Film Editing	Arthur Schmidt
Best Visual Effects	Ken Ralston,
	George Murphy,
Steven Rosenbaum and Allen Hall	

ACADEMY NOMINATIONS

Best Supporting Actor	Gary Sinise
Best Cinematography	Don Burgess
Best Original Score	Alan Silvestri
Best Art Decoration	Rick Carter
	and Nancy Haigh
Best Make-up	Daniel C. Striepeke,
Hallie D'Amore and Judith A. Cory	
Best Sound	Randy Thom,
Tom Johnson, Dennis Sands	
and William B. Kaplan	
Best Sound Effects Editing	
Gloria S. Borders and Randy Thom	

BEST PICTURE

Forrest Gump

STARS OF 1994

Tom Hanks
Jim Carrey
Arnold Schwarzenegger
Tom Cruise
Harrison Ford

1994 Blockbusters

The Lion King
True Lies
The Santa Clause
The Flintstones
Dumb and Dumber

THE WORLD

- Nelson Mandela becomes President of South Africa
- Russia invades Chechnya
- Ceasefire agreed in Northern Ireland
- First woman priest ordained in UK

FORREST GUMP was based on the best-selling book by Winston Groom and became the third-highest grossing film of all time. The novel was a survey of 30 years of American history through the eyes of a simpleton, who had an IQ of 75 and yet became a football star, a war-hero, a ping-pong champion and a millionaire shrimp businessman. His picaresque odyssey was a satire on the American Dream and a sentimental celebration of innocence, conservatism and family values. "I imagined," said Robert Zemeckis, "Norman Rockwell painting the baby boomers."

Gump sat an Alabama bus stop and regaled strangers with the story of his life. He was raised by a single mother, who had prostituted herself with a headmaster in order to get him into a good school. She had an endless supply of homely banalities, such as "You've got to put your past behind you before you move on", "Stupid is as stupid does" and "Life is a box of chocolates. You never know what you're gonna get." (It was typical of the essential softness of the screenplay that the aphorism was changed. The actual line in Groom's book is "Being a fool is no box of chocolates"; but that, presumably, wouldn't have looked so good on the posters.)

> " I don't know if we each have a destiny or if we're floating around accidental like on a breeze. But I think maybe it's both. "
>
> *Forrest Gump*

Gump did the best with what God has given him. "I'm not a smart man," he admitted, "but I know what love is." He was born with a crooked spine, but one day the braces on his legs fell apart and he found he could run faster than anybody. He met famous people and participated in major events. Zemeckis edited Tom Hanks into existing newsreel footage in the same way that Woody Allen had edited himself into *Zelig*, a story of another nonentity.

Gump taught Elvis Presley how to gyrate his pelvis, he chatted with John Lennon on television and was seen shaking hands with Presidents Kennedy, Johnson and Nixon. ("The best thing about meeting the President," he said, "is the food.") He fought in Vietnam and won a Congressional Medal of Honour for bravery, because he was too dumb to know that what he was doing was dangerous. ("The good thing about Vietnam," he said, "is there's always something to do.") He proudly showed the war-wounds on his buttocks to President Johnson.

Gump, inadvertently, took part in a Civil Rights Movement at Alabama University and made a political gesture without realising he had done anything of the sort. He addressed an anti-war demonstration in Washington but nothing that he said was heard; somebody pulled the plug on the microphones. He became a long-haired hippie and attracted a cult following when he ran across America. He didn't run for any reason, he just liked running. He was responsible for the aphorism, "Have a nice day" and the bumper-sticker slogan: "Shit happens." If it hadn't been for him, Watergate might never have been exposed.

Gump, redeemer, entrepreneur, a holy fool in an insane world, remained unscathed. He was a Capraesque hero with plenty of heart but no brains. He was an innocent at large in the worst of all possible worlds. His moral compassion and innate sense of what was right never wavered. Colour blind, classless, asexual, oblivious to what was going on round him, he kept his innocence while America lost hers. Forrest Gump had nobility, purity, humanity, fortitude, sincerity. He believed in nothing, he stood for nothing, he was totally guileless. Blessed are the stupid for they shall inherit the earth.

Tom Hanks affected a Southern drawl, a crew cut, a ramrod posture and a glazed look.

"Life is a box of chocolates. You never know what you're gonna get." Rebecca Williams and Tom Hanks as Forrest Gump.

Robin Wright played the childhood sweetheart he idolised. Physically and sexually abused by her father, beaten up by the Black Panthers and into drugs, flower-power, promiscuity and rebellion in a big way, she symbolised all that was rotten with America. She ended up totally haggard and dying of AIDS, although the word AIDS was never mentioned.

Gary Sinise played Gump's commander officer in Vietnam whose life Gump saved. He was furious. Every member of his family had fought and died in war. There was a quick, comic montage of shots depicting his ancestors being killed. "I was meant to die with honour in the field. You cheated me of my destiny." The lieutenant lost his legs and, with the aid of computer technology, Sinise's legs were completely erased.

Actors who play mentally challenged characters, almost invariably, win Awards: John Mills in *Ryan's Daughter*, Dustin Hoffman in *Rain Man*, Leonard DiCaprio in *What's Eating Gilbert Grape?* and Nigel Hawthorne in *The Madness of King George*. Hanks, who won an Academy Award for his performance in *Philadelphia*, won the Award for the second year running, which was something nobody had done since Spencer Tracy in 1937 and 1938.

The film has been very well worked out on all levels and manages the difficult feat of being an intimate, even delicate tale played with an appealingly light touch against an epic background.

Variety

The film hedges its bets so carefully in all directions that it can be read virtually any way you want. But it definitely earns one PC rating – Pernicious Crap.

The Sunday Telegraph

Forrest Gump is a black comedy that white-washes its hero.

The Sunday Times

So *Gump* will appeal to almost everybody but the acutely, irredeemably cynical.

The Guardian

1995 • Batman Forever

CREDITS

Batman/Bruce Wayne — Val Kilmer
Harvey Two Face — Tommy Lee Jones
The Riddler/Nygma — Jim Carrey
Dr Chase Meridian — Nicole Kidman
Robin/Dick Grayson — Chris O'Donnell
Alfred Pennyworth — Michael Gough
Police Commissioner — Pat Hingle
Spice — Debi Mazar
Sugar — Drew Barrymore

Studio — Warner
Director — Joel Schumacher
Producers — Tim Burton
Peter MacGregor-Scott
Screenplay — Lee Batchler
Janet Scott-Batchler
Akiva Goldsman
Photography — Stephen Goldblatt
Music — Elliot Goldenthal

AWARDS

ACADEMY AWARDS

None

ACADEMY NOMINATIONS

Best Cinematography
Stephen Goldblatt
Best Sound — Donald O. Mitchell,
Frank A. Montano,
Michael Herbick and Peter Hiddal
Best Sound Effects Editing
John Leveque
and Bruce Stambler

BEST PICTURE

Braveheart

STARS OF 1995

Tom Hanks
Jim Carrey
Brad Pitt
Harrison Ford
Robin Williams

1995 Blockbusters

Apollo 13
Toy Story
Pocahontas
Ace Ventura: When Nature Calls
Casper

THE WORLD

• Jacques Chirac becomes French President
• Assassination of Yitzhak Rabin
• Peace agreed in Bosnia

BATMAN FOREVER was the third film in the present *Batman* cycle. Warner Bros decided that the Tim Burton/Michael Keaton version had been too dark, too macabre, too creepy, too nihilistic, so they engaged a new director, new stars and ordered new costumes. The new film was a marketing exercise aimed entirely at children; it was totally devoid of narrative drive, surprise and any emotional involvement. There were no thrills, not even on the high-wire in the circus sequence. The heroics were meaningless. The only good things about *Batman Forever* were the garish colours of Barbara Ling's designs and the photography of Stephen Goldblatt.

Val Kilmer in his dual role of billionaire philanthropist and flying rodent failed to characterise either role. Bruce Wayne was bland and inexpressive. Batman was never anything more than a flying costume. Bruce was in love with Dr Chase Meridan, a crime psychologist, but she, alas, was in love with Batman. "Do you want to get under my cape?" he asked. She let him play with her doll but she never found out his true identity.

> ❝ Was I over the top?
> I never can tell. ❞
>
> *The Riddler*

Robin was no longer the Boy Wonder of the camp 1960s television show but a strong adolescent with a short haircut and an ear-ring, haunted by the death of his three brothers in a circus accident for which the villainous Harvey Two Face was responsible. He became Batman's friend and partner. They had a mutual interest in motorbikes, which came as no surprise to the cognescenti, who outed them both many years back. The rubber costumes emphasised every muscle, every nipple, every buttock and their codpieces.

All the main characters had split personalities and lived double lives. Jim Carrey had the role of nerd-inventor transformed into madman transformed into The Riddler, each characterisation more whacko than the last. Carrey had the manic elasticity of a cartoon figure. In his portrayal of The Riddler, he had spiky red hair and pranced about in a tight-fitting, lime-green body-suit with question marks all over it. The question was what did all this glitter and sequins mean? He fell in love with Batman and ended up in the madhouse thinking he was Batman. Carrey was very agile, very stylised, very camp and not really evil; certainly not evil in the way Jack Nicholson's Joker had been evil. The Riddler, with his bowler hat and cane, was essentially a vaudeville song-and-dance man in need of a song and choreography by Bob Fosse.

Tom Lee Jones played Two-Face, the former district attorney turned maniac, terrorising Gotham, whose fate he decided on a flip of a coin. His face was cleft in two, one side scarred with acid. He had two bimbos in tow, played by Drew Barrymore and Debi Mazar, both wasted. Lee Jones cackled like the Demon King in pantomime and was completely sidelined by Carrey.

Michael Gough, the one constant actor in the series, played Bruce's butler in his familiar dry, British manner. "Can I persuade you to take a sandwich with you?" he asked his master – an offer which was refused because Batman was going to pick something up at a fast food chain, a key sponsor of the film.

Whether you enjoy *Batman Forever* depends on your capacity for high intensity junk.
The Financial Times

It doesn't have much on its mind except employing yours for two hours.
The Sunday Times

A 130-minute film so unencumbered by suspense and sexual tension does indeed seem like forever.
Screen International

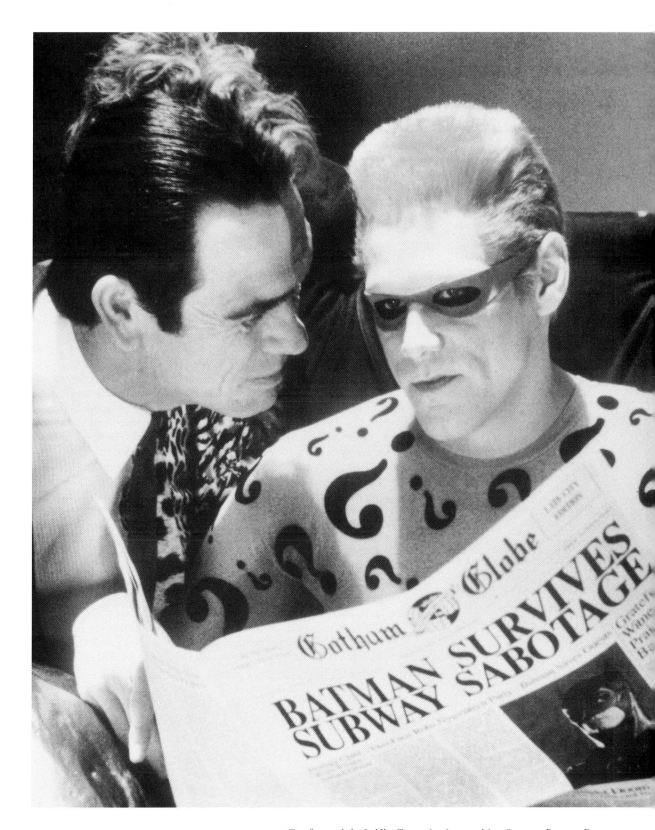

Two-face and the Riddler. Tommy Lee Jones and Jim Carrey in Batman Forever.

1996 • Independence Day

CREDITS

Captain Hiller	Will Smith
President Whitmore	Bill Pullman
David Levinson	Jeff Goldblum
Marilyn Whitmore	Mary McDonnell
Julius Levinson	Judd Hirsch
Russell Casse	Randy Quaid

Studio	Twentieth Century Fox
Director	Roland Emmerich
Producer	Dean Devlin
Screenplay	Dean Devlin
	Roland Emmerich
Photography	Karl Walter Lindenlaub
Music	David Arnold

AWARDS

ACADEMY AWARDS

Best Visual Effects   Volker Engel, Douglas Smith, Clay Pinney and Joseph Viskocil
Best Sound   Chris Carpenter, Bill W. Benton, Bob Beemer and Jeff Wexler

BEST PICTURE

The English Patient

STARS OF 1996

Tom Cruise
Mel Gibson
John Travolta
Arnold Schwarzenegger
Sandra Bullock

1996 Blockbusters

Twister
Mission Impossible
The Rock
Eraser
The Hunchback of Notre Dame

THE WORLD

- Divorce of Prince and Princess of Wales
- IRA resume campaign in Northern Ireland
- Dunblane killings in Scotland
- Cloning of Dolly, the sheep

INDEPENDENCE DAY, described by Variety as "the biggest B movie ever made," was simple-minded, patriotic jingoism for popcorn-audiences nostalgic for the alien invasion movies of the 1950s and the disaster movies of the 1970s. The advance publicity was excellent. The trailer had the unforgettable image of the White House being blown to smithereens. "We treated the aliens as a natural disaster," said Roland Emmerich.

A number of 15-mile wide massive metal spaceships, fearsome, menacing objects, hovered in strategic positions above world cities. "What happens if they turn hostile?" asked somebody. "God help us," was the reply." The only people who were really pleased to see the aliens were UFO watchers and hookers who took their placards of welcome to the top of a tall skyscraper. They were the first to be blown apart. The aliens were not nice guys like the ones cinema audiences had met in *ET* and *Close Encounters of the Third Kind*.

> " We treat the aliens as a natural disaster. "
>
> *Roland Emmerich*

Could the Americans negotiate a truce and live in peace or was this the end of the world as they knew it? It was the end of the world as they knew it. Washington, New York and Los Angeles were left in ruins. The American air force was destroyed. "It is important," said the President of the United States, addressing the nation, "for everyone not to panic." But who could save the planet? Who would save the human race from extinction? "Let's nuke the bastards!" said the President, launching a totally unsuccessful nuclear attack. The crisis was seen always entirely from an American perspective with just a handful of token flashes in Arabic, Russian, Japanese and English.

A space ship and its alien pilot had been recovered and were kept in a secret military installation in the Nevada desert, which was so secret that even the President knew nothing about it. The place was run by a mad scientist (who else?) and there was a bit of grisly horror when, under an autopsy, the alien pilot came back to life.

Independence Day celebrated the US's military power and technology. There were four heroes: the President, a Jewish computer genius, a black pilot and an alcoholic crop-duster. The pilot (Will Smith, suave, cocky) was a top dog fighter pilot but his career was on hold because he was living with an erotic dancer. He gunned down an alien plane, captured the pilot, a slimy, smelly alien, whom he greeted with a punch and then dragged across a desert in his parachute. The alcoholic crop-duster (Randy Quaid) was so alcoholic he was liable to dust the wrong field. He claimed he had been abducted and sexually assaulted by the aliens, so he was naturally keen to have his revenge. He died in the service of his country.

The President (Bill Pullman) was a Clintonesque figure, young, liberal, idealistic, a good guy, who had made his name in the Gulf War, but was now regarded as something of a wimp. The President emerged the hero of the hour. He rallied his troops with an oration, second only to Henry V's "Saint Crispin Day" speech and Dylan Thomas's poem *And Death Shall Have No Dominion*.

"We are fighting," he said, "for our right to live, to exist, and should we win the day, the 4th of July will no longer be known as an American holiday but as the day when the world declared in one voice we will not go quietly into the night and vanish without a fight. We're going to live on, we're going to survive." The President led them into battle.

The computer genius (Jeff Goldblum) was a divorcee whose wife had walked out

The White House under attack from aliens in Independence Day.

on him to work and sleep with the President. He decided to feed a virus into the alien mother ship's control system and destroy it. His chess-playing father (Judd Hirsch), who hadn't spoken to God in a long time, decided this was time for everybody to hold hands and start praying. "I'm not Jewish," observed the Minister of Defence. "Nobody's perfect," was the instant retort.

The actors played a supporting role to the special effects. The rolling balls of fire, which engulfed the panicking citizens who were attempting to escape them, were impressive. So, too, was the image of Air Force 1, the President's plane, taking off and narrowly escaping the flames.

Firmly located between art and trash, virtuosity and insignificance, *Independence Day*'s success is in being bigger but never better than its audience. Its mediocrity is its greatest triumph. This may be the most cheerful film about the apocalypse ever.
Sight and Sound

It may be film-making by numbers, but the numbers are the right ones and they fall into place with a satisfying clunk.
The Sunday Telegraph

The movie is fatuous, simple-minded, jingoistic and fun.
The Independent on Sunday

Apocalypse of the feelgood kind.
The Financial Times

1997 • Men in Black

CREDITS

Agent K	Tommy Lee Jones
Agent J	Will Smith
Dr Laurel Weaver	Linda Fiorentino
Edgar	Vincent D'Onofrio
Agent Zed	Rip Torn

Studio	Amblin
Director	Barry Sonnenfeld
Producer	Walter F Parkes
	Laurie MacDonald
Screenplay	Ed Solomon
Photography	Don Peterman
Music	Danny Elfman

AWARDS

ACADEMY AWARDS

Best Make-up	Rick Baker and
	David LeRoy Anderson

ACADEMY NOMINATIONS

Best Art Decoration	Bo Welch
Best Set Decoration	Cheryl Carasik
Best Original Musical or Comedy	
Score	Danny Elfman

BEST PICTURE

Titanic

STARS OF 1997

Harrison Ford
Julia Roberts
Leonardo DiCaprio
Will Smith
Tom Cruise

1997 Blockbusters

The Lost World
Liar Liar
Jerry Maguire
Star Wars (reissue)
Ransom

THE WORLD

• Tony Blair becomes British Prime Minister
• Hong Kong returned to China
• Death of Diana, Princess of Wales
• Scotland says yes to devolution

THE NATIONAL paranoia of being invaded from outer space continued. This time the premise was that the aliens were already here, disguised as humans and working in New York, mainly, as you would expect, in the Manhattan area. There was a secret service unit facilitating the immigration.

"Men in Black" is a term used to describe government agencies involved in cover-ups. The men wear black suits, black ties and black shades. They look like FBI men. Tommy Lee Jones was cast as a top agent whose job was to monitor, sort out undesirables and, in extreme circumstances, eliminate them. Will Smith played a young New York cop whom he had singled out to be his partner and successor. The agents had no names. They were known simply as K and J. The actors gave the ciphers their characters.

Jones was an ultra-cool operator, totally unimpressed by either aliens or special effects; it was all part of the daily routine. Jones' minimalist, humourless performance was in a different and better key to his over-the-top Harvey Two-Face

> " Protecting the earth from the scum of the universe. "
>
> *Slogan*

in *Batman Forever*. Informed the world was coming to the end, he merely asked when. Faced with a group of aliens disguised as illegal Mexican immigrants, he told them to put up their hands and their flippers. Jones was the film's anchor.

Smith, who had just saved the planet in *Independence Day,* was back on the same job. Agile, personable, his performance was in the hip, bumptious, smart-arse Eddie Murphy manner. J was decidedly put out when he was given a teeny-weeny weapon until he actually fired it and the recoil hurled him across the floor. The best visual gag (all the better for being played out in the background of a scene) was when J was delivering a baby alien in the back of a car and the enormous tentacles grabbed him by the waist and waved him about all over the place.

Barry Sonnenfeld, former cameraman to the Coen Brothers and director of the stylish *Addams Family* films, described *Men in Black* as an action film without any action. He might have added it was an action film without any story. It was all bits and pieces. What story there was involved a big bad bug, who arrived by flying saucer and took over a farmer's body, intending to destroy Earth. (Vincent D'Onofrio played the possessed farmer as a parody of Frankenstein's lumbering monster blundering around.) He finally turned into a giant cockroach and the only way he could be annihilated was for K to get inside him and blow him up from within. The downside of being a man in black was all the goo, slime and viscous he was liable to get in his face and all over his clothes.

The special effects were by Industrial Light and Magic Factory, who produced a wide range of tentacled, bug-eyed, reptilian aliens. The head of one human was opened and inside was a wizened old baby man, part-ET, part-Yoda, manipulating pulleys and levers. There was a nice joke about back-room extra terrestrials, Wurm Guys, lazy buggers, lolling about all day, drinking coffee and smoking, who, when it seemed as if Earth was about to be destroyed, skedaddled, taking trolleys of duty-free cigarettes with them. The aliens were cut seamlessly into the live action footage. The film's big revelation was that Stephen Spielberg is an alien. Sadly, Linda Fiorentino, so erotic in *The Last Seduction*, was completely wasted as a medical examiner in a morgue.

Men in Black was based on an obscure 1990 Malibu comic book strip by Lowell Cunningham. The film, quirky and zany, did not have the political agenda of *Mars Attacks!* It was just a straightforward down-the-middle, commercial Sci-Fi comedy and it managed to edge *Jurassic Park – The Lost World* out of top place.

"More secretive than the C.I.A. More powerful than the F.B.I." Will Smith and Tommy Lee Jones as Men in Black.

It may be a mere snack of a film – light, inconsequential, but it has the advantage of not pretending to be anything else.
The Independent

It's so much fun, in fact, it's almost over before you realise you've been watching a great idea for a movie in desperate search of a plot.
Time Out

Sonnenfeld, a nimble hand at visual eccentrics and blunderbuss farce but a bad man at shaping and sustaining.
The Times

The film appears to promise but does not quite deliver the slam-bang finale that most summer movies consider *de rigeur.*
Screen International

1998 • Titanic

CREDITS

Jack Dawson	Leonardo DiCaprio
Rose Dewitt Dukater	Kate Winslet
Cal Hockley	Billy Zane
Kathy Bates	Molly Brown
Ruth Dewitt Dukater	Frances Fisher
Captain Smith	Bernard Hill
Bruce Ismay	Jonathan Hyde
Fabrizio De Rossi	Danny Nucci
Spice Lovejoy	David Warner
Brock Lovett	Bill Paxton
Old Rose	Gloria Stuart
Thomas Andrews	Victor Garber

Studio	Lightstorm, Paramount Twentieth Century Fox
Director	James Cameron
Producer	James Cameron, Jon Landau
Screenplay	James Cameron
Photography	Russell Carpenter
Music	James Horner

AWARDS

ACADEMY AWARDS

Best Picture	James Cameron Jon Landau
Best Director	James Cameron
Best Cinematography	R. Carpenter
Best Art/Set Decoration	Peter Lamont and Michael Ford
Best Costume Design	Deborah Scott
Best Sound	Gary Rydstrom, Tom Johnson, Gary Summers and Mark Ulano
Best Film editing	Conrad Buff, James Cameron and Richard Harris
Best Sound Effects	Tom Bellfort and Christopher Boyes
Best Song	'My Heart Will Go On' by James Horner and Will Jennings
Best Original Score:	James Horner

ACADEMY NOMINATIONS

Best Actress:	Kate Winslett
Best Supporting Actress:	Gloria Stuart

BEST PICTURE

Shakespeare in Love

STARS OF 1998

Julia Roberts • Hugh Grant
Tom Hanks • Bruce Willis
Eddie Murphy

1998 Blockbusters

Armageddon • *Saving Private Ryan*
Deep Impact • *Doctor Doolittle*
Godzilla

THE WORLD

- President Clinton's impeachment proceedings begin
- Terrorist outrage in Omagh
- UK House of Lords abolished

O N 14 April 1912, *Titanic,* the largest and most luxurious ship ever built, sank on its maiden voyage from Southampton to New York. It had been said that God himself could not sink her and since she was unsinkable, there were not enough lifeboats. Bruce Ismay, chairman of the Line, was responsible; he hadn't wanted to take away the space from the first class passengers. When the ship hit the iceberg, the passengers went and got ice for their drinks.

Titanic was so designed that it could float with any two of her 16 watertight compartments flooded. She could float with any of her first three out of five compartments flooded. But the iceberg caused a 300-foot gash which cut all five compartments in one sweep. *Titanic* sent up flares of distress. A nearby ship presumed that they were fireworks celebrating the maiden voyage. Of the 2207 men, women and children, only 705 were saved.

James Cameron's film, the most expensive ever made, which at one time

> " Nothing on earth could come between them. "
>
> *Slogan*

looked as if it might sink the studio, went on to become one of the industry's biggest success stories. The screenplay began in the present day with the camera exploring the wreck at the bottom of the ocean. The tragedy was told through the memory of an old lady (Gloria Stuart) who sailed on the ship and so couldn't have been less than 103.

The love story was a romance out of the *Upstairs, Downstairs* drawer. The heroine was Rose (Kate Winslet), a poor little rich girl. Her mother (Frances Fisher) wanted her to marry a millionaire in order to pay off the family debts. The hero was Jack (Leonardo DiCaprio), a penniless artist, who won a passage in steerage in a game of poker. The couple met when he stopped her jumping into the Atlantic, a somewhat drastic measure she was taking to avoid marrying a man she did not love. Soon she was lying around naked so Jack could paint her. The cabin was littered with paintings by Degas, Manet, Picasso, Cezanne. The idea that these famous works of art went down with the *Titanic* was presumably a joke.

Rose's fiancé (Billy Zane) was an absolute bounder, a rotter, a cad, a brute and he was not pleased when he found he had a rival. He invited Jack to dinner, hoping to humiliate him, but Jack was able to borrow a dinner jacket from Molly Brown, who very oddly had a spare suit in her luggage. The fiancé was furious when he learned that Rose and Jack had been making love in the back seat of a car in the hold. He had Jack arrested for theft, having first got his valet (John Warner) to plant a valuable piece of jewellery in his pocket in a ridiculous set-up.

This meant that Jack was in chains when the ship started to sink and had to be rescued by Rose, who having staggered through a seemingly never-ending labyrinth of waterlogged and water-rising corridors, pluckily wielded an axe to cut him free. Despite the fact that water was lapping round their waists, they still found time to have a lingering kiss. The fiancé got murderous and, even as the passengers were scrambling for the last boats, he was pursuing Jack, firing his revolver, taking class warfare to farcical limits.

To call the film *Titanic* and then turn a great disaster, one of the most memorable tragedies of the 20th Century, second only to World War One, into a banal women's magazine love story was a gross insult to the real passengers who died. But then *Titanic* did not pretend to be a documentary like *A Night to Remember* (1958), which presented a cross-section of people from first class to steerage, and told what happened to them in a low and sober key.

That sinking feeling. Leonardo DiCaprio and Kate Winslet "colliding with destiny" in Titanic.

The re-creation of the ship, almost as big as the original, with its magnificent staircase and reception areas, was stunning. The enormous engine rooms were awesome. The actual sinking was impressive, with the water crashing through the panels of the corridors and the steerage passengers trapped behind locked gates. People slid and ricocheted down the upturned ship. The most memorable single image was of the officer (Ioan Gruffudd) on one of the boats searching for survivors among the floating dead in their life-jackets. They had frozen to death. The scene looked like an engraving by Gustave Dore, an illustration for Dante's Inferno.

Kate Winslet and Leonardo DiCaprio made an engaging couple. Schoolgirls identified with Rose and fell in love with DiCaprio. The girls went on seeing the film again and again, which was one of the main reasons for its phenomenal success at the box office. Jack's death must have taken audiences by surprise. Heroes usually survive in disaster films, especially if they have top billing.

It is one of the great achievements in popular film-making.
The Daily Telegraph

Yet for all the sluggish script and the enormous weight of the special effects, this movie behemoth still has the power to shake us rigid and touch the soul.
The Times

The regretful verdict here: Dead in the water.
Time

1999 • The Phantom Menace

CREDITS

Qui-Gon	Liam Neeson
Obi-Wan Kenobi	Ewan McGregor
Queen Amidala	Natalie Portman
Anakin Skywalker	Jake Lloyd
Senator Palpatine	Ian McDiarmid
Shmi Skywalker	Pernilla August
Jar Jar Binks	Ahmed Best
Yoda	Frank Oz
Mace Windu	Samuel L Jackson
Darth Maul	Ray Park
Studio	Lucasfilm
Director	George Lucas
Producer	Rick McCallum
Script	George Lucas
Photography	David Tattersall
Designer	Gavin Bocquet
Creatures Effects	Nick Dudman
Music	John Williams

AWARDS

ACADEMY AWARDS

None

ACADEMY NOMINATIONS

Best Sound Effects Editing   Ben Burtt and Tom Bellfort
Best Visual Effects   John Knoll, Dennis Murren, Scott Squires and Bob Coleman

BEST PICTURE

American Beauty

STARS OF 1999

Gwyneth Paltrow
Julia Roberts
Hugh Grant
Tom Hanks
Bruce Willis

1999 Blockbusters

The Sixth Sense
Toy Story
Austin Powers, The Spy Who Shagged Me
The Matrix
Tarzan

THE WORLD

• Massacre in Kosovo
• Round the world balloon flight succeeds
• Scottish parliament opens

THE PHANTOM MENACE is the first of the prequels to the *Star Wars* trilogy. The fans could not wait. They went from cinema to cinema paying to see films they did not want to see just to see the trailer again and again.

The story, a mixture of classical myth, Christianity and Zen, incomprehensible and infantile, was a pretentious allegory without drama, aimed at a very young audience. The dialogue was out of a comic book. There was no characterisation. The critical reception ranged from lukewarm to hostile. "A spent force" was the headline in The *Guardian*.

The Jedi Knights, guardians of peace and justice, were pony-tailed monks, who wielded light sabres. That was all they did. Liam Neeson managed a bit of authority. Ewan McGregor as his young apprentice (who would grow up to be Obi-Wan Kenobi) didn't do anything with a role, which was mere gymnastics, somersaulting, jumping and duelling. Natalie Portman, as the Queen, modelled eight costumes and head-dresses; she looked like a Geisha girl. Darth Maul, the bad guy with the double-bladed sword, had a tattooed red and black face and looked like the Demon King in pantomime.

The most irritating character was the sloppy, goofy, accident-prone, computer-generated Jar Jar Binks, who had a falsetto, Caribbean rap voice and a loose-limbed walk. He had a camel/horse face, floppy ears, flared nostrils, eyes on sticks, bell-bottomed legs and a prehensile tongue. He behaved like black comedians used to behave in 1930s Hollywood movies. Lucas was accused of racism. The character, which gave even greater offence, especially to the Jewish community, was the anti-Semitic caricature of a squinting, gambling slave-owner and junk-dealer called Watto, a hooked-nose, Fagin-like bumble bee.

The nine-year-old Annakin Skywalker, son of a virgin mother, the future Darth Vader, lived in a sun-baked Tunisian compound designed by Antoni Gaudi. Annakin was a slave and worked for Watto. His major scene was a Pod-race through a digitally created desert wilderness. The race was a straight crib from *Ben-Hur* and looked like any video game any child might play in a video arcade. The child's bicycle helmet made Annakin look like every child. The goggles made him look like Biggles.

The best thing about *The Phantom Menace* was not the spaceships, planes and army of metal droids, but the great monsters, the panoramic landscapes and seascapes. The architecture for the Jedi Council Chamber and the Art Nouveau bubble kingdom beneath the ocean were impressive. Jabba the Hutt (the bloated gangster slug) made a welcome guest appearance at the Pod-racing.

> "At the end of the day, our audience is between 7 and 14. I mean of course we want it for everybody. But the truth is that if the kid in you isn't there, if that part of you is gone, there is no way you are going to like this movie."
>
> *Rick McCallum*

"Every saga has a beginning." Ewan McGregor as Obi-Wan Kenobi and Liam Neeson as Qui-Gon in Phantom Menace, Episode 1 of Star Wars.

No summary can convey the spirit of the movie whose defining characteristic are pomposity, vulgarity and dreariness... Moviegoers should be allowed to make their own mistakes, of course – and there won't be a bigger one all year than paying to see this trash.

The Independent

Nothing, absolutely nothing, works this time round... *The Phantom Menace* is itself less important than the merchandising frenzy surrounding it.

The Independent on Sunday

It is all tricks and no magic, ingenuity without imagination.

The Observer

Nobody has the right to bore and disappoint us this much.

The Guardian

The *Star Wars* films aren't so much films as a franchise. Maybe they should be reviewed on the business pages.

The Sunday Telegraph

Index

PICTURE ACKNOWLEDGEMENTS

The pictures from this book are from the BFI, the Kobal
Collection and the Joel Finler Collection.

The illustrations in this book include many from stills issued to
publicize films made and/or distributed by the following: Amblin,
Archers, Columbia, Carolco Pacific Western, Goldwyn, Howard
Hughes, Lightstorm, Lucasfilm, MGM, Paramount, Rainbow,
RKO, Selznick, Touchstone, Twentieth Century Fox, United
Artists, Universal, Walt Disney Productions and Warner Brothers.
Grateful acknowledgement is given to all the producing
companies and distributors. Although effort has been made to
trace present copyright owners, apologies are made in advance for
any unintentional omission or neglect; we will be happy to insert
appropriate acknowledgement to companies or individuals in
subsequent editions of the book.